126 STRATEGIES TO BUILD LANGUAGE ARTS ABILITIES:

A Month-by-Month Resource

CATHY COLLINS
Texas Christian University

Illustrations by **Ruben Olmos**

Allyn and Bacon
Boston London Toronto Sydney Tokyo Singapore

Dedicated to my
mother and sister,
JoAnn and Wanda Zinke,
and to Stan and Michael

Library of Congress Cataloging-in-Publication Data

Collins, Cathy.
    The language arts almanac : 126 activities for teaching the most
difficult concepts in the language arts / Cathy Collins ;
illustrations by Ruben Olmos.
        p.   cm.
    ISBN 0-205-13025-9
    1. Language arts (Elementary)–United States. 2. Education,
Elementary–United States–Activity programs.   I. Title.
LB1576C5773   1992
372.6′044–dc20   91-6672
                                                                    CIP

Printed in the United States of America
10 9 8 7 6 5 4 3 2   95 94 93

Table of Contents of Activities and Skills Taught

CHAPTER 4 **December** **120**

CHAPTER 5 **January** **158**

CHAPTER 6 **February** **202**

Table of Contents of Activities by Holidays

Table of Forms

Preface

This book is designed to help you increase the effectiveness and efficiency of your language arts instruction. One of *126 Strategies to Build Language Arts Abilities'* most prominent features is that it provides new strategies to teach the more difficult communication and conceptual skills. Special elements of this book were included to increase students' retention of lesson objectives while reducing the amount of time spent in instruction. Such efficiency of class time is valuable as we move into the more frequent use of children's literature as the primary curriculum for language development. With *126 Strategies,* departures from a more holistic focus to targeted skill development can be briefer and scheduled when students' needs dictate. In addition, this book illustrates many ways the language arts can be integrated across the curriculum as each lesson is based on a social science, historical, sociological, or scientific theme.

Some of the special features of *126 Strategies,* as well as alternative ways in which the book can be used, are described below.

1. Directions for activities follow a format that teachers have found easy to use. Each lesson includes a statement of the time requirements; an itemization of strategies used to teach the concept; answer keys (when appropriate); modifications that can be used in grades K–8 to meet the needs of rapid, average, and slower learning students; and room for notations concerning individual students' needs, projects, and your ideas for using the activity again. The activity directions are sometimes in dialogue form. You do not need a script to follow, of course, but this approach provides relief from constant do-this-say-that commands and gives an idea of how the activities can come to life in a classroom.

2. Since the lessons are based on seasonal, holiday themes, instructional activities are available during these busier times of the year. In addition, due to the holiday focus and the nature of the basic skills taught, the lessons integrate into your language arts classes easily regardless of the curriculum covered during other days of the month.

3. The teaching strategies of the activities can be used in other content areas, and may broaden your instructional resource base.

4. Activities are tailored to challenge the gifted, aid the less able, and expand the interests and imaginations of all students. Supplemental activities are included for early finishers' and gifted students' use without teacher direction.

5. Activities can be used as a part of the regular curriculum or in supplemental ways (e.g., when plans have been changed abruptly or when a substitute teacher is needed).

6. A different form is included at the end of each chapter. The forms can be used in a wide variety of ways throughout the year, saving teachers' time and providing standardized ways to grade some of the more difficult language arts concepts.

7. A take-home calendar is given for each month. The daily activities can be assigned as homework or done in class, as discussed in more detail in Chapter 1. A blank calendar form is also provided, so that students can devise their own method for practicing what was learned in their language arts lessons.

8. Birthday lists of famous people are given for each month. Students can practice language arts skills by researching on or near their own birthdays. Chapter 1 discusses in more detail how to use these lists.

9. Each chapter opens with the monthly scope and sequence of instruction and a listing of the month's major events and themes.

10. Each chapter lists addresses of agencies to which students can write for information about the monthly themes and events. This book can be used when grade levels and teaching assignments change, since lessons can be used from grades K–8.

11. The book contains three tables of contents, one identifying the objective of each activity, another listing the holiday and seasonal focus of each lesson, and a third listing the forms in the book.

Suggestions for Using the Book

Because *126 Strategies to Build Language Arts Abilities* begins with activity themes for September, you can use it in the order in which it was written. When the book is used in this way, students are exposed to fourteen lessons a month designed to increase reading, writing, thinking, speaking, spelling, and hand-writing abilities. If all activities are used, by the end of the year sixty-three language arts competencies will have been addressed.

A second way of using the book is to refer to it as student needs arise. In this way *126 Strategies* becomes a reference manual—when a difficult concept appears in the language arts curriculum, activities from the book can be used to teach that concept.

Third, the book can be used as sample lessons at in-services and faculty meetings. These samples can provide a model for supervisors, lead teachers, and administrators as they demonstrate recently developed language arts strategies or create new curriculum.

College professors can use *126 Strategies* as a supplemental or basic text for graduate/undergraduate courses and as a resource in conducting in-service training sessions. School librarians responsible for teaching small groups of students can use some activities during story times. Teacher aides can refer to the book during small-group instruction and one-to-one sessions to meet in-dividual students' needs.

Acknowledgments

I extend my best wishes to you as you continue to give your students the best learning experiences to expand their thinking, listening, speaking, reading, handwriting, spelling, grammar, and composition abilities. I sincerely hope *126 Strategies to Build Language Arts Abilities'* activities assist you in many ways.

Many teachers I admire have field-tested the activities, working diligently so that other teachers receive new strategies to assist their students. I appreciate their common drive and dedication over the past two years—they are a part of this book.

I would like to thank Sandra Baker, and Catherine Hatala, who spent several days reading the first draft. Their comments and suggestions increased the quality of this book.

I would also like to extend a special word of appreciation to Ruben Olmos, who spent many evenings and weekends designing the graphics. This remarkable young man was a senior at Polytechnic High School, Fort Worth Texas, and President of that student body, at the time this book was written.

Ramona White, Penny Torres, Camille Jackson, Tammy Walker, Tanya Pierce, and Tammy Birdow spent countless hours at word processors. They also listened to and critiqued my ideas in the development stages, and shared in the joy of seeing the final results in classrooms. They believed in the worth of this project and performed many of the tedious tasks that were necessary but not fun.

Last, I dedicate this book to my mother, sister, Stan, and Michael. Their character, kindness, and devotion to others nurtured me in my work and made it possible for me to write this book.

I also owe a large debt to Ellen Silge, my copy editor. She scrutinzed every activity to ensure that all were as direct and clear as possible. She suggested and made changes in several. Her insights and creativity strengthened many activities. Thank you very much, Ellen.

In addition to these people, I am grateful to Mylan Jaixen, Deborah Reinke, Michael Bass and Joe Devlin, my publication editors who did an outstanding job in creative formatting and working diligently in light of the difficulties created by a computer virus. Mylan Jaixen believed in the project from the beginning, and was always available whenever needed. I appreciate and am grateful for his support, guidance, and expertise. Without him, this book would not exist.

CHAPTER

1 *September*

September's lessons are built on the themes of beginning school; celebrating students' birthdays; identifying the autumn equinox; as well as recognizing the first newspaper, Native American Week, National Dog Week, and the significance of several sporting events.

Other September events include: Labor Day; National Grandparents Day; the International Day of Peace; Mayflower Day; Citizenship Day and Constitution Week; World Gratitude Day; the anniversary of the discovery of the planet Neptune; Rosh Hashanah, the Jewish New Year; and National Good Neighbor Day.

Scope and Sequence of Language Arts Concepts Taught in September

Reading (Activities 1-1 and 1-2): Students will learn what main idea statements are, where they typically occur in the paragraph or in talks, and how main idea statements can help them remember more of what they read and hear.

Spelling (Activities 1-3 and 1-4): Students will learn how to use English spelling patterns to improve their spelling abilities.

Handwriting (Activities 1-5 and 1-6): Students will learn to make correct size, slant, and shape of letters in manuscript, cursive, and/or calligraphy.

Composition (Activities 1-7 and 1-8): Students will learn to create effective story openings, settings, middles, and endings when writing and speaking.

Speaking (Activities 1-9 and 1-10): Students will learn to speak before groups, and use principles of effective formal/informal speaking.

Grammar (Activities 1-11 and 1-12): Students will learn when to use the four parts of speech: nouns, verbs, conjunctions, and adjectives.

Listening (Activities 1-13 and 1-14): Students will learn skills to improve their listening ability.

Additional Activities for September

The following information can be used in a wide variety of ways to extend the lessons of September. Students can work alone or in small groups.

1. Students can write letters to obtain much information about activities in September and October. The following companies will mail this information to the students free of charge:

Good Neighbor Day Foundation
Dr. Richard C. Mattson
Drawer R
Lakeside, MT 59922

Edna Foerth Lemle
World Gratitude Foundation
777 United Nations Plaza
Suite 7-A
New York, NY 10017

Fulton County Historical Society
7th and Pontiac
Rochester, IN 46975

The Navajo Nation
Chairman's Office
Box 308
Window Rock, AZ 86515

Mountain Eagle Indian Festival
Indian Festival Committee
Bridge St.
Hunter, NY 12442

National Championship Indian
Powwow
Dallas-Forth Worth Inter-Tribal
 Assn.
Traders Village
2602 Mayfield Rd.
Grand Prairie, TX 75051

National Indian Summer Art Show
Florence Valore Miller
205 N. Montpelier Ave.
Atlantic City, NJ 08401

Florida Native American Heritage
 Festival
Tallahassee Junior Museum
3945 Museum Dr.
Tallahassee, FL 32304

United Tribes Powwow
United Tribes Educational Technical
 Center
3315 South Airport Rd.
Bismarck, ND 58501

National Society for the Prevention
 of Cruelty to Animals
National Association for the
 Advancement of Humane Educa-
 tion Center
P.O. Box 362
East Haddam, CT 06423

Galerie Triangle
3701 14th St., N.W.
Washington, DC 20010

Cloverdale Citrus Fair Association
Box 445
Cloverdale, CA 95425

Cranberry Festival
Massachusetts Division of Tourism
Boston, MA 02202

American Heart Association
Mike Rogers
7320 Greenville Ave.
Dallas, TX 75231

Pickle Packers International, Inc.
108½ E. Main St.
Charles, IL 60174

Puns Corps
Robert L. Birch
Publicity Chairman
Box 2364
Falls Church, VA 22042

National Popcorn Farmers Day, Inc.
Box 231
Ridgway, IL 62979

Committee for the Observance of
 American Newspaper Week
Box 68
Montague, MI 49437

Healthy American Fitness Leaders
U.S. Jaycees
Public Relations Dept.
Box 7
Tulsa, OK 74121

National Wildlife Federation
1412 16th St., N.W.
Washington, DC 20036

The White House
1600 Pennsylvania Ave., N.W.
Washington, DC 20500

The Chamber of Commerce in a student's favorite city

2. Students can use library resources to report and write about fairs (their origin and purposes) or to design a bulletin board about an important event in their city.

3. Students can invent a commemorative seal or song that highlights the qualities and events that make September unique.

4. Students can select one of the following activities about Queen Elizabeth I of England. She was born September 7, 1533 and began to rule England when she was 55. She died at the age of 70.

  a. Imagine what Queen Elizabeth I was like. Think about what she looked like. Write three rules she could have written for her country. Ask a friend to do the same. Then check your ideas by reading about Queen Elizabeth I in an encyclopedia.
  b. Contrast the duties of our President to England's King or Queen. Make this contrast by listing how our President leads our country. Then find out (in the library) if England's Queen leads her country in the same way.
  c. Read one or more books about the people who created our government. List three reasons why these people did not make a king or queen rule over our government.
  d. Imagine you woke up this morning and found yourself king or queen of the world! Write, tell, or draw descriptions of ten silly or serious rules you would want your subjects to follow if you ruled the world.

5. American writer O. Henry was born September 11, 1862. He is best known for stories with surprise endings. Locate one of his stories in the library, one of the fairy tales from *The Fairy Tale Treasury* by Virginia Haviland (Dell, 1980), a selection from *The Wide World All Around* by Francelia Butler, Anne Devereaux Jordan, and Richard Rolert (Longman, 1987), or ask someone to tell a fairy tale. When you finish reading or listening to the story, create your own surprise ending. Write it down or tell someone about your ending. For example, you could change the ending of "Goldilocks and the Three Bears" by changing the main characters to Golden Boy and the Four Giants and create a surprise by changing one of the events in the Goldilocks story. You could rewrite "Little Red Riding Hood" so that Little Red Riding Hood and her grandmother are wolves. You could write what would have happened if Cinderella's shoe had not fallen off as she left the ball. What would happen if Sleeping Beauty were asleep today and _____ finds her; or if Hansel and Gretel were able to live happily ever after with the witch? What surprise ending do you want to create?

6. The Constitution of the United States was signed September 17, 1787. Read or ask someone about Colonial times, Pilgrims, Native Americans, and the people who signed the Constitution. Then, as a class or small-group project, make a quilt as they did in Colonial times. At a location in the room your teacher selects, cut pieces of fabric into 6″ squares. Using fabric markers, draw pictures that represent something you have read or heard about Colonial times or a person who signed the Constitution. Then either: (1) sew the quilt squares together, putting plaid or Colonial-looking material between the pictured squares, (2) glue pictures on a large sheet to make it look quilted, or (3) take the pictured pieces to a group of senior citizens who could use them to make a real quilt. After the quilt is finished, you could hang it on the wall of the classroom or give it to someone in your community who could use it.

7. Students whose birthdays fall in September can be given a special treat to celebrate their birthdays. This assignment could be one of their choice, assigned in lieu of another lesson. Students can learn about famous people who were born on or around their own birth date and how these people are similar to themselves. If the people are alive, students can write to them by locating their address from one of the following sources or in the reference section of the library:

ABC (American Broadcasting Co.)
1300 Avenue of the Americas
New York, NY 10019

CBS (Columbia Broadcasting System)
51 West 52nd St.
New York, NY 10019

NBC (National Broadcasting Co.)
30 Rockefeller Plaza
New York, NY 10112

Mutual Broadcasting System
1755 S. Jefferson Davis Highway
Arlington, VA 22202

PBS (Public Broadcasting Service)
1320 Braddock Pl.
Alexandria, VA 22314

Motion picture companies' addresses can be found in the *International Motion Picture Almanac* in your public or university library reference section. If the people are not alive, students can find out about them through autobiographies, biographies, or encyclopedias. Sandra Baker gave November's names to her class to research the ones they wished to know more about. Her students enjoyed the activity and learned "a great deal."

These notable people were born on these September dates:

1. Rocky Marciano, Lily Tomlin
2. Jimmy Connors, Terry Bradshaw, Christa McAuliffe
3. Alan Lad, Eileen Brennan, Nicolo Amati, Edward Filene
4. Tom Watson, Daniel Burnham
5. Jesse James, Bob Newhart, Raquel Welch
6. Jane Addams, Jane Curtin
7. Queen Elizabeth I, Buddy Holly, Grandma Moses
8. Peter Sellers, Sid Caesar
9. Otis Redding, Colonel Harlan Sanders
10. Arnold Palmer, Fay Wray
11. O. Henry, Bear Bryant, Kristy McNichol

12. Maurice Chevalier, Jesse Owens

13. Claudette Colbert, Jacqueline Bisset

14. I. P. Pavlov, Margaret Sanger

15. William Howard Taft, Agatha Christie, Prince Henry Charles Albert David (second son of Prince Charles and Princess Diana of Wales)

16. Lauren Bacall, Allan Funt, Peter Faulk

17. Anne Bancroft, Roddy McDowall

18. Greta Garbo, Samuel Johnson

19. Twiggy, Cass Elliot

20. Sophia Loren, Jelly Roll Morton

21. Larry Hagman, Bill Murray, Catherine Oxenberg

22. John Houseman, Meryl Streep, Scott Baio

23. Ray Charles, Bruce Springsteen, William McGuffey

24. Jim McKay, Jim Henson, F. Scott Fitzgerald

25. Barbara Walters, Phil Rizzuto, Red Smith

26. George Gershwin, Olivia Newton-John, Johnny Appleseed, Melissa Sue Anderson

27. Jayne Meadows

28. Al Capp, Ed Sullivan, Brigitte Bardot

29. Gene Autry, Madeline Kahn

30. Johnny Mathis, Angie Dickinson

The Calendar

The calendar for September like those for the other months, can be used in a wide variety of ways. Because the calendar contains activities involving the concepts taught this month, it can be a homework assignment for the entire class, and students can be given a bonus/reward if all homework is completed by the end of the month. Students can write answers in each square, and parents can verify.

Alternatively, the calendar can be used as a "sponge" activity (an activity that can be completed in less than 15 minutes and is a valuable learning experience), or for students who come to school early and those who may stay for a few minutes after school is dismissed. You can ask the class to complete one activity from the calendar each day. The calendar can also be used by a classroom officer who selects an activity already studied. This officer asks classmates to do the activity together, as a daily review of language arts concepts.

Students can be divided into teams to generate as many answers to each day's activity as possible. This teamwork can occur near the end of the month to review major concepts. The team with the most correct answers wins.

Finally, this calendar can be mounted in a learning center where students

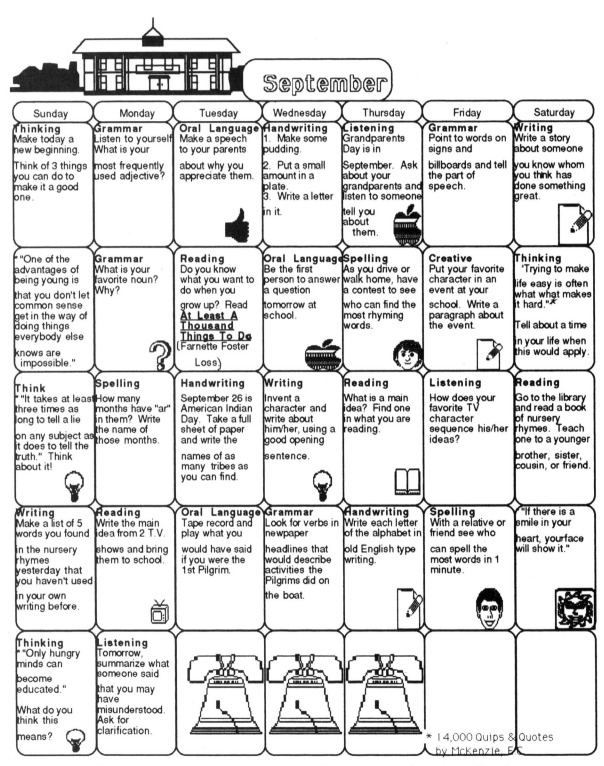

September

Sunday	Monday	Tuesday	Wednesday	Thursday	Friday	Saturday
Thinking Make today a new beginning. Think of 3 things you can do to make it a good one.	**Grammar** Listen to yourself. What is your most frequently used adjective?	**Oral Language** Make a speech to your parents about why you appreciate them.	**Handwriting** 1. Make some pudding. 2. Put a small amount in a plate. 3. Write a letter in it.	**Listening** Grandparents Day is in September. Ask about your grandparents and listen to someone tell you about them.	**Grammar** Point to words on signs and billboards and tell the part of speech.	**Writing** Write a story about someone you know whom you think has done something great.
* "One of the advantages of being young is that you don't let common sense get in the way of doing things everybody else knows are impossible."	**Grammar** What is your favorite noun? Why?	**Reading** Do you know what you want to do when you grow up? Read <u>At Least A Thousand Things To Do</u> (Farnette Foster Loss)	**Oral Language** Be the first person to answer a question tomorrow at school.	**Spelling** As you drive or walk home, have a contest to see who can find the most rhyming words.	**Creative** Put your favorite character in an event at your school. Write a paragraph about the event.	**Thinking** 'Trying to make life easy is often what what makes it hard."* Tell about a time in your life when this would apply.
Think * "It takes at least three times as long to tell a lie on any subject as it does to tell the truth." Think about it!	**Spelling** How many months have "ar" in them? Write the name of those months.	**Handwriting** September 26 is American Indian Day. Take a full sheet of paper and write the names of as many tribes as you can find.	**Writing** Invent a character and write about him/her, using a good opening sentence.	**Reading** What is a main idea? Find one in what you are reading.	**Listening** How does your favorite TV character sequence his/her ideas?	**Reading** Go to the library and read a book of nursery rhymes. Teach one to a younger brother, sister, cousin, or friend.
Writing Make a list of 5 words you found in the nursery rhymes yesterday that you haven't used in your own writing before.	**Reading** Write the main idea from 2 T.V. shows and bring them to school.	**Oral Language** Tape record and play what you would have said if you were the 1st Pilgrim.	**Grammar** Look for verbs in newpaper headlines that would describe activities the Pilgrims did on the boat.	**Handwriting** Write each letter of the alphabet in old English type writing.	**Spelling** With a relative or friend see who can spell the most words in 1 minute.	"If there is a smile in your heart, yourface will show it."
Thinking * "Only hungry minds can become educated." What do you think this means?	**Listening** Tomorrow, summarize what someone said that you may have misunderstood. Ask for clarification.					

* 14,000 Quips & Quotes by McKenzie, E.

This calendar created in collaboration with Frances Dornan, Valarie McGarry, George Russell.

add their own ideas or questions on post-a-note paper or notecards. When another student answers a classmate's idea, they sign their name.

Teachers and students may wish to cover each day with post-a-notes so each day's activity is uncovered and discussed at the end of each day.

The following blank calendar can be copied and distributed to students. They can use it to record special homework assignments you make.

In addition, throughout the school year, you may wish to read the book *Over and Over* by Charlotte S. Zolotte, published by Harper and Row. This book contains a listing of children's literature that introduces months and seasons of the year.

Reading Skill Development: Using Main Ideas to Enjoy Reading More and Comprehend Better

TIME REQUIRED

Teacher Directed Page (Activity 1-1): 25–35 minutes

Student Discovery Page (Activity 1-2): 30–40 minutes

TEACHING STRATEGIES

There are three instructional strategies in this activity. Students will learn more than one method and select which one they prefer to use. The first strategy is to allow student choice. Students choose which method they want to use to find main idea statements. The second strategy is that students share with classmates the thinking process they used to find a main idea. This strategy reinforces learning through "think alouds," and makes thinking "public." The third strategy is to give students three examples of a concept and to have students tell how these examples are alike and different.

ACTIVITY 1-1 _____

BACK TO SCHOOL: LEARNING TO READ BETTER AND REMEMBER MORE

[OBJECTIVE] STUDENTS, TODAY YOU WILL LEARN THE PURPOSE AND THE LOCATIONS OF MAIN IDEAS IN ORAL AND WRITTEN COMMUNICATION. YOU WILL LEARN TO USE THESE TO REMEMBER MORE OF WHAT YOU READ AND HEAR. YOU WILL KNOW YOU HAVE LEARNED IF YOU ANSWER AT LEAST EIGHT OF TEN STEPS IN THE "POT OF GOLD" **[ACTIVITY 1-2]** CORRECTLY.

Today we will learn three ways to remember the most important things a writer tells us. All three help us find where authors write the main ideas they want us to learn.

The first method is to find the sentence that tells what the other sentences in the paragraph have in common. To find this sentence, find the sentence that does *not* describe just *one* thing or does *not* just tell when, where, or why something is being done. Instead, the main idea sentence is the most general statement about the subject.

SUNDAY	MONDAY	TUESDAY	WEDNESDAY	THURSDAY	FRIDAY	SATURDAY

MONTH _____ YEAR _____

A second way to find the main idea is to study the first and last sentences of a paragraph very carefully. Most authors put the main ideas in the first or last sentence of their paragraphs.

A third method is to draw a table or picture in your mind that has a flat top and four legs like the one I'm drawing on the board now. **[Use Figure 1-1.]** On each leg you place a sentence from the paragraph that is a specific fact about the subject. Once all these "detail sentences" have been placed beneath the tabletop, if only one sentence remains, that will be the main idea. This sentence goes on the tabletop.

In some paragraphs there will be no main idea statement. When this occurs, you should think of a statement that combines or summarizes all the other points in the paragraph. For example, consider the following paragraph. **[Diagram this paragraph, allowing the students to tell you where each sentence goes and why (see Figure 1-2.]**

My grandfather cooks ham very well. He bakes pies too. He cooks my favorite, pizza, whenever I come over. He also makes wonderful steaks, his favorite thing to cook.

[Have the students make up a main idea statement, since this paragraph has none. One example of a correct answer is: My grandfather is a very good cook.]

Now let's practice using these three methods of finding main idea statements. Remember, some paragraphs do not have main idea statements. **[You can use the following examples on an overhead projector or you can ask students to use the first three paragraphs from the next story or book they are going to read silently.]** Look at these three samples (or the first paragraphs in the book to be read today). What is the main idea in the first paragraph? Tell us how you know this is the main idea. Which of the methods we learned did you use to find the main idea? Where is the main idea for the second paragraph, and how did you find it? **[Correct answers for the sample paragraphs are given at the end of this activity.]**

FIGURE 1-1

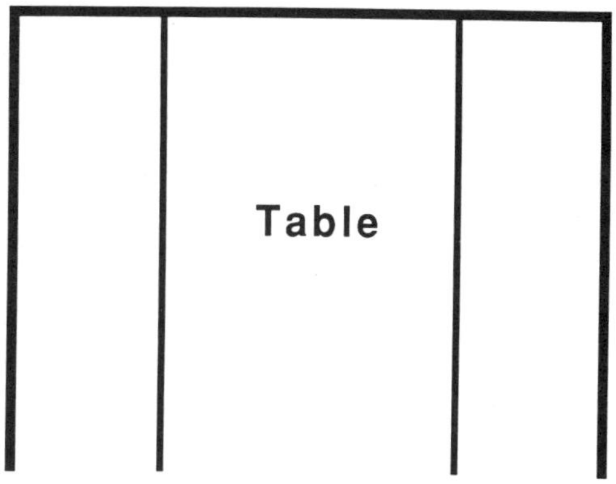

FIGURE 1-2

(My grandfather is a very good cook.)

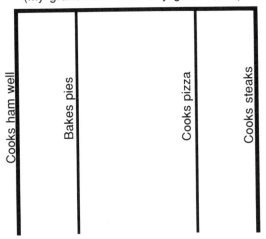

1. It is not hard to make good chocolate fudge. You take cocoa, sugar, and milk and put them in a pan. You stir these things together, then boil them into a syrup. The syrup will become thick after about four minutes. Pour the fudge into a pan that has been greased with butter or margarine. Let the fudge cool. Cut into squares.

2. We watched the monkey's keeper come with dinner. They got bananas and sweet potatoes. They liked the bananas best. The monkeys had fun stealing bananas from each other. One monkey climbed high in the cage with a banana in its mouth. At the zoo, monkeys are so much fun to watch!

3. The size of the pupil controls the amount of light that enters the eye. In bright light the pupil is smaller than it will be in darkness. The human eye really is remarkable in many ways. As another example, the lens changes its thickness to view distant objects better. Because of this, we see things from a few inches to hundreds of miles away. The pupil also makes it possible to see about 150 colors!

[Pass out Activity Sheet 1-2.] Now, on this sheet we are going to practice finding main ideas. You will read paragraphs from your story or book. You will write the main idea from the first paragraph you read in the square marked 1, and this is the first answer to your Pot of Gold. You will then read the second paragraph and write its main idea in the second square. **[You may have students who finish first grade the papers of other students or award a prize for the first, second, and third students who score 100.]**

ANSWER KEY

1. It is not hard to make good chocolate fudge.

2. At the zoo, monkeys are so much fun to watch!

3. The human eye really is remarkable in many ways.

GRADING CRITERIA: _____

_____

EARLY FINISHERS

You may wish to make a second copy of the Pot of Gold handout and allow early finishers to identify main ideas in a chapter of their library book. Early finishers or students who do not need to complete this activity could look up the definition of literacy, as September 8 is International Literacy Day. (This is the day the United Nations celebrates the ability to read and write. It is also designed to reaffirm our country's desire to help all people learn to read and write.)

MODIFICATIONS FOR GRADE LEVELS AND STUDENT ABILITY LEVELS

For Kindergarten, First Grade, and Slower Learning Groups, you will use pictures instead of text to teach main ideas. _For Second through Eighth Grades, Average or Slower Learning Groups,_ you can select one method of recognizing main ideas each day, rather than introducing three methods at once. _For Gifted Students,_ you can direct students to identify the main idea in single paragraphs and then in several sequential paragraphs.

STUDENTS WHO WILL BE WORKING ON OTHER PROJECTS OR LESSONS: _____

_____

NOTES FOR FUTURE USE: _____

_____

ACTIVITY 1-2

POT OF GOLD

Name_____   Date_____

Main Ideas Lead You to the <u>Pot of Gold:</u> Reading Better And
Remembering More

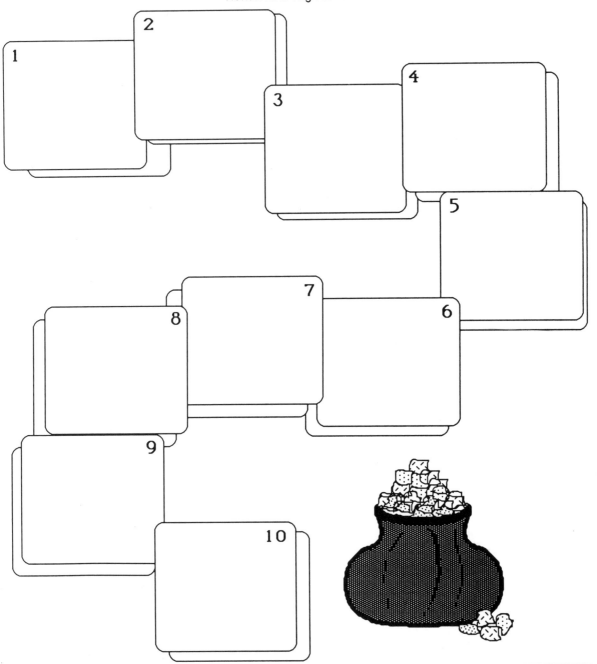

Spelling Skill Development: Using Spelling Patterns to Improve Spelling Ability

TIME REQUIRED

Teacher Directed Page (Activity 1-3): 20–60 minutes; can be extended into two days if all modifications are followed

Student Discovery Page (Activity 1-4): 20–40 minutes

TEACHING STRATEGIES

Students learn by teacher modeling how to improve spelling ability by using word parts.

A by-product of this activity is that it generates a list of students' birthdays.

ACTIVITY 1-3

YOUR BIRTHDAY CAKE TO CELEBRATE SPELLING SUCCESS

[OBJECTIVE]   TODAY YOU WILL LEARN TO RECOGNIZE SOME OF THE MAJOR SPELLING PATTERNS OF OUR LANGUAGE. YOU WILL KNOW YOU HAVE LEARNED THESE SPELLING PATTERNS WHEN YOU MAKE A SCORE OF 75% OR MORE CORRECT ON THE TEST OVER THE WORDS ON THE BIRTHDAY CAKE OF ACTIVITY 1-4.

I want to know the month and date you were born. We will use these dates to learn to spell many words. In English, words with similar sounds can be spelled alike. Let me show you what I mean. In the word "birthday" the spelling of the last sound, "ay," is spelled the same in every day of the week and for other words that end in the /ay/ sound (such as "clay," "gray," "play," "stray," "stay," and "tray.") By knowing this spelling rule (an /ay/ sound at the end of a word can be spelled -ay), you can spell many new words.

There are many similar spelling patterns in the English language. In the words "Have a Happy Birthday" there are several spelling patterns such as -ave, -ap, -ir (which is one of the spellings of the sound /ir/), and -ay. Which words in our spelling book, or in a story you wrote have these patterns?

[Pass out Activity 1-4.] Put your name on the page I've given you. Also put the month and day of the year you were born. **[For kindergarten, first, and second grades you can do this section as a whole-class language experience approach by writing student birthdays on the board with students' names. The next step you take will depend on the age and ability level of your students. You can have them identify the word parts in the months or you can identify them.]** Each time you identify a word part, it is written on one of the candles of your cake. You will then find as many words in your spelling book or in the words you've written that fit that pattern as you can. Write each one on the line that corresponds to the number of the candle. **[You can give a reward to the person who has the most words at the end of 20–40 minutes. On the next day you can pair students and let them give each other a test over the words their partner wrote on Activity 1-4.]**

[You can reuse this activity throughout the year by replacing the word parts on the cake with: -ab, -ack, -ad, -ade, -ag, -ail, -ain, -ake, -all, -am, -ame, -amp, -an, -and, -ank, -ap, -ar, -ark, -ash, -at, -ate, -ave, -aw, -eak, -eal, -eam, -ear, -eat, -ed, -eed, -eep, -ell, -en, -end, -est, -ew, -ice, -id,

-idem, -ig, -ight, -ill, -im, -ime, -in, -ind, -ine, -ing, -ink, -ip, -it, -ive, -ob, -ock, -od, -og, -oke, -old, -one, -op, -ope, -ore, -orn, -ot, -ow, -ub, -uck, -uff, -ug, -um, -ump, -ung, -unk, -ush, and -ut.]

ANSWER KEY

-ave

-an

-ap

-ar

-ay

-ir

-ar

-er

GRADING CRITERIA: _____

MODIFICATIONS FOR GRADE LEVELS AND STUDENT ABILITY LEVELS

While there are some directions for modifications in this lesson, you can adopt the lesson by introducing as many words and spelling patterns as you feel appropriate. _For Kindergarten, First Grade, Second Grade, and Slower Learning Groups,_ this activity and Activity 1-4 will be whole-class language experiences. You will write each student's birthday on the board or overhead transparency, writing the full spelling of each month. _For Third through Eighth Grades, Average or Slower Learning Students,_ the students can identify the word parts in the spellings of each month. _For Gifted Students,_ word parts in the days of the week can also be used.

STUDENTS WHO WILL BE WORKING ON OTHER PROJECTS OR LESSONS: _____

NOTES FOR FUTURE USE: _____

ACTIVITY 1-4

HAPPY BIRTHDAY TO YOU!
YOUR BIRTHDAY CAKE FOR SPELLING SUCCESS

DIRECTIONS

Place one of the spelling patterns we studied in class on each candle. On the line that corresponds to the candle's spelling pattern in the cake, list as many words from your spelling book or writing that contain that spelling pattern as you can find. The person with the most words at the end of the lesson wins.

GOOD LUCK!

Handwriting Skill Development: Learning to Make Letter Shapes

TIME REQUIRED

Prerequisite: 10 minutes to receive a sample of each child's writing of the letters of the alphabet to be used in this activity

Teacher-Directed Exploration (Activity 1-5): 15–30 minutes

Student Discovery Page (Activity 1-6): 30 minutes for the scavenger hunt and 10 minutes for grading handwriting and awarding prizes.

TEACHING STRATEGIES

Four teaching strategies will be used. First, students will learn by using a point system to depict the amount learned. Second, they will be taught through a comparison of postinstructional work to preinstructional samples. Third, students will use self-evaluation, awarding themselves one point for each improvement. Last, students will work in cooperative learning teams.

ACTIVITY 1-5

AN AUTUMN SCAVENGER HUNT LEADS TO HANDWRITING IMPROVEMENT

[OBJECTIVE] TODAY YOU WILL IMPROVE YOUR HANDWRITING BY LEARNING TO MAKE THE CORRECT SLANT, SIZE, AND SHAPE OF IN-DIVIDUAL LETTERS. YOU WILL KNOW YOU HAVE IMPROVED YOUR HANDWRITING THROUGH COMPARISONS OF YOUR PRELESSON WRITING TO YOUR POSTLESSON SAMPLE.

[Hand out Activity 1-6.] You will have a scavenger hunt as you learn to improve your handwriting. Write each of the following letters on the lines on top of the sheet I've given you (Activity 1-6). **[Write the letters you want students to learn on the chalkboard or overhead transparency and have them copy them on the first few lines of Activity 1-6.]** Watch how I make each letter. Notice the size of each part of the letter. Notice the direction of the first stroke I make. This determines the slant of the letter. Notice how large the circle is and the length of each straight line. **[Allow students 5 minutes to practice on the top section of Activity 1-6].**

Now that you have practiced your handwriting, you are going to work on it a little longer and complete a special activity. Autumn is the season in which the length of daylight and nighttime hours is almost equal. Daylight lasts about 12 hours and 8 minutes; nighttime lasts about 11 hours and 52 minutes. The autumn season begins on or about September 23 with the autumn equinox. It is on this day that the sun crosses the equator, and the day and night are equal length. To celebrate the autumn equinox, we are going to divide into teams and have a scavenger treasure hunt. The group that finds the most items on their list wins. The team that has the most improved handwriting on the list will receive a prize also.

Before you begin your scavenger hunt, you will have 10 minutes to think of five objects a group could find, but would really have to search for on our school grounds. **[You may wish to write five things on the board that you want all groups to find instead.]** You will describe each of these items in a separate sentence. Write these sentences on the middle section of your sheet. Use what you just practiced in handwriting, so you can improve your handwriting. When you've finished, raise your hand so I can read them. **[When you read them, you are checking to be sure each item can be found on the school grounds, so all groups will have an equal chance on the scavenger hunt. You will also be checking handwriting.]**

Now we will divide into groups of four. Each group will receive four lists made by members of another group. **[Divide into teams and exchange lists.]** Each group has 20 minutes to find the twenty items on the four lists you have received. **[Dismiss the groups and tell them that the first group to find all items or the most items in the allotted time wins. Have each group appoint a timekeeper and specify where groups are to meet at the end.]**

[Once the time has elapsed, check the number of items each group found. The group who found the most items wins. Give the first prize. Then hand each student his or her prelesson writing sample.] Now that you have your prewriting sample, compare your handwriting on Activity 1-6 to the sample. Score one point for each letter in Activity 1-6 that has a better shape than similar letters on the prewriting sample. Record this score on the line marked "Points for Improved Shape" on the bottom of Activity 1-6. Then count the number of improvements in letter size in the same way, and put the count at the bottom of the same page. **[The total number of improved size of letters would be computed in the same way and written on the line designated "Points for Improved Size." The same process would occur for scoring "Points for Improved Slant."]** Now total the number of improvements (or add these to the number made by the other members of your team. **[Compare the totals. The group that has the most points wins the second award.]**

ANSWER KEY

The correct shape of manuscript letters should adhere to the system your district has selected. The correct slant of manuscript is vertical. The correct shape of cursive letters should adhere to the system your district has selected. The correct slant is at a 45-degree angle.

MODIFICATIONS FOR GRADE LEVELS AND STUDENT ABILITY LEVELS

For Kindergarten and First Grade, use only one type of letter, such as *c, o,* and *a,* and do not practice writing sentences. *For Second Grade and Slower Learning Groups,* the sentences to be used on the scavenger hunt could be dictated or written on the board. Students would then copy them. *For Third through Eighth Grades, Average or Slower Learners,* you can modify the lesson based on the number of letters you introduce in practice. *For Gifted Students and/or Good Writers,* you could modify this lesson to introduce calligraphy, by inviting a parent or friend to teach it, or use word processing for parts of the lesson.

You may wish to use the newsletter on page 23 for additional handwriting practice. You could select certain students to handwrite the newsletter as opposed to having it typed. You could also use the newsletter as an award for the most improved or best handwritten set of statements in this activity.

STUDENTS WHO WILL BE WORKING ON OTHER PROJECTS OR LESSONS: _____

NOTES FOR FUTURE USE: _____

ACTIVITY 1-6

HANDWRITING TREASURE HUNT

AaBbCcDdEeFfGgHhIiJjKkLlMmNnOoPpQq

Form to Grade Handwriting Improvement

Name_____   Date_____

Items to be Located on the Treasure Hunt

1. _____
2. _____
3. _____
4. _____
5. _____

Learning Points Grading Sytem

Points For Improved Shape_____
Points For Improved Size_____
Points For Improving Slant_____

Total Points_____
Total Group Points_____

write it down

Composition Skill Development: How to Build a Good Story

TIME REQUIRED

Teacher Directed Page (Activity 1-7): 10–20 minutes for three consecutive days or as a unit. The information in this lesson can be used in several different ways over many days if you prefer.

Student Discovery Page (Activity 1-8): As much time as you wish to extend for students to complete their creative writing stories and newspaper stories. It is suggested that you teach openings, middles, and endings of stories on separated days.

TEACHING STRATEGIES

Students will apply what they learn to an event that occurred in class. This strategy enables them to use new ideas and knowledge more readily in their own lives. Students will also use imagery and visualization to "see" a good story. Each student will write a Class Tribune to take home. Students choose two of their friends' stories to include in their Class Tribune.

ACTIVITY 1-7 _____

BACK TO SCHOOL NEWSLETTER

[OBJECTIVE] YOU WILL LEARN HOW TO WRITE OPENING, BEGINNING, MIDDLE, AND ENDING SECTIONS OF A STORY. YOU WILL KNOW YOU HAVE LEARNED WHEN YOU ARE PROUD OF YOUR STORY AND YOU IDENTIFY ONE SECTION OF STORIES THAT YOU WRITE MORE CLEARLY.

We are going to learn how to write good stories. You will know that you have learned when others tell you that one part of your story was so well done that, because of it, they wanted to read more.

After we finish our lesson, you may want to write a second story for homework. Tomorrow you will write a story for a Class Tribune newspaper to take home. You will also revise your story in pairs.

We are writing a newspaper to celebrate American Newspaper Week, which is the week of September 25th. On September 25, 1690, the first American newspaper was published. Also, 243 years later, on September 4, 1833, the first boy was hired as a newscarrier. Before then, all newscarriers were men. To celebrate people who have founded and worked on newspapers, we will write our class newspaper and learn to write good newspaper stories.

Let's learn how to write a good opening sentence.

To write a good opening sentence in a story, you can do one of three things:

1. *Begin the first paragraph with a question that states your main idea.* For example, if I want to write about the things I most appreciated about my teachers, I could begin my story with a question such as: "Was your favorite teacher just like mine?"

2. *Personalize the first sentence by using the word "you/I."* You can also personalize your opening sentence by referring to a common idea. For example,

I could begin my first sentence by saying: "You may have a favorite teacher, and then again you may not," or "We all have had a favorite teacher who taught us more than the subject. I wonder what makes some teachers 'Great.'"

3. *Say something that sounds strange, not logical.* For example, "My favorite teacher didn't know how to talk."

After you have written a good opening, you can:

1. *Describe the setting, characters, and several acts that lead to the main point of your writing.*

2. *Tell the readers what you are going to tell them.* For example, if I combined a beginning with one of the opening sentences above, my story could start like this: "Was your favorite teacher like mine? I want to describe the things he did that were important to me."

3. *Tell a mini-story that introduces the main point you will make in your writing.* For example, "We all have a favorite teacher. My favorite teacher caused me to become a teacher myself! I write this story to show how teachers do many things to help their students become the best."

To make the middle of your writing more interesting, you can:

1. *Make the main points in an outline form.* To do this, at the beginning of each paragraph you can use words such as "First," "Second," "Next," and "Finally."

2. *You can give one of your main points in one paragraph and then support that point with several paragraphs;* or

3. *You can make two main points and support each with a paragraph of details and facts. Then you can show how these two main points, in combination, lead to the final point you will make.* For example, in the middle of your writing you could state that, in students' opinion, good teachers listen well. In your second paragraph you could state that the best teachers spend more time helping students. You combine these two points for your third paragraph by saying that these two qualities come together to make one of the most important qualities of outstanding teachers (for example, "A good teacher supports students so they can learn rapidly").

To write better endings to your story, you can:

1. *Restate the main point and find a quotation by a famous person to support that point;* or

2. *Summarize the main points;* or

3. *Give the main point and then tell the readers what they could do with the information in the future.* For example, you could end your writing by saying: "Great teachers do specific things that make them special to their students. You might ask your friends if they like the same things about their teachers that I do."

Now let's practice what we've learned. You will have _____ minutes to write a story based on the following suggestions or on a topic of your choice. You will write your first draft today. It could become your lead story in the Class Tribune. Write a good opening, beginning, middle, and ending to your story.

1. *Characters.* You may select one or more characters for your story:

your favorite teacher or person

a girl and/or boy who have ESP

a girl and/or boy who can read minds

a girl and/or boy with superhuman strength

a dog, cat, or other animal who can talk

a person who is only one inch tall

a cowgirl or cowboy in the Wild West in 1890

a good Samaritan who stops a bank robbery

a lost dog looking for its owner 1,000 miles away

2. *Situations.* You may select one or more for your story:

the police need help solving a baffling case

the student never missed a question on a test

a strange voice was heard at the back of the cave

the matchbox was just the right size for a bed

the horses were getting restless

someone overheard a robbery plot

it seemed as if the animal had been walking for days

3. *Facts.* Examples you can include in your middle section:

a small, twin-engine plane keeps losing altitude

someone is groping around in a dark area and one last match is the only hope

two candy bars, chewing gum, and stale potato chips

_____

GRADING CRITERIA: _____

_____

EARLY FINISHERS

Early finishers could type, handwrite, or use word processing to complete the newsletter.

MODIFICATIONS FOR GRADE LEVELS AND STUDENT ABILITY LEVELS

For Kindergarten, First Grade, Second Grade, and Slower Learning Groups, the newspaper and student discovery activities are completed as a language-experience activity. Students dictate the newspaper to you to write. *For Third through Eighth Grades, Average and Slower Learning Students,* the activity can be completed as is or you can teach only one section a day. Students who need additional practice could write several stories as homework. *For Gifted Writers,* this activity could be read independently. Then these students could create more extensive writings to submit for publication in a national journal. A list of appropriate journals can be found in *Helping Students Improve Their Creative Writing and National Journals That Publish Student Works,* which can be purchased from Educational Research Dissemination, P.O. Box 161354, Fort Worth, TX 76161.

NOTES FOR FUTURE USE: _____
_____

ACTIVITY 1-8

NEWSPAPER STORIES

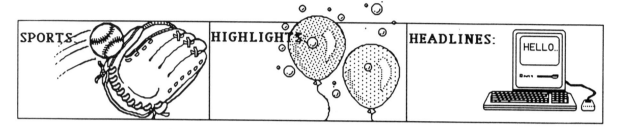

SPORTS   HIGHLIGHTS: HEADLINES: HELLO..

CLASS TRIBUNE

DATE:		PLACE:		PRICE:	

BIRTHDAYS
THIS MONTH:

_____
_____
_____
_____
_____

LEAD STORIES:

_____
_____
_____
_____
_____
_____
_____
_____
_____

Bozo The Clown

WANTED FOR

_____
_____
_____
_____
_____
_____

Skill Development: How to Speak Before Groups

TIME REQUIRED

Teacher Directed Page (Activity 1-9): 30 minutes per day for several days, if you wish

Student Discovery Page (Activity 1-10): 30 minutes

TEACHING STRATEGIES

Students will learn to use brainstorming as a method of learning. Younger students will learn to work in pairs, while older students also use peer teaching and editing.

ACTIVITY 1-9 _____

SPEECHES FOR SPECIAL DAYS: LEARNING HOW TO SPEAK BEFORE A GROUP

[OBJECTIVE]   YOU CAN DEVELOP CONFIDENCE TO SPEAK BEFORE GROUPS. TODAY YOU WILL LEARN THE RULES OF EFFECTIVE FORMAL AND INFORMAL SPEAKING. YOU WILL KNOW YOU HAVE LEARNED TO SPEAK BETTER IF SOMEONE COMMENTS POSITIVELY UPON YOUR SPEECH OF IF YOU PRESENT YOUR POINTS CLEARLY.

Learning to speak before a group is not difficult. Today you will learn to speak before a group and not be afraid. To begin, let's brainstorm about what makes a good speaker. Think of a person to whom you really enjoy listening. Think of someone in your family, a close friend, or someone on television who speaks well. What makes this person's speaking so interesting? **[Brainstorm with the students and write their suggestions on the chalkboard or overhead transparency. Hand out Activity 1-10.]** From the list we made together, write two or three characteristics you most want to develop. Write these on the first three lines of the page I've given you (Activity 1-10). In a few minutes you will have an opportunity to practice these qualities. You will know you've learned to be a better speaker if by the time you finish giving your speech people understand you and you made your points clearly.

Today we will learn rules for good speeches and talk about ways of developing self-confidence.

TEN STEPS TO IMPROVE YOUR SPEAKING

1. *Choose your topic by selecting something you know a lot about.* Select something for which others compliment you.

2. *Jot down a few notes in advance of your talk.*

3. *When you begin your speech, build on things others have told you that you do well.* For example, if others have told you that you are a very happy person, smile often; if people have told you that you have a good sense of humor, add a joke as an example; or if people have commented that you remember details well, include at least three specific points in your talk.

4. *If you get nervous, think about how much you want to help the people to whom you are talking and how many good things you want them to know.* This will help you to be less nervous.

5. *Speak slower than you would in normal conversation.* It takes longer for a large group of people to comprehend a speech than if you were in a small group. This is because they cannot see your gestures and facial expressions easily.

6. *When your audience appears to be losing interest, modify your speech.* To do so, you can give a summary of your key points. You can also use one of the techniques you learned about writing good story endings (Activity 1-7).

7. *Practice giving your speech aloud.* Do not read your notecards.

8. *Before you begin, try to notice something about the audience or the location that you can include in your speech.* Because of this, the audience will more easily feel that your speech was made specifically for them.

9. *To relax, remember that you will give a better speech if you enjoy giving it.* You have something important to share. Most people do not know about your points. The people in your audience will not be critical if you are prepared. Your audience is giving their time and attention. For this reason, you should not try to think on your feet, or use only charm and personality to earn their affection and respect.

10. *End your speech with a one- to three-point summary.* You could close with a catchy quotation or statement that pulls your main points together.

DEVELOPING CONFIDENCE

1. When giving a speech, pick out a few people on *both* sides of the room and look at them. Turning your head back and forth will make it seem as if you are looking at all of the audience. **[Either ask the class to tell other ways they increase their confidence, or follow suggestion 2 or 3.]**

2. [Ask a student to stand in front of the group for 30 seconds. The student leaves the room and the group changes three things. The student then returns.] You have 30 seconds to find three changes we have made. **[This exercise reduces the student's fear of standing before a group.]**

3. Each of you will tell us something important you have learned. It can be something funny, something important to you, something of interest from television or a book, or a skill or hobby you have. **[In this way students build confidence and learn how much easier it can be to speak before a group when a person has something important to say.]**

Now you will prepare a speech, using a special event from the following list or a topic of particular interest to you. You may write a description of the topic, a story based on your own experiences, or a make-believe story related to the topic.

TOPICS

Labor Day: The first Monday in September. It was made a public holiday, by Public Law 90-363, in 1894.

National Grandparents Day: This is a day to celebrate our grandparents, held the first Sunday in September that follows Labor Day.

International Day of Peace: The third Sunday of September is the opening day of the regular sessions of the United Nations General Assembly and is observed as the International Day of Peace. It is designed to commemorate and strengthen the ideals of peace for all nations.

Mayflower Day: Anniversary of the departure of the Mayflower, from Plymouth, England, September 16, 1620.

Citizenship Day: September 17 is Citizenship Day and a part of Constitution Week.

World Gratitude Day: September 21 is the day set aside for the purpose of uniting all people to create a world community.

Anniversary of the Discovery of the Planet Neptune: Neptune was first observed on September 23, 1846. Neptune is 2,796,700,000 miles from the sun, it is the eighth planet from the sun, and it takes 164.8 years to revolve around it. Neptune is 1,000 miles in diameter (as compared to the Earth's diameter of 7,927 miles).

Rosh Hashanah or the Jewish New Year: On or about September 24 is the beginning of ten days of repentance and spiritual renewal for Jewish people.

National Good Neighbor Day: September 27 is set aside to build a nation and world that cares. The purpose is to enhance our appreciation for and understanding of all of Earth's peoples.

GRADING CRITERIA

You may wish to use the form that appears at the end of this chapter.

EARLY FINISHERS

Those who finish early can write letters to their favorite local celebrities and ask them what they did to improve their speaking ability. They could also write to the movie star and comedian Steve Allen (in care of McGraw-Hill Publishers, 1221 Avenue of the Americas, New York, NY 10020), because he wrote a book entitled *How to Give a Speech* (1987). The students could ask Mr. Allen to help them solve a problem they have in giving speeches.

MODIFICATIONS FOR GRADE LEVELS AND STUDENT ABILITY LEVELS

For Kindergarten and First-Grade Students, do not do Activity 1-9, and complete Activity 1-10 as an oral activity in which students make one outline together. When Activity 1-10 is completed, a student can volunteer to give the speech composed by the class to the rest of the class. *For Second-Graders and Slower Learning Groups,* guide students to complete one speech as a class. Then have them work in pairs, writing a speech for themselves. Once the paired speeches are written, one of the pair can give the speech before the class. *For*

Third-Graders through Eighth-Graders, students can do this activity as written and/or they can make their own list of skills for better speeches. For Gifted and Self-Directed Students, you can tape record their speeches. Then, one or more students can be selected to transcribe and mail their speeches to the World Gratitude Society (where awards are given), the United Nations General Assembly, or The White House, to share their thoughts (address given on page 3). Students can also do library research about their topics. Activity 1-10 can also be used as an introduction to, or review of, outlining skills, notetaking, and/or formal writing of reports.

NAME _____ DATE _____

ACTIVITY 1-10

LEARNING TO GIVE GOOD SPEECHES

What the best speakers you know do: _____

_____

_____

_____

Title of Your Speech:

_____

_____

Outline of Three Main Points
and Two Details to Support
Each Main Point

Introductory Sentence:

I.

   A.

   B.

II.

   A.

   B.

III.

   A.

   B.

Concluding Statements:

- -

Comments you wish to make about the speeches made by others
in your class:

  1.

  2.

  3.

  4.

  5.

Grammar Skill Development: Teaching the Parts of Speech

TIME REQUIRED

Teacher Directed Exploration (Activity 1-11): 20 minutes if used as an overview, or it can become a week-long unit

Student Discovery Page (Activity 1-12): 20–40 minutes

TEACHING STRATEGIES

Students will learn to use a retelling of what they have learned to increase their use and retention of information. They will also tell the reason for the answers they give, which will strengthen their thinking skills. The third teaching strategy is to use a game to practice the lesson's objectives.

ACTIVITY 1-11

NATIVE AMERICAN POWWOW GAME

September is the month in which we honor Native Americans. Many tribes, such as the Potawatomi, Navajo, Seminole, Miccosukee, and Creek celebrate their heritage in special ways. Nationally, September 2 has been designated as Native American Day. To celebrate, ceremonial dances are held in Taos, New Mexico (September 29 and 30); the Trail of Courage Rendezvous occurs in Kansas (September 19–20); Arizona holds a Navajo tribal fair and powwow; New York holds a Mountain Eagle Indian Festival; Texas hosts the National Championship for Tepee Construction and Native American food; New Jersey celebrates the National Indian Art Show; Oklahoma hosts an Indian Day; Florida has a Native American Heritage Festival; and North Dakota has a United Tribes Powwow.

One of the strongest Native American traditions is to share important information and beliefs with other members of the tribe. These traditions are shared through oral stories, with older tribal members telling stories to younger relatives. In this way, younger members learn the most important facts about their tribe.

Today you are going to learn how to use this important method of learning. That is, as the Native Americans learned long ago, if you tell someone else what you have learned, you will remember it longer.

[OBJECTIVE] YOU WILL LEARN THE PURPOSE AND CORRECT USAGE OF SEVERAL PARTS OF SPEECH. YOU WILL KNOW YOU HAVE LEARNED WHEN YOU COMPLETE THE NATIONAL DOGS WEEK WORD-PARTS GAME WITH 80% SUCCESS.

Now you are going to learn three or four things about English words. If after our lesson you can tell a classmate about these words, you will have learned well today.

One reason there are so many words in our language is that each can do only specific types of things to help people know your thoughts. If you understand the things each word does, you can select the exact word you need. People will also enjoy listening to you more.

To learn four kinds of words, read or listen to the next paragraphs and remember them. You will tell a story about what you learned when we finish.

Conjunctions are the English words that connect two words and thoughts together.

1. Conjunctions join two words together so they describe one thing. The main conjunctions are "and," "or," "nor," and "but." When you use conjunctions, you can use fewer words. For example, because our language has conjunctions, you can say "My dog is black and white." If our language did not have conjunctions, you would have to say "My dog is black." "My dog is white."

2. Conjunctions can come between two nouns, two verbs, two adjectives, and two phrases. For example, a conjunction could come between the words "dog" and "cat" because these two words are nouns. When you see two words joined together by "and," they are both the same type of word. For example, you will never say: "The dog and running" because "dog" is a noun and "running" is a verb. "Dog" and "running" are not the same type of word.

3. Conjunctions make it possible for us to say things in less time. You can combine all the adjectives you want to say about something in one sentence. This is important because listeners will not become bored.

4. Conjunctions should not be the first word in a sentence.

To see if you understand what conjunctions are, identify the conjunctions in this sentence: "Which do you like best as pets, cats or dogs?"
Nouns are words that do these three things.

1. Nouns are the names of people, places, things, ideas, and feelings.

2. Nouns are the only English words that can be capitalized in the middle or at the end of a sentence.

3. Nouns are the only words that can be described by numbers, colors, and sizes (one *dog*, more *dogs*, brown *dog*, biggest *dog*).

To see if you understand what nouns are, identify all the nouns in this sentence: "The largest dog Bill ever saw was in the yard."
Verbs are the English words that do these three things:

1. Verbs tell what a noun is doing or are one of the words "is," "am," "was," "were," "seems," "looks," "feels."

2. Verbs are the only words that can end in *ed* to show that what you are talking about already happened.

3. Verbs are the only words that match the number of nouns in a sentence. Verbs are often singular to show that only one noun is being discussed (for example, an *s* is added to the verb), or plural to show that more than one noun is being discussed (an *s* is not added to the verb).

To see if you understand what verbs are, identify the verbs in this sentence: "The dogs ran past the baby who was asleep."
Adjectives are the English words that do these three things:

1. Adjectives describe nouns.

2. Adjectives tell what the noun is like, so you know exactly which noun is being described.

3. Adjectives take the form of numbers like "three," and tell how many nouns there are.

To see if you understand what adjectives are, identify all the adjectives in this sentence:

"Four large, brown dogs were playing together in the green meadow."

Check your answers to the four sentences:

Conjunctions—or

Nouns—dog, Bill, yard

Verbs—ran, was

Adjectives—four, large, brown, green

Now let's pretend you are at an Indian powwow. You are the oldest member in your tribe. You are responsible for telling the other members what you learned. Turn to a classmate and tell that person what you just learned. When you finish, your partner will tell you what he or she learned about conjunctions, nouns, verbs, and adjectives.

ANSWER KEY

The answers to the National Dogs Week Game (Activity 1-12) are:

1. large (or big), adjective

2. and, conjunction

3. is, verb

4. ran, verb

5. dogs, noun

6. or, conjunction

7. small (or short), adjective

8. and, conjunction

9. puppy, noun

10. green, adjective

11. correct as is

12. correct as is

GRADING CRITERIA: _____

_____

MODIFICATIONS FOR GRADE LEVELS AND STUDENT ABILITY LEVELS

Research suggests that teaching parts of speech may not improve writing ability. Many teachers, however, value Activities 1-11 and 1-12 and teach the parts of speech for a variety of other reasons. Activities 1-11 and 1-12 (and Activities 5-11 and 5-12) provide a concise means of introducing the parts of speech. Such instruction strengthens students' knowledge base and improves oral speaking ability. You can direct both activities orally. Activity 1-12 can be completed individually or in pairs, teams, small groups, or (for younger grades) as a whole class. *For Kindergarten, First, and Second Grades and Slower Learning Groups,* you can teach only one part of speech, turning this activity into an introduction and overview lesson. *For Third through Eighth Grades, Non–self Directed Students, Average, or Slower Learning Students,* you can teach Activity 1-11 and work Activity 1-12 with the students divided into teams or small groups. *For Gifted Students and Self-directed Students in Grades Two through Eight,* you can allow students to act as the teacher for both activities. You may decide to allow the "winning students" of this activity to have the award of writing for Indian arrowheads or to receive Native American music recordings, using these addresses:

Southwestern Minerals, Inc.
7008 Central Avenue, S.E.
Albuquerque, NM 87108

Museum of the American Indian
Heye Foundation
Broadway at 155th Street
New York, NY 10022

NOTES FOR FUTURE USE: _____

_____

NAME _____   DATE _____

NATIONAL DOGS WEEK WORD-PARTS GAME

National Dogs Week is the fourth week in September. We will use this event to improve your grammar. The objective of this activity is to help you learn what conjunctions, nouns, verbs, and adjectives are. You will know you have learned well if you score 9 of 12 correctly on the National Dogs Week Word-Parts Game on the back of this page.

The purpose of this game is to test your ability to recognize if sentences are correct and to name the four parts of speech we've studied. Begin at section number 1. Each number has two blanks. If the sentence is correct, you do nothing in the blanks and move on to the next number. If the sentence is not complete, you write a word to make the sentence complete in the first blank. Write this word beside number 1. In the second blank you write the name of the part of speech of the word you added. Continue until you finish all twelve sections.

Your teacher will tell you what to do when you finish. Your teacher may ask you to meet with one or more of your classmates to discuss your answers. Your teacher may give you the answer key to grade your own. You may write to one of the companies for information about next month's activities, or to the National Society for the Prevention of Cruelty to Animals:

Norma Terris Human
Education Center
P.O. Box 362, East
Haddon, CT 06423

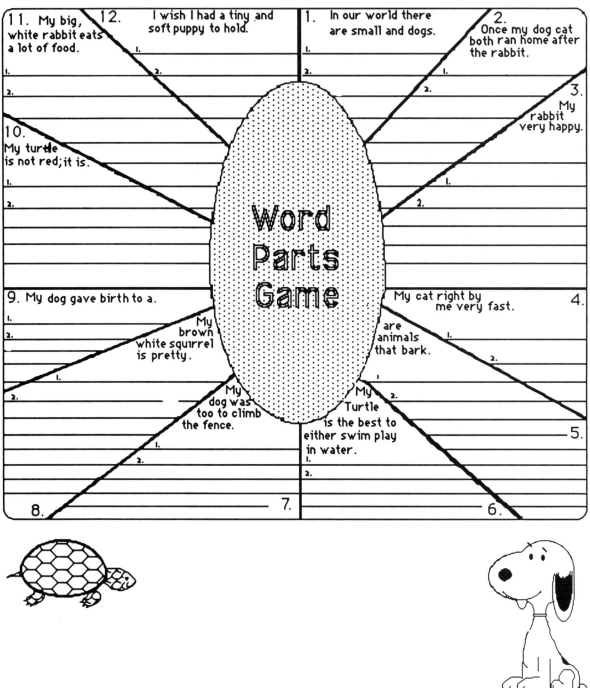

11. My big, white rabbit eats a lot of food.

1. _____

2. _____

12. I wish I had a tiny and soft puppy to hold.

1. _____

2. _____

1. In our world there are small and dogs.

1. _____

2. _____

2. Once my dog cat both ran home after the rabbit.

1. _____

2. _____

3. My rabbit very happy.

1. _____

2. _____

10. My turtle is not red; it is.

1. _____

2. _____

Word Parts Game

9. My dog gave birth to a.

1. _____

2. _____

My brown white squirrel is pretty.

1. _____

2. _____

My cat right by me very fast.

_____

are animals that bark.

1. _____

2. _____

4. _____

My dog was too to climb the fence.

1. _____

2. _____

My Turtle is the best to either swim play in water.

1. _____

2. _____

My _____

2. _____

5. _____

8. _____

7. _____

6. _____

Listening Skill Development: Learning to Listen Carefully to Details and to Follow Directions

TIME REQUIRED

Teacher Directed Exploration (Activity 1-13): 30 minutes

Student Discovery Page (Activity 1-14): to be done as part of the teacher-directed activity

TEACHING STRATEGIES

Students will learn through examples and nonexamples of a concept. Students will learn a second strategy of comparing their own preinstructional work sample to a postinstructional sample. Also, students will learn by setting their own goal as to how they want to improve their listening skills by October.

ACTIVITY 1-13 _____

SEPTEMBER'S SPORTS CENTER AND LISTENING SKILLS CONTEST

[OBJECTIVE] YOU WILL LEARN SIX METHODS TO INCREASE YOUR LISTENING SKILLS. YOU WILL KNOW YOU HAVE IMPROVED WHEN THE SECOND DRAWING YOU DO IS BETTER THAN THE FIRST.

There are eleven types of sports celebrated in September. As you learn about these sports events, you will develop skills that improve your listening ability. You will begin by making a drawing. Then you will make a second drawing after you've worked on your listening skills. If your second drawing is better than the first, you'll know you have improved your listening ability.

Let's begin by dividing into pairs. Each person in the pair will receive a picture from me. You are going to try to draw the picture your partner describes without seeing the picture and by using the oral directions your partner gives. Your partner will not tell you what the object is. Descriptions will include sentences that tell how to draw a line or how to make a circle at a certain point. Once you finish drawing your picture, you will describe a picture to your partner. **[Duplicate enough copies of Figure 1-4 or pictures from textbook you are using so every student has one picture].** Begin now. **[Allow 5 minutes per person for the drawing and a few minutes to compare their results with the original.]**

[Hand out Activity 1-14.] How similar your drawing was to what your partner wanted you to draw may be related to how well you can listen to instructions. This page (Activity 1-14) will give you tips about good listening. **[Give older students 5–10 minutes to go over the material; for younger or slower learning students, go over the six steps as a whole group.]**

Now, to practice using good listening skills, you are to find a picture in your textbook of an easy object to draw and describe it to your partner, just as we did before. Your partner must not know what the picture is. Once the first person finishes his or her picture, the second person will describe a picture to the first person. Practice using the skills of listening for key words, picturing in your mind what is being said, and asking the person questions. **[Allow a few minutes to find a picture and 5 minutes per person for drawing.]** Compare

FIGURE 1-4

Compare the second picture to the first you drew. If it is better, you will have improved your ability to listen.

To complete our work today, on a piece of paper write today's date. Now set a goal that you could accomplish by the end of the month to become a better listener. When you write your goal, describe what you want to improve upon and how you want to improve it. When you finish, turn it in to me. I will give it back in one month to see if you reached your goal.

GRADING CRITERIA: _____

MODIFICATIONS FOR GRADE LEVELS AND STUDENT ABILITY LEVELS

For Kindergarten, First Grade, Second Grade, and Slower Learners, instead of breaking into pairs, students stay together for the entire activity and you model a drawing for the entire class, such as orally describing an umbrella for them to draw. Then, after you teach the lesson, students draw one sports object from Figure 1-4 or a textbook picture as you describe it to them. Then, the person who does the best job can be designated as the leader and describe another object for the class. You can continue in this manner, using each of the objects from the Sports Center figure or other textbook pictures until most students have demonstrated that they have increased their listening skills. *For Third through Eighth Grades,* students can do the activity without modifications.

NOTES FOR FUTURE USE: _____

ACTIVITY 1-14

LISTENING SKILLS

Now we are going to learn six steps to improve your listening ability. When we are finished you will draw a second picture to see if it looks more like the intended object. If it does, your listening skills have improved.

SIX STEPS TO IMPROVING LISTENING SKILLS

In the future you can improve your listening ability by doing the following six things:

1. As soon as you begin to listen, try to hear the sentence that tells what the subject is, ask yourself what the total focus of the person's talk is. Pick the most important details the person will say.
2. Pay close attention to all words that tell directions such as north, south, east, west or up, down, here, there, over, under, above. As soon as you hear such a word picture it in your mind.
3. Listen for the words that signal order, such as first, second, last, after, before and also. Try to put yourself in the place of the person speaking and in, your mind, perform the order of the activities he/she is describing.
4. As you listen picture what is described. This mental picture will help you distinguish the most important details and how they relate together. As you hear each detail tie it to the detail immediately preceeding it. The person talking had a very important reason for putting these details together and you have to be thinking what that reason is.
5. Pay special attention to words such as and, or, but, yet, and because. These words tell you how two ideas are related to each other.
6. Ask questions of the person talking to clarify the points being made.

Now to practice using good listening skills, find a picture in your textbook and describe it to your partner. They will do the same for you.

Healthy! Exciting! Educational!

Enjoyable! Friendly! Great!

fun! *!nuƒ*

The following form can be used to assess students' progress as they work Activity 1-9 and at several additional times throughout the year.

NAME _____   DATE _____

FORM TO GRADE SPEECHES

Name of Speaker_____   Date of Speech_____

Place a check in each blank that describes the speech.

_____Spoke loudly enough
_____Spoke slowly enough
_____Looked at audience

_____Related enough details to
keep interest but not too
many
_____Appeared to be relaxed
_____Appeared to have confidence
and to know the subject
_____Good introduction that
made you want to listen
_____Good closing; helped you
remember the main points
_____Did not read notecards
_____Had practiced the speech enough
and had good expression
_____Tone of voice was good; it was
not too nasal

_____Voice was easy to listen to
_____No nervous gestures, such as
using hands in distracting
ways or using a word or phrase
over and over ("uh', O,K.,
"Do you understand?", etc.)
_____Speech met its purpose of
informing, persuading or
entertaining
_____Speaker seemed to have a special
style or talent in giving
speeches and that special
talent was_____
_____Speech was just the right length
_._Speech was well organized and
the speaker stuck to the
important points
_____Pitch was good as voice was not
too high or too low

Strengths and special qualities of the speaker:

Improvements you suggest:

Methods to improve that you suggest:

_____
Rater's Signature

CHAPTER
2 *October*

October is a month of exciting and diverse holidays. As a matter of fact, October has a greater number and variety of events than any other month of the year. Many events help people remember important historical happenings. Others, such as Halloween, are celebrated just for fun.

During this month we will use Columbus Day, the end of daylight savings time, National Poetry Day, United Nations Day, Fire Prevention Week, Charlie Brown's birthday, and Halloween as our lesson themes.

Scope and Sequence of Language Arts Skills Taught in October

Speaking (Activities 2-1 and 2-2): Students will learn to engage in effective oral discussion.

Grammar (Activities 2-3 and 2-4): Students will learn rules to improve their grammar in conversation and writing.

Composition (Activities 2-5 and 2-6): Students will write details using who, what, where, when, why, and how for Charlie Brown's birthday celebration.

Reading (Activities 2-7 and 2-8): Students will read a selection and then learn how to compare and contrast ideas and details while reading.

Listening (Activities 2-9 and 2-10): Students will study different reasons for listening, especially discerning fact from opinion.

Spelling (Activities 2-11 and 2-12): Students will learn to build words by using Greek and Latin roots.

Handwriting (Activities 2-13 and 2-14): Children will use picture associations to improve letter shape.

Additional Supplementary Activities for October

The following activities can be used in a wide variety of ways to extend the lessons of October.

1. Students can write to any of the following businesses to receive more information about the special events that occur in October.

Walt Disney World Anniversary
Publicity Department
Walt Disney World
Box 40
Lake Buena Vista, FL 32830

National Fire Protection Association
Batterymarch Park
Quincy, MA 02269

American Food Service Association
4104 E. Cliff
Denver, CO 80222

The local fire department

National Pretzel Bakers' Institute
800 New Holland Ave.
Box 1433
Lancaster, PA 17603

International Apple Institute
c/o HJK & A
Helen Sullivan/Judi Lewis
2233 Wisconsin Ave.
Washington, DC 20007

Zoofest
North Carolina Zooligical Park
Route 4, Box 83
Asheboro, NC 27203

Spectacle of the Geese
Convention and Visitors Bureau
207 N. Main St.
Fond de Lac, WI 54935

Universal Children's Day
UNICEF
No. 3 United Nations Plaza
New York, NY 10017

National Book Council
175 Fifth Ave.
New York, NY 10010

The White House
1600 Pennsylvania Ave.
Washington, DC 20500

2. Students may use library resources to find details about Columbus's voyages, identify causes of the Great Chicago Fire, locate information about Charles Schultz, or learn why Walt Disney was so successful and what was so unusual about his death.

3. The following activities can be used by students with special needs and for students who have inadequate prelesson abilities to complete an October lesson successfully.

1. At the beginning of the month, start with the word "Halloween" and see how many different words can be made using the letters in this word. Students must complete the papers in class; they cannot be taken home. At the end of the month the child with the most words receives a reward. Require each word to have a definition. If a student doesn't know the meaning of the word, the word cannot be counted.

2. Have the children make a bulletin board of such items as cats, witches, ghosts, pumpkins, scarecrows, and haunted houses. You could require that everything put on the bulletin board have a capital letter as its main part.

3. Students whose birthdays fall in October can be given a treat to celebrate their birthdays. This assignment could be one of their choice, assigned in lieu of another lesson; or students can be given time in class to learn about a famous person born on or around their birth date.

The following notable people were born in October on the dates given:

1. Julie Andrews, Jimmy Carter, Tom Bosley
2. Mahatma Gandhi, Groucho Marx, Sting
3. Chubby Checker, Gore Vidal
4. Charlton Heston, Rutherford B. Hayes
5. Ray Kroc, Bob Geldof
6. Carole Lombard, Janet Gaynor
7. Yo-Yo Ma, Ludmila Turischeva, John Cougar Mellencamp
8. Rona Barrett, Jesse Jackson
9. John Lennon, Jackson Browne
10. Helen Hayes, Martina Navratilova, David Lee Roth, Tanya Tucker
11. Eleanor Roosevelt, Jerome Robbins, John Candy, Daryl Hall
12. Luciano Pavarotti, Joan Rivers
13. Lenny Bruce, Margaret Thatcher, Marie Osmond
14. Lillian Gish, Ralph Lauren, Harry Anderson
15. Jim Palmer, Lee Iacocca, Linda Lavin
16. Oscar Wilde, Angela Lansbury, Noah Webster, Suzanne Somers
17. Rita Hayworth, Evel Knievel, Margot Kidder
18. Pierre Elliott Trudeau, Erin Moran, George C. Scott, Vincent Spano
19. Martha Jefferson, John Le Carre, Robert Reed
20. Bela Lugosi, Joyce Brothers
21. Dizzy Gillespie, Whitney Ford
22. Annette Funicello, Catherine Deneuve, Jeff Goldblum
23. Sarah Bernhardt, Johnny Carson
24. Bill Wyman, Kevin Kline
25. Pablo Picasso, Minnie Pearl
26. François Mitterand, Jaclyn Smith, Pat Sajak
27. Theodore Roosevelt, Carrie Snodgrass
28. Jonas Salk, Bruce Jenner, Charlie Daniels
29. Fanny Brice, Richard Dreyfuss
30. Charles Atlas, Grace Slick, Emily Post
31. Dan Rather, John Keats, Barbara Bel Geddes, David Ogden Stiers, Dale Evans

The October calendar can be used in many ways, as discussed in Chapter 1.

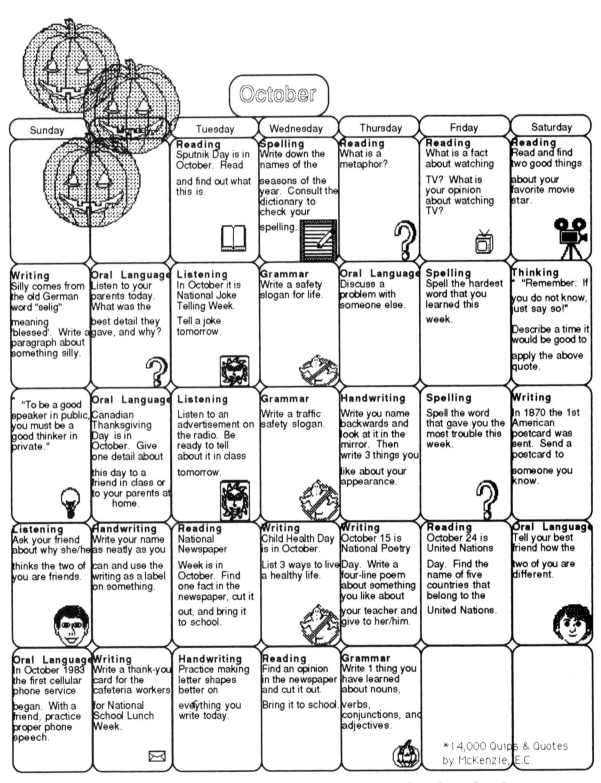

October

Sunday	Monday	Tuesday	Wednesday	Thursday	Friday	Saturday
		Reading Sputnik Day is in October. Read and find out what this is.	**Spelling** Write down the names of the seasons of the year. Consult the dictionary to check your spelling.	**Reading** What is a metaphor?	**Reading** What is a fact about watching TV? What is your opinion about watching TV?	**Reading** Read and find two good things about your favorite movie star.
Writing Silly comes from the old German word "selig" meaning 'blessed'. Write a paragraph about something silly.	**Oral Language** Listen to your parents today. What was the best detail they gave, and why?	**Listening** In October it is National Joke Telling Week. Tell a joke tomorrow.	**Grammar** Write a safety slogan for life.	**Oral Language** Discuss a problem with someone else.	**Spelling** Spell the hardest word that you learned this week.	**Thinking** " "Remember: If you do not know, just say so!" Describe a time it would be good to apply the above quote.
" "To be a good speaker in public, you must be a good thinker in private."	**Oral Language** Canadian Thanksgiving Day is in October. Give one detail about this day to a friend in class or to your parents at home.	**Listening** Listen to an advertisement on the radio. Be ready to tell about it in class tomorrow.	**Grammar** Write a traffic safety slogan.	**Handwriting** Write you name backwards and look at it in the mirror. Then write 3 things you like about your appearance.	**Spelling** Spell the word that gave you the most trouble this week.	**Writing** In 1870 the 1st American postcard was sent. Send a postcard to someone you know.
Listening Ask your friend about why she/he thinks the two of you are friends.	**Handwriting** Write your name as neatly as you can and use the writing as a label on something.	**Reading** National Newspaper Week is in October. Find one fact in the newspaper, cut it out, and bring it to school.	**Writing** Child Health Day is in October. List 3 ways to live a healthy life.	**Writing** October 15 is National Poetry Day. Write a four-line poem about something you like about your teacher and give to her/him.	**Reading** October 24 is United Nations Day. Find the name of five countries that belong to the United Nations.	**Oral Language** Tell your best friend how the two of you are different.
Oral Language In October 1983 the first cellular phone service began. With a friend, practice proper phone speech.	**Writing** Write a thank-you card for the cafeteria workers for National School Lunch Week.	**Handwriting** Practice making letter shapes better on everything you write today.	**Reading** Find an opinion in the newspaper and cut it out. Bring it to school.	**Grammar** Write 1 thing you have learned about nouns, verbs, conjunctions, and adjectives.	*14,000 Quips & Quotes by McKenzie, E.C.	

This calendar created in collaboration with Frances Dornan, Valarie McGarry, George Russell

Oral Speaking Skill Development: Working More Effectively in Groups and Having Productive Discussions

TIME REQUIRED

Teacher Directed Exploration (Activity 2-1): 10–15 minutes

Student Discovery Page (Activity 2-2): 30–40 minutes.

TEACHING STRATEGIES

The cooperative learning teams approach is used, wherein students assume responsibility to help others learn the rules of effective discussions. They will use imagery to increase their retention. More advanced and older students will also create a symbol to help them remember each rule. The last teaching strategy is self-evaluation, designed to heighten students' awareness of the continual need to improve their discussion skills.

ACTIVITY 2-1

COLUMBUS DAY: DISCOVERING NEW ORAL SPEAKING ABILITIES

[OBJECTIVE]   YOU WILL LEARN NINE DISCUSSION RULES AND USE SELF-ASSESSMENT TO COMPLETE CLASS DISCUSSIONS AND SMALL-GROUP PROJECTS MORE SUCCESSFULLY.

Today you will learn how to have more effective discussions. As you learn, you will be much like Columbus, whose work led to the discovery of America in October 1492. Today you will explore new ways of talking and listening, and you will discover new oral speaking abilities.

Let's begin by listing all the things you have enjoyed and done to create good discussions in class. **[List these on the board or follow the suggestions given in the Modifications Section. Next, divide the students into small groups and appoint or elect a leader for each group. Once these groups are formed, present Rules That Lead to Good Discussions on page 46.]** You will work together in your groups to create a symbol to remind yourselves of each rule. For example, you could draw an ear to depict Rule #1. **[If you prefer, students could read and paraphrase each rule statement. Students could then write a sentence to help them remember to use this rule in discussions.]**

Now each of your groups will share with the rest of the class the symbols (or statements) you created. Hold up your rule sheets, please, and your leader or other spokesperson can tell us which symbol (statement) your group is most proud of.

[Hand out Activity 2-2.] Now you can put the rules for good discussion into practice in your groups. As you talk about the topic **[(a) a topic you select, related to a content area you are studying; (b) the subject of Columbus Day, such as what person living today is making as much contribution to our world as Columbus did and why?; or (c) a current event or issue at school for which students have a lot of background knowledge.]**

During the discussion you will complete the lefthand columns of Activity 2-2 group work evaluation. Complete the columns by placing the names of group

---

RULES FOR GOOD DISCUSSIONS

1. Only one person talks at a time.

2. Ask questions if you do not understand what someone else said.

3. State your main point first. Watch the people in your group. If they do not look like they have a question about what you said, stop. If they do have a question, answer it. Do not say more than is necessary.

4. If someone disagrees with you, try to understand that person's point by asking a question.

5. Try to be sure everyone gets a chance to talk. Ask quieter people in the group what their opinion is.

6. Summarize the conclusions you reach. Ask if there is anything left out of the summary.

7. Evaluate yourself as a group member after each group meeting. Set a goal to improve your group discussions.

---

members in each column. Under each person's name, write a comment about the way in which the person followed each rule. If a person did not follow a rule, write a suggestion to help that student follow the rule in the future. Then complete the bottom section of the form by describing the most important improvements your group made in your discussion. **[Depending on the abilities and age of your students, more structures can be added to this section of the lesson by guiding students as they complete each column. If students are more advanced and have good rapport, they could read each others' comments before they are turned in to you.]**

[Following this 10–15 minute discussion period, distribute Activity 2-2.]

GRADING CRITERIA: _____

MODIFICATIONS FOR GRADE LEVELS AND STUDENT ABILITY LEVELS

For Slower Learners or Younger Students (K, 1, 2), you can begin this lesson with a short discussion about what people can do when they work in a small group that can make that group more successful. Then the entire activity is completed in one large group, orally. You can read each sentence on Activity 2-2 orally to the younger students. *For Gifted Students or Grades Three through Eight:* Students begin this lesson by writing qualities they like about small-group work and discussions they've had in the past. They then discuss how problems that occur in small-group work can be overcome. They can also write a scenario of an effective small-group discussion. The scripts could be read to their classmates or to students in other classes.

NOTES FOR FUTURE USE

The "Our Group Work Evaluation" form and/or Activity 2-2, "Discovering My Best Discussion Skills," can be reused during small-group sessions throughout the year. With reuse, students will more rapidly increase their speaking abilities.

ACTIVITY 2-2

DISCOVERING MY BEST DISCUSSION SKILLS:
USING THE EXPLORATION SKILLS OF COLUMBUS

Just like great explorers of the past, good group members discover new ideas, solve problems. Judge how much you contributed to your group's work.

My Evaluation

Discussion skill you are exploring	Date	Date	Date	Date
1. How much did you contribute to the group? How can you improve?				
2. Are your comments helping other members in the group? Grade yourself as compared to other group members.				
3. What was the best thing you did to help the group today?				
4. How can you do this more often in the future?				

Discussion skill you are exploring	Date	Date	Date	Date
5. Which rule will help your group improve?				

Bonus Question: What will you do to help yourself during small-group work in the future? Check one, and if you already have an idea of how you can improve, write it down in the blanks after the statement you checked.

_____Bring more information and printed materials to our discussion. To do this I will... _____

_____
_____

_____Add to someone else's idea, politely. To do this I will... _____

_____
_____

_____Explain my ideas more clearly but simply. To do this I will... _____

_____
_____

_____Make my sentences shorter and allow others to ask me questions if they need to. To do this I will... __

_____
_____
_____

_____Rearrange the order of my ideas so people understand what I mean. To do this I will... _____

_____
_____

Grammar Skill Development: Fire Prevention Week and Preventing Grammar Errors

TIME REQUIRED

Teacher Directed Exploration (Activity 2-3): 5–10 minutes to pass out work and explain instructions. Students will read ten sentences and correct grammar errors for an additional 20–30 minutes.

Student Discovery Page (Activity 2-4): This requires use of the form from Activity 2-3. Students will write complete sentences for 25–30 minutes. The teacher will grade this work in class orally for 5–10 minutes.

TEACHING STRATEGIES

Students will learn through nonexamples and by predictive, high-level thinking as a monitoring strategy.

ACTIVITY 2-3 ───────────────────────────────────

[OBJECTIVE] YOU ARE GOING TO LEARN RULES TO IMPROVE YOUR CONVERSATION AND WRITING. YOU WILL HAVE LEARNED THE RULES WHEN YOU ANSWER EIGHT OR MORE SENTENCES CORRECTLY ON ACTIVITY 2-4.

In October a week is set aside to help peope learn more about eliminating fires. We will use this event to learn why people speak differently and why it is important that you select words that make it easy for others to understand you.

[Pass out the "Preventing Grammar Mistakes" form (Figure 2-1).] In this activity you will practice hearing word choices that make it easy for others to understand you. There are ten basic rules that you will learn.

In the blank after each rule, write a sample sentence that shows how you can use the rule correctly when you talk and write. [Younger students will tell the teacher orally; and only a few rules will be used. Statements will be written on the board for students to copy onto their sheets. You will do the first one yourself to model what students are to do.]

Rule #1 says, "Use the correct form of "is," "are," "was," "were." [Write: They were here.] The way I'll remember this rule is that I will use "were" for plural subjects and actions in the past. I will use "is" for singular in the present, "are" for plural in the present, and "was" for singular in the past. [Have students complete the exercise by writing a sentence to illustrate each rule on Figure 2-1.]

[Pass out "Firefighters' Approach to Eliminating Problems" (Activity 2-4).] It is as easy to recognize and correct written grammar errors as it is to recognize a fire. All you have to do when you write is to notice if some words look strange; read these words and the sentence aloud. As you do, listen for which words sound strange. The words will probably sound strange because they are breaking a rule in our language. Think about the rules we've just learned and how the sentence might be improved. Rewrite it using new words. Let's practice this skill with the "Firefighters' Approach to Problems: Eliminating Grammar Mistakes." Read each sentence quietly, but orally, to yourself. Circle the words you believe are wrong. Then rewrite the sentence with a word that would be correct. [For younger students, complete the activity orally as a group, except for the bonus question. On the bonus, allow three or four students to

suggest an answer. You may wish to give a surprise reward to students who answer the bonus question correctly.]

ANSWER KEY (For Firefighters' Approach to Eliminating Problems)

1. were

2. omit "he"; "taught" for "learns me"; take out "here" or "this here"

3. "am not" for "ain't"

4. omit "there"

5. "it's" for "its"

6. "doesn't" for "don't"

7. "Those" for "Them"

8. "I"; "likes" to "like"

9. omit "there"; "shows" for "showing"; "is" for "are"

GRADING CRITERIA: _____

_____

MODIFICATIONS FOR GRADE LEVELS AND STUDENT ABILITY LEVELS

For Kindergarten, First, Second, and Third Grades and Slower Learning Groups, complete the activity orally, as described in the activity. *For Fourth through Eighth Grades,* students write in a journal as a replacement for Activity 2-4. *For Gifted Students,* have them create and distribute pamphlets that describe ways to prevent a fire and what to do in case of a fire.

STUDENTS WHO WILL BE WORKING ON OTHER PROJECTS OR LESSONS: _____

_____

NOTES FOR FUTURE USE: _____

_____

FIGURE 2-1

Preventing Grammar Mistakes Chart

Name_____   Date_____

1. Use the correct form of "is," "are," "was," and "were".
    _____

2. Do not use the words "no" and "never" in the same
    sentence._____
    _____

3. Do not use "my sister she."_____
    _____

4. Use "it's" and "its" correctly (it is = it's; its means
    something belongs to it)._____
    _____

5. Do not use "this here" and "that there" (Use "this" alone
    and "there" alone.)_____
    _____

6. Use "a" and "an" correctly. ("A: comes before words that
    do not begin with a vowel; "an" comes before words that
    begin with a vowel.)_____
    _____

7. Use pronouns "he," "she," "we," "I," and "they" as the
    subject._____
    _____

8. Use "us," "me," "him," "her," and "them" as objects._____
    _____

9. Do not use "he don't," "she don't," "it don't"; instead use
    "he doesn't," "she doesn't," and "it doesn't."_____
    _____

10. Do not use "ain't"; instead use "is not," "am not," or
    "are not."_____
    _____

ACTIVITY 2-4

FIREFIGHTERS' APPROACH TO ELIMINATING PROBLEMS: PREVENTING MISUNDERSTANDINGS

Directions: Circle the part of the sentence that appears strange. Then rewrite each sentence using correct grammar.

1. We was getting ready to go to the movies when the fire broke out in the field.
_____
_____

2. My brother he learns me how to put out grease fires in pans. You put this here baking soda on the grease. It will put out the fire.
_____
_____

3. I ain't going to play with matches!
_____
_____

4. We saw that there film on putting dirt on campfires.
_____
_____

5. Its good to practice fire drills.
_____
_____

6. My sister don't know if we've ever had a fire at school.
_____
_____

7. Them people should not have crossed there street just to watch the fire.
_____
_____

8. Me likes fireplaces.
_____
_____

9. That there sign showing what can happen if someone are smoking a cigarette near gasoline.
_____
_____

Bonus Question: Can you make a sentence that uses two rules from the <u>Preventing Grammar Mistakes</u> Chart?
_____
_____

Composition Skill Development:
Charlie Brown's Birthday

TIME REQUIRED

Teacher Directed Exploration (Activity 2-5): To discuss Charles Schultz, Peanuts, and details using "who," "what," "where," "when," "why," and "how," 10–20 minutes; 15–30 minutes to work Activity 2-5 in groups

Student Discovery Page (Activity 2-6): 30–40 minutes, depending on whether or not students correct each other's stories

TEACHING STRATEGIES

Students will use a paired-teaching strategy and writing samples. If students grade each other's writing, students will also use symbols and imagery to aid recall. Students will use high-level thinking when they give reasons to support their answers.

ACTIVITY 2-5 _____

[OBJECTIVE]   TODAY YOU WILL LEARN TO IMPROVE YOUR WRITING BY VIVIDLY DESCRIBING WHO, WHAT, WHERE, WHEN, WHY, AND HOW. YOU WILL KNOW YOU HAVE IMPROVED YOUR WRITING WHEN OTHERS CAN IDENTIFY THE DETAILS IN YOUR WRITINGS.
[Show the Peanuts comic strips in Figure 2-2 to the class; point to the different cartoon frames. Ask what details they provide. Answers appear on page 57.] Who is this? What is this? Where is this? (and so on). **[Show the picture of Charles Schulz in Figure 2-3 and ask the same type of questions.]** Charles Schulz is the author of Peanuts, and he was born in October. He, like all writers, has to use details in stories.

Today you will learn to use the questions who, what, where, when, why, and how to write details in your stories so you can become better writers.
[Write "who," "what," "where," "when," "why," and "how" on the board.] These questions are used in writing. It is important for writers to use sentences in their writing that answer these questions. These types of details help the reader understand exactly what is being explained.
You can pick out details when you read or listen to someone. You can learn to select the clearest details when you write and speak. The following information will help you.

HOW TO USE BETTER DETAILS

1. Details tell us about pictures and stories. They tell us who, what, where, when, why, and how.

2. Details are very important in a story because they help express the author's exact meaning and feelings.

3. Details make people, places, and/or events come alive.

4. Details help readers feel as the characters feel.

5. Details help ideas flow easily and connect naturally.

FIGURE 2-2

Reprinted with permission of Charles Schulz from *The Peanuts Jubilee.* United Media, 200 Park Ave.,
New York, New York 10166.

FIGURE 2-3
Writer/Artist Charles Schulz at Work

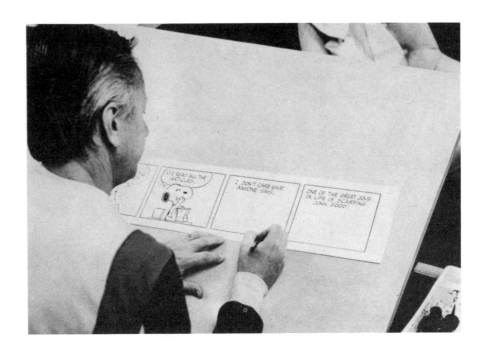

6. Details that tell who, what, where, when, why, and how should usually be written in separate sentences.

[For younger students, you now read a story and have them raise their hands when they hear a detail. You ask a student to tell what the detail was and how he or she knew it was a detail. For second to fourth graders, have students cut out the flashcards in Figure 2-4. Students will hold up the flashcard that shows the type of detail they believe you just read. For above fourth grade, you can proceed to the following step without this intermediate learning step.]

[Divide the class into groups of six. Give a copy of Figure 2-4 to each group.] Cut out these flashcards and give one to each person in your group.

Now, using the type of detail on your card, each of you will write the best detail you can, using what you have learned. Each group will then put its sentences together to create a story.

For example, if your card says "who" on it, you will make up a character and write who the main character of the story will be and who he or she is.

[Each group reads their cards to each other. Each group uses the details to write a story. Each group can read its stories to the rest of the class, if you desire. As they read, the class can pick out the details from each other's invented story by raising the card that names each detail type when they hear it. In this way, the skill of identifying details when listening will be strengthened.]

[Pass out Activity 2-6. Students will complete the activity alone or as a large group, depending on their age and ability.]

ANSWER KEY FOR ACTIVITY 2-6

"Home Wanted"

1. what; who; where; when

2. why

3. who

4. what; why

5. what

6. when

7. where

8. who; where

9. what

"Stupid Kid!"

1. who; what; where; when

2. why

FIGURE 2-4

3. what

4. when

5. what or how

6. why

"Pay To The Order of Me"

1. who; where; when

2. what

3. when

4. how; where

5. why

6. what

7. what

8. what; where

9. how

GRADING CRITERIA: _____

_____

MODIFICATIONS FOR GRADE LEVELS AND STUDENT ABILITY LEVELS

For Younger Grades, allow students to write sentences instead of stories, or complete the entire activity as a language experience approach.

ACTIVITY 2-6

USING CLUE CARDS FOR WRITING:
WRITING GOOD DETAILS

Person with the "Who" Card: Describe someone or something. Write three sentences to describe all the important things about that person or thing, but do not tell what happened to him, her, or it.

Person with the "What" Card: Think of something that could happen to a character in a story. Write about that event, making it as interesting, scary, or funny as you can. Write three sentences to describe what happened. Only tell what happened; do not tell where, how, when, or why it happened.

Person with the "When" Card: Think of a time that an event could take place. This could be long ago, now, in the future, in the morning, afternoon, evening, fall, spring, summer, or winter. Write three different sentences to help everyone know when something occurred. Do not tell what occurred.

Person with the "Why" Card: Think of an interesting event that happened to you. Write three sentences that clearly describe why something happened without telling what the thing was, where it was, or when it was. You may want to begin your first sentence with "It happened because . . . ."

Person with the "How" Card: Think of how something important happened in your life. Write three sentences to describe how this thing happened, the steps that led up to it, or created it, but do not tell what it was.

Person with the "Where" Card: Think of a setting or place where many different things could happen. It could be a real or make-believe place. Write three sentences about this place. Use interesting details, but do not tell what happened there.

Reading Skill Development: Finding Comparisons and Contrasts in Literature

TIME REQUIRED

Teacher Directed Exploration (Activity 2-7): 15–25 minutes

Student Discovery Page (Activity 2-8): 10–15 minutes (If time permits and students do an extra activity, add 10–15 minutes.)

TEACHING STRATEGIES

Students will learn by using concrete objects to introduce a concept. Another strategy is to practice metacognition as they read. The type of metacognition to be studied is the ability to recognize when something read does not make sense.

ACTIVITY 2-7 _____

[OBJECTIVE] YOU WILL LEARN TO READ A SELECTION AND COMPARE AND CONTRAST DETAILS AND IDEAS WHILE YOU READ. IN THIS WAY YOU CAN REMEMBER MORE OF WHAT YOU READ.

During the month of October several events occur, such as World Food Day and National Poetry Day. We are going to celebrate these events by using poems about food to help us learn to comprehend more of what we read. **[For younger students, read a version of the Cinderella story. Then complete this lesson on a second day by reading to the middle of the book *Prince Cinders*.]** Can you tell me three similarities and three differences between the Cinderella story and *Prince Cinders?* **[List these on the board.]** What do you think the ending of *Prince Cinders* will be? **[Solicit several responses.]** The reason you can predict the ending is because you were paying attention to likenesses and differences. This helps you learn. **[Read the rest of *Prince Cinders*.]**

In the future when you read, remember what we just learned about likenesses and differences. If, while you learn, listen, and read, you picture the ways in which the material is like or unlike something you learned before, your mind will store the information better. What you are learning will be stored in two places: in "ways the story is different from anything I have read before" and in "how this subject is just like what I already know".

You must practice learning to think about similarities and differences in the things you read. To practice, and to celebrate National Poetry Day, World Food Day and National Children's Book Week we are going to do two activities. **[Distribute copies of Figure 2-5].** Read each poem carefully and pause to think about how it is just like something you've read before or how it is different from anything you've read before.

When you've finished, you may begin Activity 2-8, which I'll give you when you bring the poems page to me.

_____

GRADING CRITERIA: _____

_____

MODIFICATIONS FOR GRADE LEVELS AND STUDENT ABILITY LEVELS

For Younger Students, complete Activities 2-7 and 2-8 orally. *For Older Students,* Activity 2-8 will help them think as they read. You may require that all students read the same passage or book.

NOTES FOR FUTURE USE: _____

_____

FIGURE 2-5

Peter Prangle

Peter Prangle,
The prickly prangly pear picker,
Picked three pecks
Of prangly prickly pear, from
The prickly pear trees
On the pleasant Prairies.

Author Unknown

Cookout Night

Paper cups and paper plates.
Pickle jar.
Popcorn in a crackly bag.
Salt and pepper?
Here they are.

Paper napkins! Who forgot?
"I didn't, you did."
"I did not."
Besides what difference does it make?
Look at all the grass around
For wiping our faces on.......

Nothing's ever impolite:
Not outdoors on a cookout night.

Dorothy Aldis

FIGURE 2-5 (Continued)

This Little Morsel

But this little morsel of morsels here-
Just what it is, is not quite clear:
It might be pudding, it might be meat,
Cold, or hot, or salt, or sweet;
Baked, or roasted, or broiled or fried;
Bare, or frittered, or pudding, or pied;
Cooked in a saucepan, jar, or pan;
But it's all the same to Elizabeth Ann.
For when one's hungry it doesn't much matter
So long as there's something on one's platter.

Walter De La Mare

ACTIVITY 2-8

NATIONAL CHILDREN'S BOOK WEEK:
LEARNING TO THINK WHILE READING

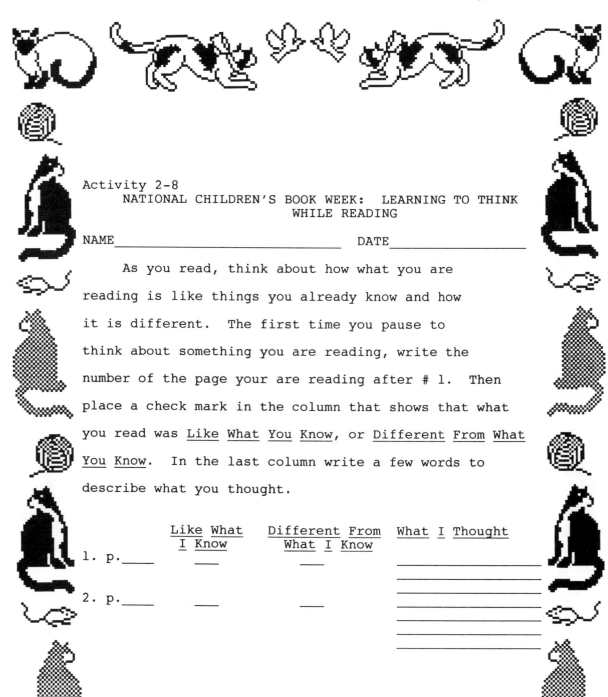

Activity 2-8
    NATIONAL CHILDREN'S BOOK WEEK: LEARNING TO THINK
                            WHILE READING

NAME_____   DATE_____

    As you read, think about how what you are
reading is like things you already know and how
it is different. The first time you pause to
think about something you are reading, write the
number of the page your are reading after # 1. Then
place a check mark in the column that shows that what
you read was Like What You Know, or Different From What
You Know. In the last column write a few words to
describe what you thought.

	Like What I Know	Different From What I Know	What I Thought
1. p.____	___	___	_____
			_____
2. p.____	___	___	_____
			_____
			_____
			_____
			_____

TYPE OF THOUGHT

LIKE WHAT I KNOW

DIFFERENT FROM WHAT I KNOW

NEW THOUGHT I HAD

4. P____
5. P____
6. P____
7. P____
8. P____
9. P____
10. P____

Listening Skill Development: Learning to Recognize Facts

TIME REQUIRED

Teacher Directed Exploration (Activity 2-9): 30–40 minutes

Student Discovery Page (Activity 2-10): can be completed as a 30 minute class activity.

TEACHING STRATEGIES

The first teaching strategy is to give students the opportunity to form sentences of facts about themselves, family, school, or community and to form their own opinions about why they think about certain topics. The second strategy is to have the students work in teams to decide whether sentences are factual or opinionated. Finally, students will learn by completing an individual project.

ACTIVITY 2-9 _____

LISTENING FOR FACTS

[OBJECTIVE] TODAY WE WILL LEARN HOW TO DETERMINE IF STATEMENTS PEOPLE MAKE ARE FACTS OR OPINIONS. YOU WILL KNOW YOU HAVE LEARNED TO MAKE THIS DISTINCTION WHEN YOU CORRECTLY IDENTIFY FIVE STATEMENTS ON TELEVISION (OR IN BOOKS) AS EITHER FACTS OR OPINIONS.

As we grow, we learn to listen for different purposes. We use listening every day for enjoyment and work.

Today we will be listening to a variety of different things: poems, a story, a tape. While you listen, you will learn to make better decisions by recognizing when someone is giving his or her opinion or stating a fact that can be proven.

[Write the column headings "Fact" and "Opinion" on the board.] Divide a piece of paper into two columns, and label them with these headings. Can you give statements that describe one of these headings? Write the statements you hear in the correct column. **[For younger and less vocal groups, you say one of the sentences that appears below and ask them to write it in the most appropriate column on their paper. You then write it in the correct column on the board. Continue reading (or eliciting) statements in a random order without telling from which column it came, until all statements have been discussed.]**

Facts are:

1. Statements about something that happens that can be proven.

2. Something that occurred that can't be changed just because you want it changed.

3. Statements that usually contain exact dates, times, places, and details that could be checked.

4. Statements of something you personally experienced, tested, touched, tasted, heard, said, saw, or smelled.

Opinions are:

1. Statements about something that happens that does not seem possible and you cannot prove.

2. Statements that usually contain words like "I feel," "in my opinion," "the most."

3. Statements that are not based on positive knowledge but on unsupported statements of preference.

4. Statements that exaggerate what occurred.

[You can continue the lesson by using *Grandfather Tales* by R. Chase or one of the following suggestions. While you read *Grandfather Tales* to the class, students write items from the tales appropriately in columns they have labeled "Fact" and "Opinion." Grade their work orally, as the *Tales* create exciting discussion and thinking.]

[Then either have students watch a 15-minute TV segment (with commercials) or read a book or newspaper editorial that you have brought and copied. Again, students write statements of fact and opinion in labeled columns as appropriate.]

Daylight Savings Time will end this month. As homework, I want you to find out more about this time change. Talk with an adult about it or look in newspapers or research books. Prepare two statements of fact about Daylight Savings Time and two statements of opinion about it. Be ready to share your opinions with the class tomorrow.

[Immediately following this activity, or as an activity for a subsequent day, pass out Activity 2-10 (which you have laminated to be used for many other types of activities at later times). You will need to have prepared a list of numbered, randomly ordered statements describing and exemplifying facts and opinions. These statements can be taken from the earlier discussions in this activity, from examples students have turned in or from textbooks or other sources. The Daylight Savings Time statements can be quickly numbered and used for this activity.] Take a crayon and write "F" (for FACT) and "O" (for OPINION) randomly on the squares of your Bingo board. I will read numbered statements that describe or exemplify facts or opinions. If the sentence is a fact or tells about facts, use a crayon to write its number in one of the squares you have marked "F." If the statement is an opinion or tells about opinions, write its number in a square marked "O." Try to make a Bingo vertically, horizontally, or diagonally. Call out "Bingo" when you have a line.

[To check a Bingo, the child must tell the number the statement and *why* it was a fact or opinion. A student will not be correct unless the categorization and reason are correct.]

GRADING CRITERIA: _____

MODIFICATIONS FOR GRADE LEVELS AND STUDENT ABILITY LEVELS

For Kindergarten, give the correct answer immediately after each Bingo statement you call so students will learn more rapidly. Ask a student to tell how he or she knew each Bingo was a fact or an opinion. *For Older Students and Gifted Learners,* allow them to bring fact and opinion statements from television shows, commercials, or books they read the night before. They then mark each other's statements as either fact or opinion and write on the back of the paper how they knew the statement was a fact or an opinion. These statements are then collected and used as the items for the Bingo game.

STUDENTS WHO WILL BE WORKING ON OTHER PROJECTS OR LESSONS: _____

_____

NOTES FOR FUTURE USE: _____

_____

ACTIVITY 2-10

		FREE		

United Nations Day Teaches Us How to Make Spelling Easier

TIME REQUIRED

Teacher Directed Exploration (Activity 2-11): 10–15 minutes

Student Discovery Page (Activity 2-12): as much time as desired

TEACHING STRATEGIES

Students are involved in preparing their own transfer of learning experiences and in using a game to spell word parts.

ACTIVITY 2-11 _____

[OBJECTIVE]   TODAY WE WILL LEARN TO BUILD WORDS BY USING GREEK AND LATIN ROOTS. YOU WILL KNOW YOU HAVE LEARNED WHEN YOU SCORE TWELVE OR MORE CORRECT ON ACTIVITY 2-12.

The United Nations began in October 1945. Each October we set aside a day to celebrate this beginning. It is a special day dedicated to better understanding and appreciating people from all countries. One problem in reaching this goal is that language differences cause us to misunderstand each other.

Today words from other languages have become a part of English, such as the Eskimo word "igloo," the Japanese word "judo," and the Hawaiian word "luau." Because these words are foreign they are not spelled the way English words are spelled. Such new words make it more difficult to learn to spell.

When words from Greek and Latin became a part of the English language, they were spelled very similarly to English words. Moreover, every time a Greek or Latin word appears, it will always have the same meaning, unlike English words, such as "run" (*run* home and home*run* and a *run* in a lady's hose). Therefore, by learning the meanings and spellings of parts of English words that have come from the old Greek and Latin languages, we can improve our spelling and reading abilities.

For example, the Greek word part *"tele"* means "far" and is always spelled "tele." So by learning "tele" you can spell and understand many words, such as telephone, telegraph, television, telemarketing, teletype, and telescope.

[Hand out copies of Figure 2-6.] Look at the words in our language that came from other languages on the United Nations Spelling Key (Figure 2-6). You are to find three words in any of your textbooks or library books that have one of these word parts. Use the meaning of that foreign word part to help identify the meaning of the English word. When you've finished the United Nations Spelling Key, you will find a partner and test each other.

[On the next day, or as an activity for those who finish early, distribute Activity 2-12, United Nations Word Building Game. This activity will teach students some of the most commonly used foreign word parts. Students can then have a contest to see who can find the most words that have these word parts in other books. This will significantly increase the students' retention of the lesson's objective.]

_____

ANSWER KEY FOR ACTIVITY 2-12

1. telephone

2. biology

3. democracy

4. automobile

5. autobiography

6. instruction

7. refund

GRADING CRITERIA: _____

_____

MODIFICATIONS FOR GRADE LEVELS AND STUDENT ABILITY LEVELS

For Younger Students and Slower Learners, both exercises can be completed orally. If you prefer, substitute for this activity a lesson in which students give you five foreign or domestic words they want to learn, as a large-group activity. *For Older Students and Gifted Learners,* allow them to complete the Activity 2-12 and locate other examples of English words that use the word parts in this lesson. They can locate other words in their content area textbooks, spelling books, and dictionaries. At the end of Activity 2-12 students can share their words and ask classmates to tell the meanings. You can also allow a group of gifted learners to prepare a spelling test for each other, composed of the words they located.

STUDENTS WHO WILL BE WORKING ON OTHER PROJECTS OR LESSONS: _____

_____

NOTES FOR FUTURE USE: _____

_____

FIGURE 2-6

UNITED NATIONS SPELLING KEY

Name_____Date_____

Directions: Find three words that contain each foreign word part below. Find these words in your textbooks or the dictionary. After you've found three words, write the meaning of each word. You will then be tested over how many new words you can now spell.

	English Word	Meaning of Word
-ful (means full of)	1.	
	2.	
	3.	
-hood (means all the members in a group)	1.	
	2.	
	3.	
-ish (means to like something)	1.	
	2.	
	3.	
-ness (means an example of being)	1.	
	2.	
	3.	
bi- (means two or twice)	1.	
	2.	
	3.	
ob- (means being against something)	1.	
	2.	
	3.	

ACTIVITY 2-12

UNITED NATIONS WORD BUILDING GAME

100

Directions: Many of the words in our language have been built by combining words from other languages. By learning to spell a few foreign words you can spell many new English words. Combine these word parts by thinking of the English words that would be composed of the meaning in these parts. For each of the ten problems find the word parts represented by the letters and combine them to make an English word.

Foreign word parts meanings and spellings	English words you can now spell
A). tele- (far) and B) -phone (sounds)	1.
C). bio- (life) and D). -logy (study of)	2.
E). demo- (people) and F). -cratic (rule)	3.
G). y- (inclined to)	
H). auto- (self) and I). -mobile (move)	4.
J). auto- (self) and K). bio- (life) and	
L). -graph (write) and M). -y (inclined to)	5.
N). -in (into) and O) -struct (the building up of) and	
P). -ion (act of)	6.
Q). re- (back again) and R). -fund (together)	7.

Spelling Test Given to You by a Friend
1.
2.
3.
4.
5.
6.
7.
Grade_____

If you finish early, how many other words can you find by combining the Greek and Latin word parts in A-Q? Write the two letters that could go together to make another English word below. The person who finds the most words will win.

Handwriting Skill Development: Halloween's Special Surprise

TIME REQUIRED

Teacher Directed Exploration (Activity 2-13): 35 minutes

Student Discovery Page (Activity 2-14): 20–30 minutes

TEACHING STRATEGIES

Students are taught to picture the shape of letters before they write them. They are also taught to associate the shape to a visual image. Older students will also use the strategy of rehearsal and review.

ACTIVITY 2-13 _____

ROAMING GHOST'S HALLOWEEN SURPRISE

[OBJECTIVE] TODAY YOU WILL LEARN TO USE VISUAL IMAGES TO IMPROVE HANDWRITING. YOU WILL PRACTICE EACH ALPHABET LETTER AND WILL KNOW YOU HAVE IMPROVED YOUR LETTER SHAPES WHEN YOU DO NOT GO BEYOND THE OUTLINE WHILE TRACING AND YOU CAN WRITE THE CORRECT LETTER SHAPE WITHOUT AN OUTLINE.

Today you will learn how to create a picture in your mind of something you are trying to learn. When you make a picture of it in your mind like that, you will learn faster because your mind is working harder to learn.

First, you are going to learn how to picture the shape of an animal's body or an object to remind you of the correct shape of a manuscript letter. To practice, you will have the letter and object in front of you. You will look at each picture, and, as you trace it, you will picture the letter shape in your mind.

[Pass out Activity 2-14. After 20–30 minutes, continue as follows.] Now you will have a special Halloween treat. You will learn how to picture in your mind the events of a story just as you did when you wrote the alphabet. I am going to read a special Halloween story. You will picture each thing that happens. If you have learned how to picture well, you will be surprised at the end of the story.

[Before you begin, distribute two sheets of orange construction paper and a pair of scissors to each student. Read the story to your class, but practice making the jack-o-lantern first so you can more easily guide the class.]

Once there was a little ghost named "Roaming." Each day he skipped from one mossy riverbank to the next, singing gaily, and pausing to nap under a toadstool. He would feast on seeds and wild berries, and sip honey from wildflowers. At night, he crawled under a broad leaf, and into a milkweed pod to make his bed. He was sheltered from the dew and the rain. He wasn't lonely because Peto, his wee pet bat, went everywhere with him. Roaming and Peto had many friends.

Now, it was near that time of year when real people begin to think of Halloween and when ghosts and bats begin to think of surprising people. Roaming had been thinking what fun it would be to build a house before Halloween so he could invite all his friends over for a celebration. So he started the morning in search of something with which to make a house. He found it! He found a piece of paper, something like the one I just gave you.

"Ah," said Roaming, "the very thing!" Then he pulled and he tugged and he pushed and he sat on his new-found house material until the paper was folded in half with the longest side becoming the shortest. **[The paper should be folded like this: ◿]** (Do with your paper now what you picture in your mind that Roaming did to his.) **[Do not give any clues. Allow students to succeed or partially succeed depending on their imaging abilities.]** Taking his little scissors from his vest pocket, and working very slowly and carefully, he cut the two corners off the side of his house that was not folded. When he had finished, he had a house that looked like one-half of a circle. (Now, make your paper look like you think Roaming's looked.) **[⌐]**

Roaming was very proud of his work and pulled it up against a tall weed to have a better look at it. "Oh my, of course!" thought Roaming. "It must have a tall door about one inch from the left end of the folded side." He wanted to make his door tall so his friends, the witches, could fly in. So he cut it to within one inch of the roof of his house. **[Make your door so it looks like Roaming's.]**

[⌐∏⌐] "Now I want a window so Peto and I can see outside." Roaming cut a window in his house about one inch from the top right side of his roof. His window was on the opposite side of the house than his door. (Make your window where Roaming made his.) **[∏ □]**

By this time Peto, who had not squeaked a single squeak, was becoming very interested in the new house. Suddenly he became very concerned. He did not know how he was going to get in and out of the house. "Where do I come in?" he asked, with a twitch of his wee bat wings.

Roaming laughed and with a twinkle in his eye he cut another door, a very tiny, wee little door right in the center of the folded side of his house. Peto's door was special because it was so small he was the only one that could use it. Roaming made it about the size of one-half of a dime. (Make Peto's door just as Roaming did.) **[∏ₙ □]**

The next day was Halloween! All the animals in the forest were excited because Roaming had invited them to his new house for a party. Roaming and Peto were excited too, and when they opened up their house for all their friends to see, it was all a-glow! There, sitting right in the middle of the living room, was . . . what do you suppose? Yes, the very thing to make a real Halloween! **[Ask students to guess as you _slowly_ unfold the paper as you read the last line]** . . . a Jack-o'-lantern just like yours!*

[Students either sing or read the poems on Figure 2-7 now. If they only read the songs,] imagine (image) the words and picture each verse until you can identify the Christmas carol to which the poem could be sung.

*An adaption of "Toby's Surprise" by Jody Bernhardt.

FIGURE 2-7
by the class of Miss Colleen Pilant*

Hallowe'en is becoming a forgotten holiday. We dedicated followers of the Great Pumpkin must do something to rekindle the Hallowe'en spirit. Let us not rest until the universe resounds with Pumpkin Carols.

The Great Pumpkin

I'm dreaming of the Great Pumpkin,
Just like I do this time each year;
　　When he brings nice toys
　　To good girls and boys
Who wait for him to appear.
I'm dreaming of the Great Pumpkin
With every Pumpkin card I write.
May your jack-o' lanterns burn bright,
When the Great Pumpkin visits you
　　tonight.

Pumpkin Bells

Dashing through the streets
In our costumes bright and gay,
To each house we go,
Laughing all the way.
Hallowe'en is here,
Making spirits bright:
What fun it is to trick-or-treat
And sing Pumpkin carols tonight.
Oh, Pumpkin bells! Pumpkin bells!
　　Ringing loud and clear,
Oh, what fun Great Pumpkin brings
　　When Hallowe'en is here!

Deck the Patch

Deck the patch with orange and black,
　　Fa-la-la-la-la la-la-la-la,
Take along your goody sack;
　　Fa-la-la-la-la la-la-la-la.
Don we now our gay apparel,
　　Fa-la-la-la-la la-la-la-la,
Troll the ancient Pumpkin carol,
　　Fa-la-la-la-la la-la-la-la.
See the great one rise before us,
　　Fa-la-la-la-la la-la-la-la,
As we sing the Pumpkin chorus;
　　Fa-la-la-la-la la-la-la-la.
Follow him as he ascends,
　　Fa-la-la-la-la la-la-la-la,
Join with true Great Pumpkin friends,
　　Fa-la-la-la-la la-la-la-la.

The Twelve Days of Hallowe'en

On the first day of Hallowe'en,
My true love gave to me:
　　An owl in an old, dead tree.
On the second day of Hallowe'en,
My true love gave to me:
　　Two trick-or-treaters,
　　An owl in an old, dead tree.

　　Three black cats . . .
　　Four skeletons . . .
　　Five scarey spooks . . .
　　Six goblins gobbling . . .
　　Seven pumpkins glowing . . .
　　Eight monsters shrieking . . .
　　Nine ghosts a-booing . . .
　　Eleven masks a-leering . . .
　　Twelve bats a-flying . . .

*Miss Pilant has retired but was teaching at St. Claire Elementary School (St. Claire, CA) when these poems were written.

[If they sing the songs,] pay close attention to your favorite verse, because you will use that verse to strengthen your memory and imagery skills in a moment. [A record that can be used for these poems is *A Tribute to Christmas,* which contains all the Christmas carols without words. This record can be ordered from:

Image VII
P.O. Box 6900
Vancouver, B.C.
Canada V6B 4B5]

Now on a new sheet of paper describe what you learned today. You will make visual images in your mind when you read to help you understand in the future. You should picture letters in your mind as you write, as well. As you write what you've learned, also concentrate on making letters correctly. When you finish, let me read it. I'm interested in reading about what you've learned today.

GRADING CRITERIA: _____

MODIFICATIONS FOR GRADE LEVELS AND STUDENT ABILITY LEVELS

All students may use markers, map colors, or chalk in place of pen or pencil. *For Kindergarten, First, and Second Grade,* enlarge Activity 2-14 and introduce the story and Activity 2-14 together. Also use other ways to say "inches" in the directions, such as showing how much to cut by holding up your hand and spacing your fingers, or by making a model as you tell the story. *For Older and Gifted Students,* allow students to turn Activity 2-14 over and write each letter shape from memory. Students can also write the name of the image that helped them write the letters correctly.

ACTIVITY 2-14

THE ANIMALS THAT CAME TO ROAMING'S HALLOWEEN PARTY

<u>Directions</u>: The shape of each object can help you remember the shape of letters. As you trace each letter, think about each animal's shape. You may use a pen, pencil, crayon, chalk-ola or marker. You will know you've improved your handwriting if you do not go beyond the outline of at least 21 of the 26 letters!

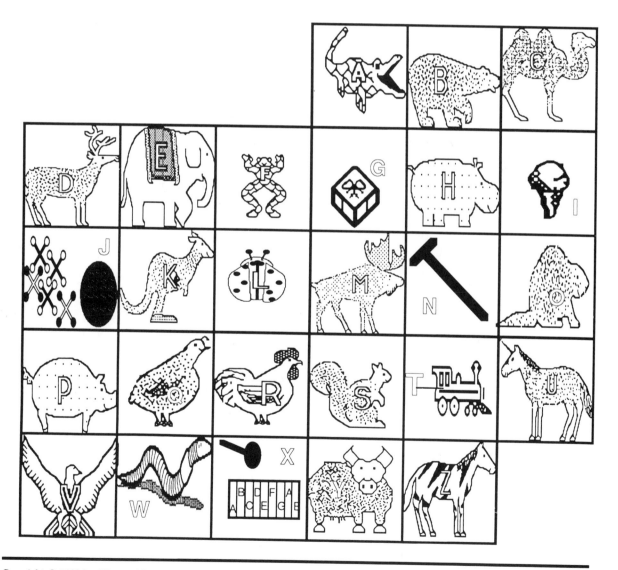

Class Monitoring Record

The Class Monitoring Record can be used in many ways to assess students' thinking growth in language arts abilities and to monitor and grade students' work.

You list students' names on one of the axes in the order in which they are seated in class. On the second axis you will write descriptions of daily work you will be checking as you walk around the room. Then put the class monitoring record on a clipboard or other hard surface so you can write on it as you walk.

Following are a few of the ways the Monitor can be used. Each increases the effectiveness of the time spent to monitor students' work.

1. You can grade random samples of items on homework papers while students work on a classroom assignment.

2. You can record daily grades of +, −, and OK as you monitor oral speaking and thinking ability during a class discussion.

3. The form can become a method of checking written work for a full six-week period. You set aside a time in the morning for moving from desk to desk to check written work and/or marking attendance on the form, while providing individualized instruction by noting special concerns for each student.

4. The form can become a means of helping students develop better work habits. For example, you create a contest whereby students receive a point for each day they begin their work on time and a second point if they complete at least 75 percent of the assignment before the bell rings. You could then mark the first point on the Class Monitoring Record from your desk as soon as an assignment is made and the second as you walk around the room during the last 5 minutes of class.

5. Because one axis contains 26 spaces and one contains 32, some columns can be used to indicate which students need to bring permission slips, fees, and forms from home.

THE CLASS MONITORING RECORD

CLASS _____

3 *November*

November is a very busy month for most of us. With the end of the second grading period, the Thanksgiving holiday, and Christmas just around the corner, much has to be completed in language arts classes. In the November activities, students will write their own Thanksgiving story to share with the rest of the class, present a play, and interview people.

The major themes of November's activities are "National Family Week," "National Children's Book Week," "World Hello Day," the anniversary of the Gettysburg Address, Thanksgiving, and the celebration of Mark Twain's birthday.

Scope and Sequence of Language Arts Skills Taught in November

Composition (Activities 3-1 and 3-2): The students will write formal letters and other types of business correspondence that follow conventions and deliver a clear message.

Reading (Activities 3-3 and 3-4): Students will learn to use story maps to relate subtopics.

Spelling (Activities 3-5 and 3-6): When spelling, students will use mneumonics as learning tools to improve their spelling.

Handwriting (Activities 3-7 and 3-8): When writing in cursive or manuscript, students will learn the correct spacing between words and sentences.

Listening (Activities 3-9 and 3-10): Students will develop question-asking skills as they learn to conduct effective interviews.

Grammar (Activities 3-11 and 3-12): Students will learn proper punctuation and capitalization and how they are used to convey meaning.

Speaking (Activities 3-13 and 3-14): Students will learn to become more interesting speakers by creating images with exact vocabulary in their informal and formal speaking.

Supplementary Activities and Projects

1. Students may write to one of the following companies or agencies for free information about the special events in this month.

National Children's Book Week
The Children's Book Council, Inc.
Mr. John Donovan, President
67 Irving Pl.
New York, NY 10003

American Music Week
American Music Center
Griselle Colon, 250 W. 54th St.
Suite 300
New York, NY 10019

World Hello Day
The McCormick Brothers
Box 993
Omaha, NE 68101

North American International
 Livestock Exposition
Kentucky Fair and Exposition
Box 37130
Louisville, KY 40098

National Author's Day
Mrs. Sue Cole
191 N. Cole
St. Macon, IL 62544

YMCA Arts and Crafts Fair
Ms. Betty Williams
304 Squires Student Center
Blacksburg, VA 24060

New York City Marathon
New York Convention and Visitors
 Bureau
2 Columbus Circle
New York, NY 10019

Anniversary of Gettysburg Address
Soldiers National Monument
Gettysburg National Travel Council
35 Carlisle St.
Gettysburg, PA 17325

2. Students may write to notable people born in November. Students whose birthdays fall in November may write to, or read, biographies/autobiographies on one or more of the following people born on their birthdate.

Notable November Birthdays

1. Barbara Bosson, Robert Foxworth, Betsy Palmer

2. Daniel Boone

3. Charles Bronson, Michael Dukakis

4. Loretta Swit, Ralph Macchio

5. Tatum O'Neal, Roy Rogers, Paul Simon

6. James Naismith, Sally Field, Lori Singer

7. Marie Curie, Billy Graham

8. Patti Page, Morley Safer

9. Benjamin Banneker, Lou Ferrigno, Carl Sagan

10. MacKenzie Phillips, Roy Scheider

11. Jonathan Winters, Demi Moore

12. Nadia Commanici, Elizabeth Cady Stanton, Stefanie Powers

13. Robert Louis Stevenson, Rod Serling

14. Brian Keith, MacLean Stevenson

15. Marianne Moore, Ed Asner

16. Lisa Bonet, W. C. Handy

17. Danny DeVito

18. Linda Evans

19. Dick Cavett, Jodie Foster, Dan Haggerty

20. Alistair Cooke, Bo Derek, Richard Dawson

21. Goldie Hawn, Marlo Thomas

22. George Elliot, Jamie Lee Curtis, Rodney Dangerfield, Mariel Hemmingway

23. Boris Karloff

24. Carlo Collidi, Scott Joplin

25. Marc Brown, John Larroquette, Ricardo Montalban

26. Rich Little, Tina Turner

27. Jayne Kennedy, Eddie Rabbitt

29. Louisa May Alcott, Howie Mandell

30. Mark Twain, Shirley Chisholm, Dick Clark

3. The calendar for November can be used in the variety of ways suggested in Chapter 1.

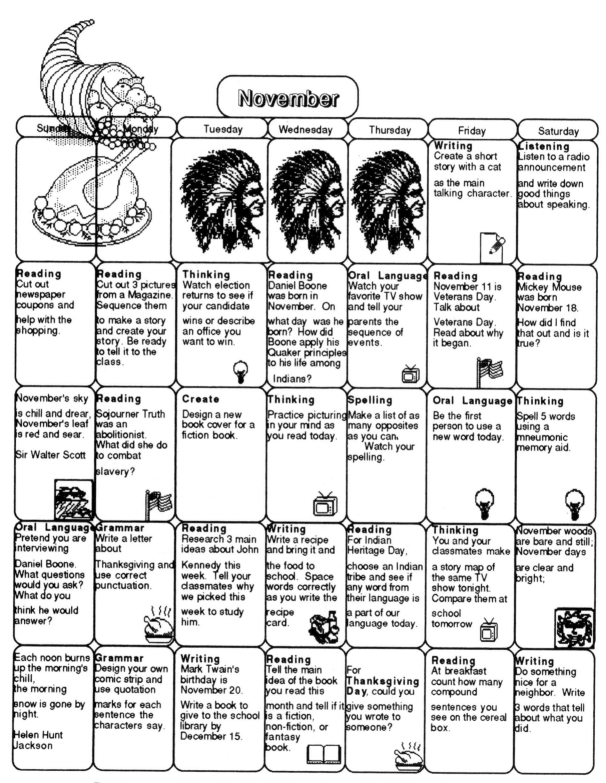

November

Sunday	Monday	Tuesday	Wednesday	Thursday	Friday	Saturday
					Writing Create a short story with a cat as the main talking character.	**Listening** Listen to a radio announcement and write down good things about speaking.
Reading Cut out newspaper coupons and help with the shopping.	**Reading** Cut out 3 pictures from a Magazine. Sequence them to make a story and create your story. Be ready to tell it to the class.	**Thinking** Watch election returns to see if your candidate wins or describe an office you want to win.	**Reading** Daniel Boone was born in November. On what day was he born? How did Boone apply his Quaker principles to his life among Indians?	**Oral Language** Watch your favorite TV show and tell your parents the sequence of events.	**Reading** November 11 is Veterans Day. Talk about Veterans Day. Read about why it began.	**Reading** Mickey Mouse was born November 18. How did I find that out and is it true?
November's sky is chill and drear, November's leaf is red and sear. Sir Walter Scott	**Reading** Sojourner Truth was an abolitionist. What did she do to combat slavery?	**Create** Design a new book cover for a fiction book.	**Thinking** Practice picturing in your mind as you read today.	**Spelling** Make a list of as many opposites as you can. Watch your spelling.	**Oral Language** Be the first person to use a new word today.	**Thinking** Spell 5 words using a mneumonic memory aid.
Oral Language Pretend you are interviewing Daniel Boone. What questions would you ask? What do you think he would answer?	**Grammar** Write a letter about Thanksgiving and use correct punctuation.	**Reading** Research 3 main ideas about John Kennedy this week. Tell your classmates why we picked this week to study him.	**Writing** Write a recipe and bring it and the food to school. Space words correctly as you write the recipe card.	**Reading** For Indian Heritage Day, choose an Indian tribe and see if any word from their language is a part of our language today.	**Thinking** You and your classmates make a story map of the same TV show tonight. Compare them at school tomorrow	November woods are bare and still; November days are clear and bright;
Each noon burns up the morning's chill, the morning snow is gone by night. Helen Hunt Jackson	**Grammar** Design your own comic strip and use quotation marks for each sentence the characters say.	**Writing** Mark Twain's birthday is November 20. Write a book to give to the school library by December 15.	**Reading** Tell the main idea of the book you read this month and tell if it is a fiction, non-fiction, or fantasy book.	For **Thanksgiving Day**, could you give something you wrote to someone?	**Reading** At breakfast count how many compound sentences you see on the cereal box.	**Writing** Do something nice for a neighbor. Write 3 words that tell about what you did.

This calendar created in collaboration with Frances Dornan, Valarie McGarry, George Russell.

Composition Skill Development: Learning the Correct Form for Business and/or Personal Letters

TIME REQUIRED

Teacher Directed Exploration (Activity 3-1): 10–30 minutes

Student Discovery Page (Activity 3-2): 10–20 minutes

TEACHING STRATEGIES

Students learn by following an explicit example and by applying their knowledge to their daily lives.

ACTIVITY 3-1

WRITING INTERESTING AND PURPOSEFUL LETTERS

[OBJECTIVE]   YOU WILL LEARN TO ORGANIZE YOUR THOUGHTS AND FORMULATE AN INTERESTING AND PURPOSEFUL LETTER. YOU WILL FOLLOW A FORMAT USED IN BUSINESS COMMUNICATIONS OR A FRIENDLY LETTER FORMAT. YOU WILL KNOW YOU HAVE BEEN SUCCESSFUL WHEN YOUR LETTER IS SO WELL WRITTEN THAT SOMEONE UNDERSTANDS THE PURPOSE OF YOUR WRITING.

[Select an apropriate sample letter for your students.] In the month of November elections are held for people who wish to hold public office. These people communicate effectively in letters and write to many people.

Today you are going to improve your ability to communicate and will learn the correct form for letter writing. Look at this example. **[Show the sample letter of Figure 3-1 or Figure 3-2 on the overhead projector, or make your own example, using the figures or a letter to the editor as a guide. Point to each part of the sample and teach its purpose. For younger grades ask students to tell what they like to read in a letter. Make a list of these on the board for students to refer to as they write.]** There are other elements that also will make your letters more interesting and easier to read.

1. A letter that follows a correct form will be easier for people to read.

2. A letter that has a clearly stated purpose, at the beginning, will be more interesting and easier to remember.

3. Letters should include information that people don't know and might want to know about you or something else. Some valuable information to include in letters about yourself is:

> — family, brothers and sisters
> — pets
> — hobbies and after-school activities
> — friends
> — your school teacher, what you are learning
> — account about a school activity
> — something humorous
> — news, something exciting that has happened
> — your goals
> — a pet peeve

FIGURE 3-1
Sample Letter to Use in K–1 Classes

FIGURE 3-2
A Sample Letter to Use in 1–2 Classes

November 4, 1991

Dear Class,

I am excited about the year that we have before us. We will all learn very much. We will meet many new people and make new friends.

Today we will learn how to write letters. Letters are one way we can tell others our thoughts and feelings.

Sincerely,

Ms. Aune

- favorite pasttime
- what you would do with a million dollars
- your favorite place to visit
- what you want to do when you grow up
- greatest accomplishment

1. You can allow students to address their letters to a penpal. You can secure penpals by locating American or foreign students of their same age, as listed with the following associations:

International Friendship League
55 Mt. Vernon St.
Beacon Hill
Boston, MA 02108

League of Friendship
P.O. Box 509
Mt. Vernon, OH 43050

Student Letter Exchange
308 Second St., N.W.
Austin, MN 55912

World Pen Pals
1690 Como Ave.
St. Paul, MN 55108

Worldwide Pen Friends
P.O. Box 6896
Thousand Oaks, CA 91359

2. Ask a colleague at another school if your students can become penpals. Each child could write letters, invitations, and thank you notes to a counterpart several times during the year.

3. Students can select a loved one to whom they would like to write. They can write to this person or can apply the principles of this lesson to a real-life political or consumerist situation. They can also write a letter to you offering suggestions for class changes.

4. For older students it is important that the skills of this lesson are applied to a higher level of thinking. Older students should learn that important writings are carefully planned and can change the course of events. They can study and discuss with you distinguishing characteristics of editorials in the newspaper. They can select an issue they favor and research it through books and interviews. they can then outline the issues and positions they want to communicate before they write. Then they can devise actions they could take to improve the situation. Issues in their neighborhood are best, but they can write to national leaders as well. The final draft of the letter can be typed.

One measure of the success of your correspondence is that a classmate can understand your message. Before you mail your letter, ask someone else to proofread it and restate its message to you.

[Hand out Figure 3-3. Use the first half only for grades 1-6; use both halves for grades 6–8. Also hand out Activity 3-2.]

[For younger grades:] In Activity 3-2 you will write an Election Day letter. You will fill in the blanks to tell your penpal or a relative or friend what your thoughts and feelings are about voting. Or you may just want to tell the person something interesting about what you have been doing recently. You will use the friendly letter format. **[Go over the elements of this format, including placement and punctuation.]**

[For older students:] In Activity 3-2 you will write an Election Day letter. You will fill in the blanks to explain how you feel about a ballot item or other issue to a candidate, an elected official, or a voter. You will use the business letter format in Figure 3-3. **[Review business letter elements and their placement and punctuation.]** In your first paragraph you will state your position—tell why you are writing the letter. In the next paragraph give reasons and details that support your position. In the last paragraph tell what you hope the person to whom you are writing will do in response to your letter. Do you hope that he or she will vote a particular way on Election Day? Should he or she present your point of view before the city council or county, state, or federal representatives? Perhaps you merely want your correspondent to respond with information for you about the issue, or tell you his or her viewpoint and opinions about it.

[Allow students to begin their Activity 3-2 letters.]

GRADING CRITERIA: _____

MODIFICATIONS FOR GRADE LEVELS AND STUDENT ABILITY LEVELS

For Kindergarten and Slower Learning First-Graders, students only draw a picture of themselves or something else to mail to a friend or relative as a type of friendly letter, and you teach only the conventions of friendly letters. *For First Grade, Second Grade, and Slower Learners,* Activity 3-1 may be structured so students have a specific model to follow. *For Third through Eighth Grades and Gifted Students,* students may research the subject they will write about and contact a company to answer their specific questions.

NOTES FOR FUTURE USE: _____

FIGURE 3-3
Forms to Follow in Business Correspondence

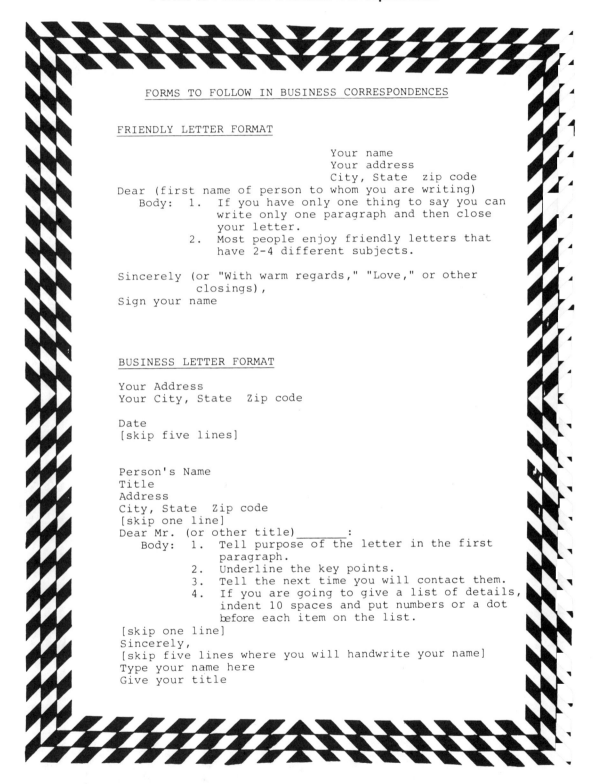

```
        FORMS TO FOLLOW IN BUSINESS CORRESPONDENCES

FRIENDLY LETTER FORMAT

                              Your name
                              Your address
                              City, State  zip code
Dear (first name of person to whom you are writing)
    Body:  1.  If you have only one thing to say you can
               write only one paragraph and then close
               your letter.
           2.  Most people enjoy friendly letters that
               have 2-4 different subjects.

Sincerely (or "With warm regards," "Love," or other
           closings),
Sign your name




BUSINESS LETTER FORMAT

Your Address
Your City, State  Zip code

Date
[skip five lines]


Person's Name
Title
Address
City, State  Zip code
[skip one line]
Dear Mr. (or other title)_____:
    Body:  1.  Tell purpose of the letter in the first
               paragraph.
           2.  Underline the key points.
           3.  Tell the next time you will contact them.
           4.  If you are going to give a list of details,
               indent 10 spaces and put numbers or a dot
               before each item on the list.
[skip one line]
Sincerely,
[skip five lines where you will handwrite your name]
Type your name here
Give your title
```

FIGURE 3-3 (Continued)

```
BUSINESS LETTER FORMAT
---------------------------
---------------------------
---------------------------


---------------------------
---------------------------
---------------------------
---------------------------
Dear ---------------------
     The purpose of this letter is to _____
---------------------------------------------------------------
     My key points are _____
---------------------------------------------------------------
---------------------------------------------------------------
---------------------------------------------------------------
     I hope you will _____
---------------------------------------------------------------


-------------------------


-------------------------------
-------------------------------
```

ACTIVITY 3-2

ELECTION DAY LETTER

FRIENDLY LETTER FORMAT

_____

_____

_____

Dear _____

_____

_____

_____

_____

_____

_____

_____

_____

_____

_____

Reading Skill Development: How to Make a Story Map

TIME REQUIRED

Teacher Directed Exploration (Activity 3-3): 20–30 minutes

Student Discovery Page (Activity 3-4): 2–5 days

TEACHING STRATEGIES

These activities involve right and left brain integration and creative thinking development.

ACTIVITY 3-3 _____

HOW AUTHORS PLAN STORIES

[OBJECTIVE] YOU WILL LEARN TO USE STORY MAPS TO IMPROVE YOUR READING AND WRITING ABILITIES.

Robert Louis Stevenson is a famous author born in November 1850. One of his most famous books is *Treasure Island.* He, like most writers, used a story map to write his books. During National Children's Book Week we are going to learn how authors write books. Most begin by making a story map. These maps help authors write good stories and can be used to help you predict what will happen next when you read. You can also use them to improve the stories you write.

Many writers think about and outline the following points before they begin to write. These points guide their writing and cause them to write in an ordered fashion:

Description of main characters

Details about the location and setting of the story

Problems that will occur in the story

Events in the plot

Point of climax

Resolution or ending

[Hand out Figure 3-4.] When you read your library book (or story) today, complete Figure 3-4. Then make the story map your author might have used as he or she wrote the book (or story).

To make your map, write a main idea or word. Make a box or circle around it if it is very important to the story. if it is a part of another idea, draw a line from that word to the bigger idea so you and everyone else can more clearly see how all the ideas in the story relate together.

To show you how to do it, let's make a map with _____.
[Select one of your favorite pieces of children's literature. Read it to the class and ask them to point out the main ideas. As each main point is given, write it on the board and connect it to other main points with a line that demonstrates which ideas are superordinate and which are subordinate. Any of the samples from Activity 3-4 can be used as the initial framework. Stop and collectively revise the map after each new idea appears.]

FIGURE 3-4
Story Outline

STORY MAP FOR _____

Description of Main Characters:

Details about location and setting of the story:

Problem that will occur in the story:

Main events in the plot:

      1.

      2.

      3.

      4.

Point of climax:

Resolution or ending:

[When finished, pass out Activity 3-4 and have students decide what type of story map they want to use as they read. Students make a story map using one of the basic forms from Activity 3-4 as they read from a story or library book. If you wish, at the end of the class students can share their maps.]

GRADING CRITERIA: _____

EARLY FINISHERS

Early finishers can make a story map of what they think will happen in the next chapter, or if the author were to write a sequel to the book. Encourage the use of a different framework for this story map.

MODIFICATIONS FOR GRADE LEVELS AND STUDENT ABILITY LEVELS

For Kindergarten, First, and Second Grades, the entire group completes one story map with you.

STUDENTS WHO WILL BE WORKING ON OTHER PROJECTS OR LESSONS: _____

NOTES FOR FUTURE USE: _____

ACTIVITY 3-4

STORY MAPS

1ST   2ND   3RD   4TH   END
EVENT   EVENT   EVENT   EVENT

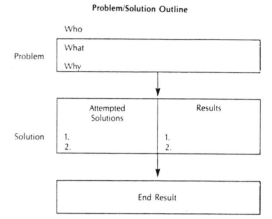

Problem/Solution Outline

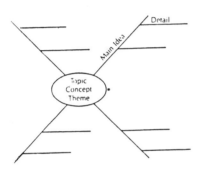

Compare/Contrast Matrix

	Name 1	Name 2
Attribute 1		
Attribute 2		
Attribute 3		

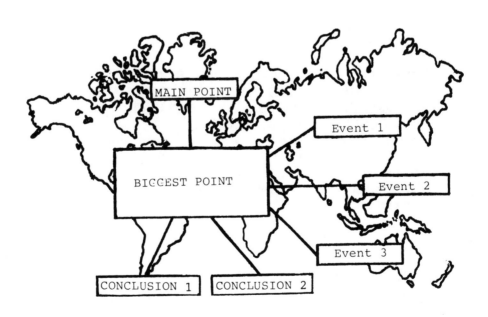

Spelling Skills Development: Learning to Use Mneumonic Devices to Spell Words Correctly

TIME REQUIRED

Teacher Directed Exploration (Activity 3-5): 45 minutes

Student Discovery Page (Activity 3-6): 40 minutes

TEACHING STRATEGIES

Students will learn to create their own mneumonic devices to improve spelling ability

ACTIVITY 3-5

STRATEGIES FOR SUCCESSFUL SPELLING

[Read the following history of American Education Week or an excerpt from it.] American Education Week was initiated after the draft boards in World War I discovered that about 25 percent of draftees were illiterate, while only 9 percent were physically unfit.

Since its inception 66 years ago, American Education Week has been celebrated to make Americans more aware of the values of education.

Today the observance of American Education Week serves to increase public understanding and appreciation of the nation's schools, to encourage parents to visit schools, and to build civic and community support to improve education.

One of the most difficult skills to learn is how to spell difficult words. In September we learned how to spell words that contain common word parts. In October we learned how to memorize parts of words that come from other countries to improve spelling ability.

This month, in celebration of American Education Week, we will learn to spell words that do not have either of these features.

[OBJECTIVE] YOU WILL LEARN TO USE MNEUMONIC DEVICES TO IMPROVE YOUR SPELLING ABILITY. YOU WILL KNOW YOU HAVE BEEN SUCCESSFUL WHEN YOU CAN SPELL FIVE WORDS THAT HAD PREVIOUSLY GIVEN YOU TROUBLE.

First, when you have trouble spelling a word, add a design to the letters that shows the meaning of the word. This helps you remember each of the letters of the word because it looks different from anything you've ever seen before. **[Use a transparency of Activity 3-6 to show the students a sample of what they can do.]**

A second strategy is to think of a clever saying about the word, such as

1. The one in once is divided by "c." (once)

2. Not all mice are nice. (mice)

3. Almost and always are spelled with one "l." (always)

4. The word "pal" is in principal. (principal)

5. All right is spelled like all wrong. (all right)

6. There is a second "o" in chocolate. (chocolate)

7. There is a liar in familiar but not in similar. (similar)

8. There is a rat in separate. (separate)

9. Watch the "e"'s in cemetery. (cemetery)

[Students complete Activity 3-6 and/or use one or more of the mneumonic strategies as they make a list of five to ten words they have misspelled in their writings.]

_____

GRADING CRITERIA: _____

_____

MODIFICATIONS FOR GRADE LEVELS AND STUDENT ABILITY LEVELS

For Kindergarten through Third Grades and Slower Learners, either omit this activity or teach only the first mneumonic device. *For Fourth through Eighth Grades and Gifted Learners,* students can do as many words as you desire.

STUDENTS WHO WILL BE WORKING ON OTHER PROJECTS OR LESSONS: _____

_____

NOTES FOR FUTURE USE: _____

_____

ACTIVITY 3-6

DURING AMERICAN EDUCATION WEEK WE WILL LEARN NEW WAYS TO IMPROVE OUR SPELLING

Directions: In this column I created mneumonic ways to remember words I misspelled these past two months at school. I'm ready for a test over all 25 words on this sheet.

1. write
2. smile
3. hop~~t~~ing
4. writing
5. Smiling
6. dance
7. joke Ha!
8. hope
9. April
10. dancing

11. half
12. TRAIN
13. too
14. doctor
15. balloon
16. school Ra-Ra!

17.
18.
19.
20.
21.
22.
23.
24.
25.

Handwriting Skill Improvement: Developing the Ability to Place Proper Space Between Letters and Words:

TIME REQUIRED

Teacher Directed Exploration (Activity 3-7): 30 minutes

Student Discovery Page (Activity 3-8): 30 minutes

TEACHING STRATEGIES

Students will learn through comparing correct and incorrect samples.

ACTIVITY 3-7

SPACING FOR GOOD HANDWRITING

[OBJECTIVE] WHEN WRITING IN CURSIVE OR MANUSCRIPT, YOU WILL LEARN CORRECT SPACING BETWEEN WORDS AND SENTENCES. YOU WILL KNOW YOU HAVE BEEN SUCCESSFUL WHEN YOU LEAVE ENOUGH SPACE TO INSERT THE LETTER "O" BETWEEN WORDS AND TWO "O"'S BETWEEN SENTENCES. A FURTHER TEST OF LEARNING OCCURS WHEN THE PRACTICE ON SPACING THAT THIS LESSON PROVIDES IS EVIDENCED IN PROPER SPACING IN YOUR DAILY WORK.

One characteristic of good handwriting is that there is equal space between words and sentences. There should be enough space for a lowercase letter "o" between words and for two "o"s between sentences.

To practice better handwriting, we will make a plaque for your room at home or to use as a gift. Your "plaque" will be like a certificate you could frame and hang. You can put the words I'm going to teach you on your plaque if you wish.

If you want, you may create a plaque with a favorite saying of your own, or you can use a quotation we've studied at school. In the process you will practice your handwriting. Tomorrow you will make a plaque and use any type of writing utensil you prefer. Let me show you how to space on large plaques and posters.

You will place the tip of your little finger between each letter in a word to be sure letters are equally spaced. To space between words, you will put your little finger and your ring finger between words. In a minute, I will show you how to do it and you'll practice. First, it is important that you practice making equal spaces between all letters every time you write. When you write on normal-size paper, your spaces are not as large as your fingertip. It is more difficult to space between letters of normal size. By practicing you will improve your spacing and your handwriting.

To begin, I'd like to tell you a little about an important event that occurred in our country this month, long ago. On November 19, 1863, President Abraham Lincoln delivered one of his most important speeches. President Lincoln wrote five copies, in his best handwriting, so he could have one to read and some to give to friends because they thought so much of the speech that they wanted their own copies. One copy hangs in the Lincoln Room of the White House. If you ever visit, be sure to look for this speech. Study President Lincoln's speech and think about how important this handwritten speech has become to our country.

At the time President Lincoln wrote it, he did not know his handwriting would be displayed for all to see. Our goal today is to improve your handwriting to the point that no matter how many pick up your writing, they will be able to read every word. Today we are going to practice spacing between words by rewriting President Lincoln's speech, The Gettysburg Address.

Before we practice writing the Gettysburg Address, I want you to use this model to remember the shape of each letter (pass out Figure 3-5 or the hand-writing model your district follows). I also want you to know a little more about why President Lincoln wrote the Gettysburg Address.

During the Civil War, for three long days and nights in July of 1863, the Northern and Southern armies fought outside the small town of Gettysburg,

FIGURE 3-5
Handwriting Models

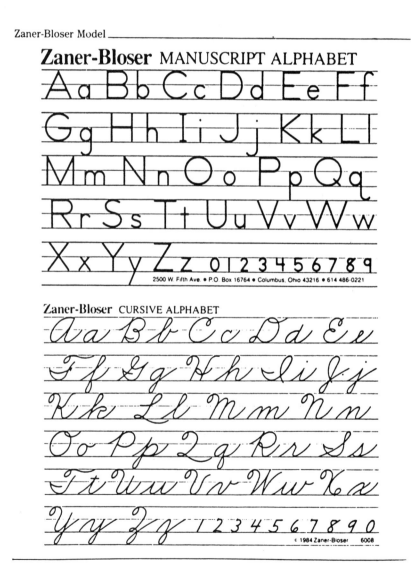

Pennsylvania. During those three days 7,000 soldiers died. After the battle ended the government purchased the land to bury these men. This land became known as the Soldiers National Cemetery. Lincoln gave the Gettysburg Address to dedicate the cemetery to all soldiers and to express his deep respect and sorrow for those who had died. This is what he wrote. **[You may wish to place the Gettysburg Address found on Activity 3-8, on an overhead projector or give a copy to each student. After you read the address aloud, have students practice writing a part of it in large, plaque-size letters.] [On the next day allow students to design their own border for a plaque. Explain that when they make large plaques or posters, they can place a lined sheet under plain paper so the lines show through or they can pencil lines in lightly on the paper where they write the plaque or poster, erasing the lines when they have finished.]**

GRADING CRITERIA: _____

MODIFICATIONS FOR GRADE LEVELS AND STUDENT ABILITY LEVELS

For Kindergarten through Third Grades and Slower Learners, the lesson may be omitted or reduced in difficulty by requiring students to write fewer lines. *For Fourth through Eighth Grades and Gifted Students,* students can experiment with different handwriting techniques.

Activity   3-8

THE GETTYSBURG ADDRESS: HANDWRITING SAMPLE AND GUIDE TO IMPROVE SPACING BETWEEN LETTERS AND WORDS

> Four score and seven years ago our fathers brought forth upon this continent a new nation, conceived in liberty and dedicated to the proposition that all men are created equal.
>
> Now we are engaged in a great civil war, testing whether that nation or any nation so conceived and so dedicated can long endure. We are met on a great battlefield of that war. We have come to dedicate a portion of the field as a final resting-place of those who here gave their lives that that nation might live. It is altogether fitting and proper that we should do this.
>
> But, in a larger sense, we cannot dedicate, we cannot consecrate, we cannot hallow this ground. The brave men living and dead, who struggled here have consecrated it far above our poor power to add or detract. The world will little note nor long remember what we say here, but it can never forget what they did here. It is for us the living, rather, to be dedicated here to the unfinished work which they who fought here have thus far so nobly advanced. It is rather for us to be here dedicated to the great task remaining before us that from these honored dead we take increased devotion to that cause for which they gave the last full measure of devotion; that we here highly resolve that these dead shall not have died in vain; that this nation, under God, shall have a new birth of freedom; and that government of the people, by the people, for the people, shall not perish from the earth.

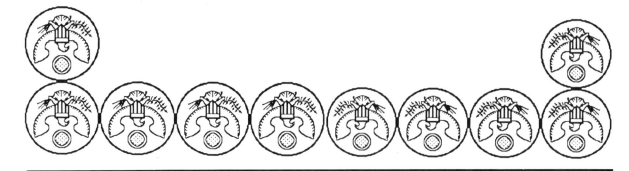

Listening Skill Development: Learning to Ask Interesting and Effective Questions and to Conduct Effective Interviews

TIME REQUIRED

Teacher Directed Exploration (Activity 3-9): 30 minutes

Student Discovery Page (Activity 3-10): as long as you desire

TEACHING STRATEGIES

Students will learn through practicing a simulated interview, teacher modeling, and applying their skills to a school or community problem.

ACTIVITY 3-9 _____

SEEKING INFORMATION THROUGH EFFECTIVE INTERVIEWS

[OBJECTIVE] YOU WILL INCREASE YOUR LISTENING SKILLS BY LEARNING TO ASK MORE INTERESTING AND EFFECTIVE QUESTIONS AND CONDUCTING INTERVIEWS. YOU WILL KNOW YOU HAVE BEEN SUCCESSFUL IF YOUR INTERVIEW PRODUCES VALUABLE INFORMATION CONCERNING A PROBLEM.

Some communities celebrate World Hello Day on November 21. These communities select a place, somewhere in the world, that they want to help. People in the two communities work together to solve a problem. As they begin, they interview many people and ask many questions.

Today you will learn to conduct good interviews and ask better questions.

[Present the information in Figure 3-6 orally for younger students. Allow older students to read Figure 3-6 as you present it to them. Then model a correct interviewing session by either showing a 10-minute segment from a TV interview show or conducting a live interview of another teacher, principal, or school secretary. When you finish, point out the Steps to Better Questions and Interviews procedures that you followed.]

[Next, younger students will work alone to draft their answer to Activity 3-10. They will then practice conducting their interview with a friend. Older students will spend the rest of the class period in small groups selecting a problem they wish to address. At home or in the next class, these older students work alone, constructing their own interview. They review and critique each other's interview sheets (Activity 3-10). They turn in Activity 3-10 for a final critique before they conduct the interview.]

[Interviews of community leaders can be conducted (1) by phone (as a last resort); (2) by parents taking students to conduct an interview after school; (3) by inviting a person to lunch at school and having students conduct an interview at that time; or (4) with principal permission, allowing students to go to a person's office to conduct an interview during school hours.]

[Once interviews are complete, small groups meet to discuss results and plan a way to help solve the problem they explored.]

FIGURE 3-6
Steps to Better Questions and Interviews

Steps to Better Questions and Interviews
1. State the purpose of the interview first. Tell the interviewee the
purpose. The purpose is:_____
2. Begin with a question seeking background information about the
purpose. This question builds trust between two people and increases
chances that both people can better understand each other.
3. Next, ask for a description of experiences that led to the present
problem. This description will be better if separate questions are
prepared and begin with the following words:
    How_____

    When_____

    Where_____

    What_____

    Who_____

    Why_____

4. Ask a person in an interview to apply a principle he is discussing
to something familiar such as a common occurrence in nature or by
giving an example. This will better ensure that you understand the
intent of the speaker.
5. Paraphrase what a person says if you aren't sure you understand
what was said.
6. Ask for an interviewee's definition of simple words that could mean
different things, such as "difficult," "happy," "good."
7. Listen carefully so you can follow up with a question.
8. Spend some time, at least 30 minutes, reading information about the
topic before you go to your interview.
9. Take notes in spaces directly below each question so the interviewer
will not have to wait too long while you write.
10. Sometimes you may want to use a tape recorder, but ask if it is
acceptable with the interviewee.
11. Write a thank you note as a follow-up of the interview.
12. After each interview, critique yourself and find ways you can
improve.

GRADING CRITERIA: _____

MODIFICATIONS FOR GRADE LEVELS AND STUDENT ABILITY LEVELS

For Kindergarten through Third Grades and Slower Learning Groups, students can interview parents, friends, or members of the school staff. The interview is designed to find a solution to a problem that the student wants to solve. *For Fourth through Eighth Grades and Gifted Learners,* students individually or in small groups decide upon a problem. Each member of the group selects two or more people to interview concerning the problem.

ACTIVITY 3-10

WORLD HELLO DAY: SOLVING A PROBLEM BY ASKING EFFECTIVE QUESTIONS AND USING INTERVIEWS

Make as many copies of this sheet as you need so you can take one sheet with you for each interview.

Name_____

Interviewee and Title_____

Phone # for Follow-up_____

Address for Thank you Note_____

_____

The purpose of this interview is to_____

_____

1. To gain background information, I will ask:_____

_____

2. Ask for description of the experience that led to the problem_____

_____

I'll listen for things that are important to the interviewee and note those here:

I'll ask specific questions:

3. How_____

4. When_____

5. Where_____

6. What_____

7. Who_____

8. Why_____

9. Ask if there is anything he or she could do to help solve the problem or any ideas about things your group could do.

10. Wrote thank you note_____mailed it_____

11. Improvements I can make before my next interview are:

a.

b.

Grammar Skill Development: Learning to Use Correct Punctuation

TIME REQUIRED

Teacher Directed Exploration (Activity 3-11): 20 minutes

Student Discovery Page (Activity 3-12): 20 minutes

TEACHING STRATEGIES

Students will role play, acting as if they are writers. They will then translate one form of writing to another.

ACTIVITY 3-11

MARK TWAIN HELPS YOU IN USING PUNCTUATION AND CAPITALIZATION CORRECTLY

[OBJECTIVE] TODAY YOU WILL LEARN HOW TO USE QUESTION MARKS AND PERIODS CORRECTLY.

[Show an overhead transparency of Activity 3-11, but cover the last half of the page.] The famous American writer Mark Twain was born on November 30. Like all writers, he had to learn to use punctuation marks and capital letters correctly. The reason punctuation and capitalization are important are because when we speak, vocal expressions, gestures, and the speed of our speech help to carry our meaning. When we write, we only have capital letters and punctuation marks to help us convey meaning.]

[Distribute a copy of Figure 3-7 to students.] As I read I want you to think of the reason each letter is capitalized or each punctuation mark is inserted. [When you come to each numbered capital letter and punctuation mark, ask the students the reason for it and then have them write this reason on a copy of Figure 3-7. The completed sheet can be used as a reference as students complete Activity 3-12 and whenever they write in the future.]

[Hand out Activity 3-12 for group or individual completion.]

ANSWER KEY FOR FIGURE 3-7

1. 1 or 11	**9.** 9	**17.** 12
2. 2	**10.** 8	**18.** 4
3. 3	**11.** 9	**19.** 11 or 13
4. 4	**12.** 10	**20.** 7
5. 5	**13.** 10	**21.** 22
6. 6	**14.** 10	**22.** 11, or 28
7. 4	**15.** 4	**23.** 16
8. 7	**16.** 11	**24.** 4

FIGURE 3-7
Huckleberry Finn and Tom Sawyer To the Rescue: They Help Me Use
Punctuation and Capital Letters Correctly

Huckleberry Finn and Tom Sawyer To the Rescue: They Help Me Use
Punctuation and Capital Letters Correctly

Mark Twain was born November   30,   1835.
1._____   2._____   3._____   4._____

_____   _____   _____   _____
I   once read Huckleberry Finn,
5._____   6._____7._____

_____
that he wrote, and he was born in   Florida,
8._____   9._____10._____

_____   _____   _____
Missouri in the   United   States of   America.
11._____   12.____   13._____14.____15.____

_____   ____   _____   ____   ____
His favorite river was the Mississippi.
16._____17.____ 18._____

_____   ____   _____
Wednesday,   his short story,
19.____20._____   21._____

____   _____   _____
"The Celebrated Jumping Frog of Calavaras County,"
22._____

_____
was published in the Reader's Digest Magazine.
23._____24._____

_____   _____
John,

1. The names of people, pets, titles, and initials are capitalized.
2. Months are capitalized.
3. Commas separate dates from years.
4. Periods end a statement.
5. The word "I" is always capitalized.
6. The titles of books are capitalized.
7. Commas often come before and after clauses (phrases) in the middle of a sentence.
8. Commas separate city and state (explain Florida is the name of a city in Missouri).
9. Capitalize cities and states.
10. Capitalize countries.
11. Capitalize the first word in every sentence.
12. Capitalize the names of rivers.
13. Capitalize the days of the week.
14. Commas come before and after an exact title if a general description comes first.
15. Capitalize the titles of short stories.
16. Capitalize the titles of magazines.
17. Capitalize the greeting in a letter.
18. Commas come after the greeting in a letter.
19. Capitalize the names of movies.
20. Capitalize the names of poems and songs.
21. Capitalize the names of holidays.
22. Commas come after a phrase that begins a sentence if that phrase is not a subject.
23. Capitalize the names of pets.
24. Capitalize the names of streets.
25. Commas separate a list of items when more than two appear in sentence.
26. Capitalize the names of mountains.
27. Commas come right before or after spoken words.
28. Quotation marks come right before and after spoken words.

GRADING CRITERIA: _____

_____

MODIFICATIONS FOR GRADE LEVELS AND STUDENT ABILITY LEVELS

For Younger Students and Slower Learning Students, you will only use quotation marks and periods and do not pass out Figure 3-7. Do Activity 3-12 orally as a group. *For Older Students and Most Able Learners,* you can use all the rules in Figure 3-7 and complete it together as a group. Use Activity 3-12 as an individual activity.

STUDENTS WHO WILL BE WORKING ON OTHER PROJECTS OR LESSONS: _____

_____

NOTES FOR FUTURE USE: _____

_____

ACTIVITY 3-12

LEARNING TO WRITE PUNCTUATION AND QUOTATIONS LIKE MARK TWAIN

Activity 3-12

Learning to Write Punctuation and Quotations
Like Mark Twain

When Mark Twain was first learning to write he worked on a newspaper. He had to set the type which means he put all the words and punctuation marks in the printer so they could print. If a writer left out a comma or put in a punctuation mark in the wrong place, Mark Twain had to correct it before he set it up to print. Let's pretend you are working with Mark Twain and you have been asked to set the cartoon printed below without the pictures. You are to write a description of what is happening and the direct words said.

The first pictures are already finished and you can use them as examples. This writer chose very good verbs to carry the meaning of the picture. Choose the most accurate vocabulary words you can. Once you've written your very best description of this cartoon, check your punctuation.

Reprinted by permission of UFS, Inc.

A boy and a girl were in the back yard with their dog. They wanted to go swimming in their pool.

"Mom!" called the girl, trying to get her mother to help her get her dog out of their swimming pool.

"Get outa there," said the boy.

Speaking Skill Development: Using Interesting Vocabulary Words

TIME REQUIRED

Teacher Directed Exploration (Activity 3-13): 30 minutes

Student Discovery Page (Activity 3-14): 90 minutes divided into more than one day. Allow five students to present each day during the week preceding Thanksgiving vacation.

TEACHING STRATEGIES

Students will be involved in higher-level thinking discussions and will generate their own writing rules.

ACTIVITY 3-13

A THANKSGIVING STORY

[Ask students to think of their favorite stories and books. Ask them to decide why they found these stories to be interesting. List their reasons on the board.]

[OBJECTIVE] TODAY YOU WILL USE INTERESTING VOCABULARY IN A THANKSGIVING STORY. YOU WILL KNOW YOU HAVE BECOME A MORE INTERESTING SPEAKER IF YOU CAN COMPLETE 90% OF ACTIVI-TY 3-14 ALONE.

[Hand out copies of Figure 3-8. Discuss with the class the Rules for Becoming a Better Speaker and Writer (Figure 3-8). Ask them to add one idea about how to use more interesting words. This idea can become number nine on the list.]

You are each going to give a 5-minute oral presentation of a story about a special Thanksgiving you remember or imagine. Use the back of the page to outline your speech, and to use the rules as you make your presentation.

Before you begin, let's practice using more vivid words. For example, tell me some vivid *sounds* you hear at Thanksgiving, such as:

basting

grating

hubbub

laughing

praying

buzzing

humming

singing

[When this discussion has ended, distribute Activity 3-14. You can use Activity 3-14 in one of three different ways. You can distribute it and discuss it, asking students to use it in the future when they write and speak. You

FIGURE 3-8
Rules for Becoming a Better Speaker and Writer

1. Use synonyms so you uo not repeat the same adjective twice. When tempted to use an adjective or adverb used previously, look up the word in a dictionary or a thesaurus to find a better word or synonym.
2. When you describe something, select words that use as many senses as possible. In this way people can picture in their minds the smells, sounds, feelings, and sights
3. Select exact words, especially very vivid verbs.
4. When describing an event, tell the most important or unusual detail first.
5. To make a special point, compare or contrast it to something familiar.
6. Ask someone else to suggest another word when when tempted to use a previously used word.
7. Practice in groups by:
   a. Describing the location of an ideal Thanksgiving.
   b. Creating one sentence to describe two people there.
   c. Describing the weather of the day.
   d. Detailing one unusual action that occurred.
   e. Telling how one thing felt.
   f. Presenting a moral or main point of the Thanksgiving story in one sentence.
8. Outline your speech,   using what you learned about outlining from September's lesson.

can ask students to evaluate each other's Thanksgiving stories in pairs. You can also ask students to evaluate each other, if speeches are given in small groups. If used in large groups, number students off 1 to 5; each student evaluates only the first, second, third, fourth, or fifth speaker of the day, according to their number.]

GRADING CRITERIA: _____

MODIFICATIONS FOR GRADE LEVELS AND STUDENT ABILITY LEVELS

For Kindergarten through Third Grades and Slower Learning Groups, allow more time in small groups for students to develop a speech. *For Third through Fifth Grades,* allow enough time for students to revise their speeches before they present them. *For Sixth through Eighth Grades,* students should write a more detailed story in a more formal manner and tell the class the story without reading from their paper. Allow each child to prepare a 5-minute presentation.

SCALE TO STRENGTHEN YOUR SPEAKING
AND WRITING VOCABULARY

Name of Speaker_____

Directions: Put an example after each rating that applied
             to the speaker's presentation.

Used a viariety of new and interesting words and comparisons
to create a vivid impression, such as _____
_____

Synonyms were provided, and they gave variety and interest,
such as _____
_____

Exact words painted vivid, clear pictures and were interesting,
such as_____
_____

Unusual expressions, word combinations, and comparisons added
zest and color to the story_____
_____

Words were descriptive but could be improved by_____
_____

Some new and interesting words to add could be_____
_____

Dull, uninteresting words were_____

Other improvements I suggest are_____
_____
_____
_____
_____
_____
_____

Rater_____

Parent Report Form

The parent report form given here can be mailed to parents prior to a parent/teacher conference at any time during the year. You can discuss other student strengths and weaknesses at the bottom of the form.

PARENT REPORT FORM

Parent Report Form

The circled words and or explanation in each section of the apple are the learning styles of _____. Becoming aware of your child's learning style helps me to meet his her needs. I hope this information is helpful to you as well.

_____   _____
signature   school room number

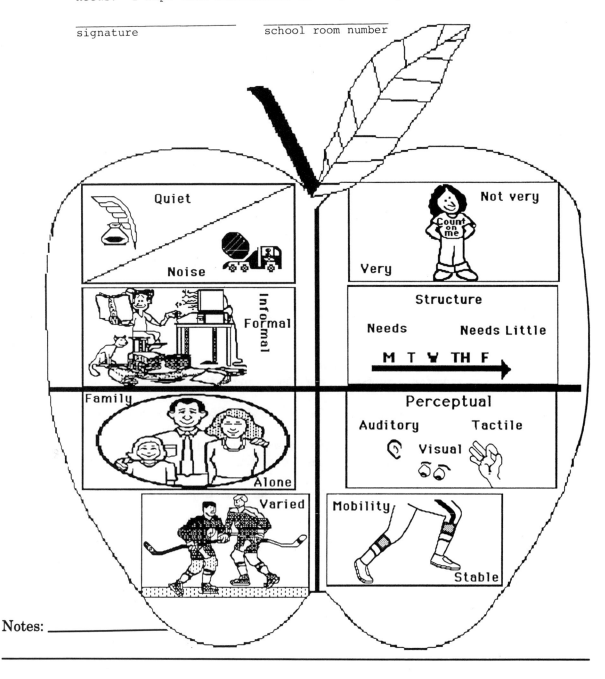

Notes: _____

CHAPTER

4 *December*

December is a month of festivities and celebrations. This month's themes center around people gathering to celebrate Christmas and Hanukkah in other countries, the anniversary of the Apollo 6 mission, the landing on Plymouth Rock, Tell Someone They Are Doing a Good Job Week, and the anniversary of the first flight of Orville and Wilbur Wright.

Scope and Sequence of Language Arts Concepts Taught in December

Reading (Activities 4-1 and 4-2): Students learn to identify their favorite types of literature.

Spelling (Activities 4-3 and 4-4): Students learn to identify why they misspell words.

Composition (Activities 4-5 and 4-6): Students increase the quality of their written expressions by brainstorming in the planning stages of their first drafts.

Speaking (Activities 4-7 and 4-8): Students learn to use transition words.

Listening (Activities 4-9 and 4-10): Students will use details and focus on main ideas so they can make correct inferences and reduce misunderstandings.

Grammar (Activities 4-11 and 4-12): Students will learn to use present and past tense of verbs.

Handwriting (Activities 4-13 and 4-14): Students will recognize mistakes in forming individual letters.

Supplementary Activities

The following projects can complement Activities 4-1 through 4-14 in many ways. Students can complete them by working alone or in small groups.

FIGURE 4-1
Following Directions for Christmas Creations

A Balloon Santa

1. Blow up a balloon and tie it to hold the air.
2. For Santa's hat, cut a sheet of crepe or construction paper long enough to go around the shell of the balloon and overlap it. Pull it together at the top and tie it with thread. Glue a band of cotton around the bottom of the hat. Glue a cotton ball to the top of the hat.
3. Paint the skin of the balloon. Let the pain dry. Paint the face.
4. Glue on cotton for eyebrows, hair, and mustache.
5. Cut a piece of white crepe paper the shape of a beard. Glue on cotton to cover it. Glue the beard to Santa's face.

A Custom Christmas Tree

1. Draw a circle on newspaper using a plate. Cut it out. Fold the circle in half. Then fold it in half again. Unfold it. Cut away one-fourth of the circle. The rest of the circle is the pattern.
2. Draw the pattern on art paper. Cut it out.
3. Pull the ends together to make a cone. Tape it in place.
4. Paint a paper towel tube brown. Let the paint dry.
5. Fit the cone over the tube. Glue it in place.
6. Cut the tube at the bottom to make the length you want.
7. Glue the trunk to a piece of cardboard for a base.
8. Paint the base.
9. Decorate the tree as creatively as you can.

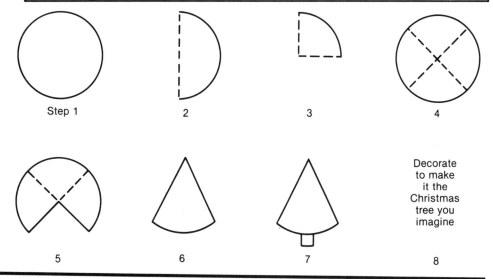

Step 1   2   3   4

5   6   7

Decorate
to make
it the
Christmas
tree you
imagine

8

1. Students make their own Santa Claus using a covered balloon for the body. The students complete the steps outlined in Figure 4-1 without teacher direction and increase their abilities to follow printed directions. Students can then create their own snowman, reindeer, or elf, using their own creative ideas.

2. Students can create their own individual Christmas trees, following the directions in Figure 4-1. Students then decorate their trees as originally as possible.

3. Two students together write a paper on what the holiday season means to them. One student can begin a story, and the second student continues it. The story can be kept in a big scrapbook at the back of the room until everyone has had time to add to it.

4. A small group of students can make a bulletin board of a Christmas street scene with houses. Under the window shutters of each house is a story and symbol of what is most important to them about the holiday season.

5. Students who have birthdays in December can find out about a famous person who was born on their birth date.

Notable December Birth Dates

1. Mary Martin, Woody Allen, Richard Pryor, Alicia Markova, Bette Midler
2. Julie Harris, Ray Ealston, Ed Meese, Alexander Haig
3. Jean Luc Goodard, Ozzy Ozbourne, Andy Williams, Maria Callas, Rick Mears
4. Thomas Carlyle, Jeff Bridges
5. Jose Carreras, Strom Thurmond, Walt Disney, Otto Preminger
6. Ira Gershwin, "Baby Face" Nelson
7. Larry Bird, Ellen Burstyn, Priscilla Barnes, Eli Wallach, C. Thomas Howell
8. Kim Basinger, Sammy Davis, Jr., Flip Wilson, Jim Morrison
9. Kirk Douglas, Douglas Fairbanks, Jr., Beau Bridges, Donny Osmond, Redd Foxx
10. Emily Dickinson, Dorothy Lamour
11. Jermaine Jackson, Brenda Lee, Donna Mills, Rita Moreno, Terri Garr
12. Connie Frances, Frank Sinatra, Dionne Warwick, Bob Barker
13. John Davidson, Christopher Plummer, Dick Van Dyke
14. Patty Duke, Lee Remick, Charlie Rich, Morey Amsterdam
15. J. Paul Getty, Alan Freed, Tim Conway, Don Johnson
16. Lisa Welmann, Leslie Stahl, Noel Coward, Jane Austen

17. Arthur Fiedler

18. Roger Smith, Steven Spielberg, Betty Grable

19. Tim Reid, Peter Ustinov, Jennifer Beals, Robert McNaughton, Cicely Tyson, Edith Piaf

20. Irene Dunne, John Hillerman, Mark Keyloun

21. Phil Donahue, Jane Fonda, Ed Nelson

22. Robin Gibb, Maurice Gibb, Lady Bird Johnson, Jim Wright, Diane Sawyer

23. Jose Greco, Susan Lucci, Harry Guardino

24. Howard Hughes, Ava Gardner

25. Sissy Spacek, Humphrey Bogart, Cab Calloway, Little Richard, Barbara Mandrell, Mike Mazurky

26. Steve Allen, Carlton Fisk, Alan King, Richard Widmark

27. Marlene Dietrich, Tovah Feldshuh, Lee Salk

28. Woodrow Wilson, Jorge Valasquez, Martin Milner

29. Ted Danson, Ed Flanders, Mary Tyler Moore, Jon Voight, Andrew Jackson

30. Bert Parks, Rudyard Kipling, Sandy Koufax

31. John Denver, Anthony Hopkins, Ben Kingsley, Sarah Miles, Donna Summer, Jason Robards

6. The December calendar can be used in any of the ways suggested in Chapter 1.

Reading Skill Development: Learning to Appreciate Literature

TIME REQUIRED

Teacher Directed Exploration (Activity 4-1): 10 minutes

Student Discovery Page (Activity 4-2); as long as you wish, extended throughout the school vacation, if possible, to encourage reading

TEACHING STRATEGIES

Students will complete a chart to expand their exposure to different types of reading materials and literary genre.

ACTIVITY 4-1

WINTER READING WHEEL TO INCREASE THE JOY OF READING

December is the month when winter officially begins. During the winter months many people spend more time reading than in the summer months.

WINTER READING WHEEL TO INCREASE THE JOY OF READING

[OBJECTIVE]   TODAY YOU WILL LEARN TO ENJOY NEW TYPES OF LITERATURE AS A METHOD OF INCREASING YOUR APPRECIATION OF READING. **[Hand out copies of the Winter Reading Wheel (Figure 4-2).]** This wheel will help you keep a picture of your reading this month. Write your initials in the innermost circle. Write the title and the author of the book you read on the spoke of the wheel. To the right of the spoke in the second inner

FIGURE 4-2
Winter Reading Wheel

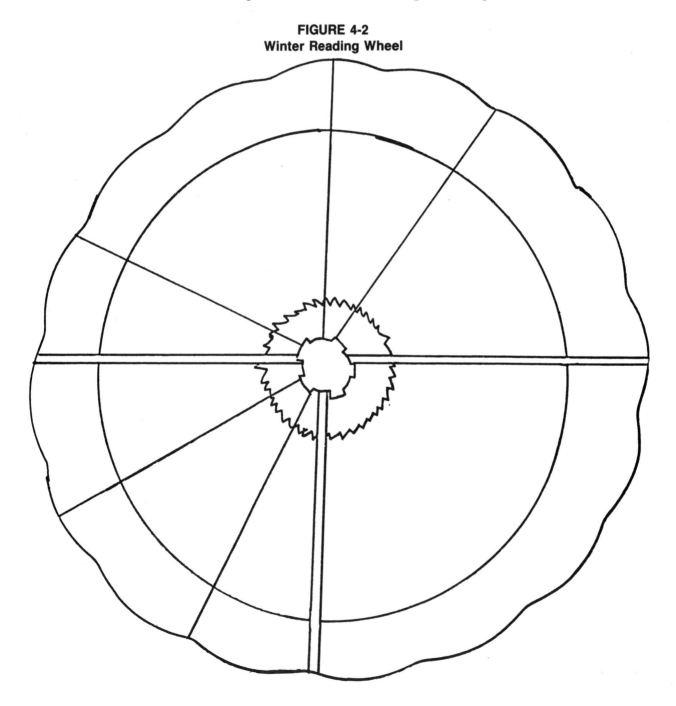

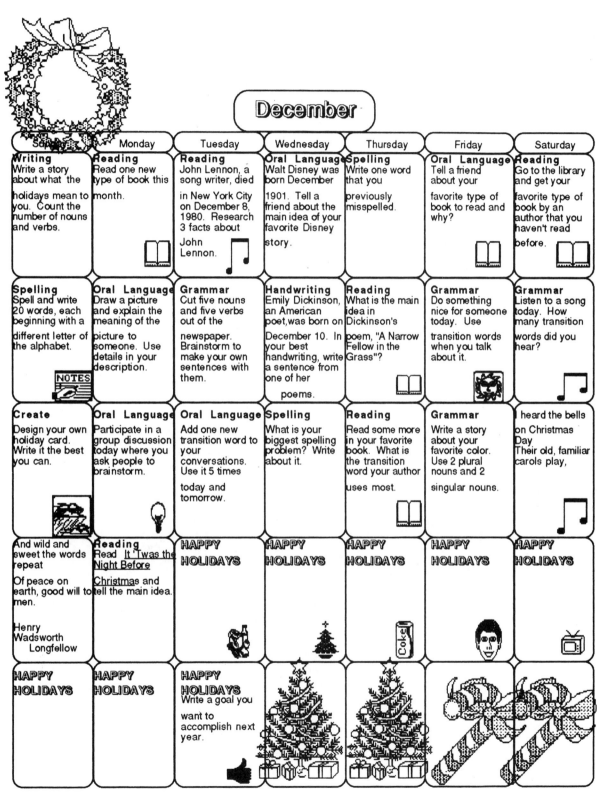

December

Sunday	Monday	Tuesday	Wednesday	Thursday	Friday	Saturday
Writing Write a story about what the holidays mean to you. Count the number of nouns and verbs.	**Reading** Read one new type of book this month.	**Reading** John Lennon, a song writer, died in New York City on December 8, 1980. Research 3 facts about John Lennon.	**Oral Language** Walt Disney was born December 1901. Tell a friend about the main idea of your favorite Disney story.	**Spelling** Write one word that you previously misspelled.	**Oral Language** Tell a friend about your favorite type of book to read and why?	**Reading** Go to the library and get your favorite type of book by an author that you haven't read before.
Spelling Spell and write 20 words, each beginning with a different letter of the alphabet.	**Oral Language** Draw a picture and explain the meaning of the picture to someone. Use details in your description.	**Grammar** Cut five nouns and five verbs out of the newspaper. Brainstorm to make your own sentences with them.	**Handwriting** Emily Dickinson, an American poet, was born on December 10. In your best handwriting, write a sentence from one of her poems.	**Reading** What is the main idea in Dickinson's poem, "A Narrow Fellow in the Grass"?	**Grammar** Do something nice for someone today. Use transition words when you talk about it.	**Grammar** Listen to a song today. How many transition words did you hear?
Create Design your own holiday card. Write it the best you can.	**Oral Language** Participate in a group discussion today where you ask people to brainstorm.	**Oral Language** Add one new transition word to your conversations. Use it 5 times today and tomorrow.	**Spelling** What is your biggest spelling problem? Write about it.	**Reading** Read some more in your favorite book. What is the transition word your author uses most.	**Grammar** Write a story about your favorite color. Use 2 plural nouns and 2 singular nouns.	I heard the bells on Christmas Day Their old, familiar carols play,
And wild and sweet the words repeat Of peace on earth, good will to men. Henry Wadsworth Longfellow	**Reading** Read It 'Twas the Night Before Christmas and tell the main idea.	**HAPPY HOLIDAYS**	**HAPPY HOLIDAYS**	**HAPPY HOLIDAYS**	**HAPPY HOLIDAYS**	**HAPPY HOLIDAYS**
HAPPY HOLIDAYS	**HAPPY HOLIDAYS**	**HAPPY HOLIDAYS** Write a goal you want to accomplish next year.				

This calendar created in collaboration with Frances Dornan, Valarie McGarry, George Russell.

circle write "F" if the book is fiction or "NF" if the book is nonfiction, or factual. In the "air" space to the right of the title spoke, write the main characters' names or a brief description of your favorite part of the book. In the wheel rim classify the book further—for example, "Autobiography" or "Poetry" or "Historical." Use a different color to shade in the different categories in the rim. You could color sports stories blue, for example. Try to make the rim of your wheel as variegated as you can. **[Using an overhead projector, demonstrate how one segment of the wheel would be filled in for a book the students have already read or heard.]** See how many spokes you can fill in this month!

[Completed wheels can be displayed in the classroom using six together in a "snowflake" formation or as wagon wheels under a Recommended Books Wagon Train that can be made from the Activity 4-2 form.]

[Hand out Activity 4-2.] This form will let you share your reading discoveries with your classmates. Fill it in for a book you read that you think others might enjoy reading.

GRADING CRITERIA: _____

MODIFICATIONS FOR GRADE LEVELS AND STUDENT ABILITY LEVELS

For Kindergarten through Third Grades and Slower Learning Groups, include on the wheels books that you read aloud. The types of literature you will encourage students to read (and include on the Winter Reading Wheel) are:

Biographies: Autobiographies

Folk literature: Fairy Tales, Folk Tales, Myths, Ballads, and Fables

Fiction: Fantasy, Science Fiction, Animal Fantasy, Historical, Contemporary Realistic, Mysteries, Adventure, and Novels

Informational: Aviation, Amusements, Sports, Games, Animals, Art, Music, Health, Personality, and Character Growth

Other Nonfiction: Historical, Humorous Works, Inventions, Machines, Occupations, Careers, Countries, Outer Space, Science, Math, Philosophy, Psychology, Our Country Yesterday and Today, Travel, and Transportation

Poetry

For Fourth through Eighth Grades and Gifted Learners, you can allow classroom officers or students in groups to select the divisions they want to place on the *Winter Reading Wheel.* Alternatively, you can allow individual students to select from the above list or to use divisions within the Dewey Decimal System in their school library to label the wheel.

You can use Activity 4-2 in a variety of ways depending on the needs of your students. The Book Recommendation form can be used by early finishers and posted in the room. Alternatively, you could design a method by which students complete a certain number of *Book Recommendation Forms,* working toward a goal they set.

NOTES FOR FUTURE USE: _____

ACTIVITY 4-2

BOOK RECOMMENDATION FORM

BOOK RECOMMENDATION

_____

Book-

Author-

Publishing Company-

Copyright Date-

Call Number in the library:

I recommend this book because:_____

_____

Here are some ways in which information about this book helped me: :__

_____

_____

_____

Below are some unsolved problems or questions that you might like about

the book:_____

_____

_____

_____

_____

Recommendation Made By-

_____

This form was adopted from one prepared for sixth grade students in Ms.

Maria D. Amigo's room.

Spelling Skill Development: Identifying Why You Misspell Words

TIME REQUIRED

Teacher Directed Exploration (Activity 4-3): 30 minutes

Student Discovery Page (Activity 4-4): 30 minutes

TEACHING STRATEGIES

A diagnostic test will be administered and individual student spelling needs will be identified and eliminated.

ACTIVITY 4-3 _____

TEST TO IDENTIFY WHY YOU MISSPELL WORDS

[OBJECTIVE] YOU WILL LEARN TODAY WHY YOU TEND TO MISSPELL SOME TYPES OF WORDS AND TO AVOID THAT PROBLEM IN THE FUTURE. YOU WILL KNOW YOU HAVE LEARNED IT WHEN YOU CAN CORRECTLY SPELL FIVE WORDS THAT YOU PREVIOUSLY MISSPELLED.

In December of 1903, the Wright Brothers flew their first plane. They had to correct all the mistakes in the plane before it would fly.

Learning to spell is very similar to creating something new, like an airplane. You must spend many years learning how to combine letters to spell correctly. It took the Wright brothers, engineers, many years to devise and combine the parts of their airplane. Just as you do not want to ride in a plane with a few engineering mistakes, you don't want to put your good ideas into words that are not spelled correctly. If you do, your ideas could be shot down before they get a chance to take off!

Further, when people see your words misspelled, they can think that if you are too lazy to correct a spelling error, you could be too lazy to tackle more difficult jobs, or that if you are not smart enough to correct your spelling, the ideas you have may not be very smart either. Some people might think that if you don't care enough to make your work as good as it can be, you may not work conscientiously on other tasks. To avoid all of these bad impressions, we will use a test to help us find out why you misspell.

[Give one of the following tests. Test 1 is for lower grades. Test 2 is for upper grades. Ask students to write each sentence or phrase you dictate. After all the sentences are dictated, show or dictate the correct spelling of the key words. Have students grade their papers. When errors are recorded, have students identify a possible cause for the misspelling by locating the error type that corresponds to the test item.]

Test 1

1. *Bunny* hops.

2. I *play*.

3. I *hear* the *bells*.

FIGURE 4-3 (Continued)

Test 2

1. *There* are *weeds*.

   (a) their, they're = confusion over homophones.

   (b) weads = using improper vowels.

2. Call the *doctor*.

   (a) docter = overuse of suffix rules.

   (b) ducture = overuse of phonics.

   (c) dockture = overuse of sight words.

3. I am *laughing*.

   (a) laffun = does not know silent letters.

4. He wants a *balloon*.

   (a) baloon for balloon = confusion in double consonants.

5. I have *none*.

   (a) nun for none = overdependence on phonics.

ACTIVITY 4-4

IN DECEMBER 1903 THE FIRST PLANE FLEW: WORKING TO MAKE SPELLING ERROR-FREE

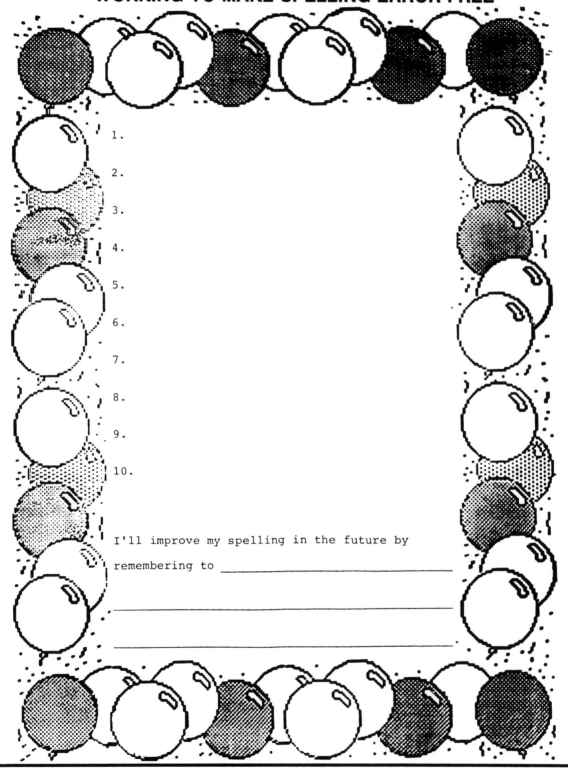

1.

2.

3.

4.

5.

6.

7.

8.

9.

10.

I'll improve my spelling in the future by

remembering to _____

_____

_____

Skill Development: Learning to Write Interesting Stories by Using a First-Person Writing Style and Brainstorming

TIME REQUIRED

Teacher Directed Exploration (Activity 4-5): 20 minutes

Student Discovery Page (Activity 4-6): 30 minutes

TEACHING STRATEGIES

The strategies are cooperative learning teams and small-group discussions.

ACTIVITY 4-5

STEPS OF SUCCESSFUL BRAINSTORMING

[OBJECTIVE] YOU WILL LEARN HOW TO WRITE MORE INTERESTING STORIES USING FIRST-PERSON WRITING AND BRAINSTORMING. YOU WILL KNOW YOU HAVE LEARNED IT WHEN YOU CAN TAKE A CLASSMATE'S STORY AND WORK WITH HIM OR HER TO IMPROVE IT AND THE IMPROVEMENT CAN BE SEEN BY THE ORIGINAL AUTHOR.

To improve your writing, you will learn to increase the number of creative and expressive ideas you use by brainstorming and by writing as if you were the person telling the story. You will write today using yourself as the subject. That is, you will say, "I did . . ."; "When I was . . .". You will also learn to brainstorm. You will know you have learned both of these skills when you work with another student in the room and both of you see improvements in each other's writing ability.

Brainstorming is a well-known, widely used problem-solving tool. It encourages participants to use their imaginations and to be creative. It helps to develop solutions to a problem. The following steps will help you be successful brainstormers.

1. *All ideas are welcomed.* No one says any idea is not good. No one needs to worry that his or her ideas are not good enough. All ideas help.

2. *Give as many ideas as you can.* The longer the list, the more likely it contains a number of workable ideas.

3. *Add to each other's ideas.* People can help each other.

4. *Think of crazy and new ideas.* One idea can trigger a useful idea for someone else. Problems are often seen in new ways as a result of a new thought.

5. *Record each idea and combine ideas at the end.* After all ideas have been given, combine and select the best.

To practice and to learn to use brainstorming when you think and write, you will learn about an important event that occurred this month. In this month, December 1791, the Bill of Rights was adopted and helped to make America a democracy. The Bill of Rights is the list of freedoms granted by our democratic government, and they are a part of our country's constitution.

[Hand out Activity 4-6. Brainstorm with the class about one or more of

the Bill of Rights questions on Activity 4-6. As students brainstorm, write their ideas on the board. Remind them to follow the steps of brainstorming. Once the brainstorming portion of the activity is complete, students write a first-person narrative. Then they share their stories with their partners or the class and suggest improvements.]

GRADING CRITERIA: _____

On the back of this page, write a first-person story about one of the numbered questions.

MODIFICATIONS FOR GRADE LEVELS AND STUDENT ABILITY LEVELS

For Kindergarten through Third Grades and Slower Learning Groups, do Activity 4-6 in small groups and pairs. After brainstorming, younger students, as a whole class, practice with you to create a list of first-person story ideas. *Older Students* can break into pairs and select their own topic and brainstorm ideas for that topic.

STUDENTS WHO WILL BE WORKING ON OTHER PROJECTS OR LESSONS: _____

NOTES FOR FUTURE USE: _____

ACTIVITY 4-6

BRAINSTORMING A BILL OF RIGHTS

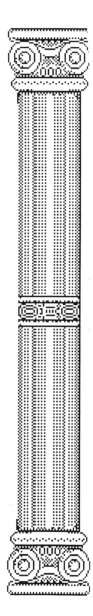

1. If our country were just beginning and you were among the representatives to establish the rules of government, what would you include in the Bill of Rights?

   _____

   _____

   _____

   _____

2. What would you include in a Bill of Rights for teachers at our school?

   _____

   _____

   _____

3. What would you include in a Bill of Rights for students at our school?

   _____

   _____

   _____

4. What would you include in a Bill of Rights for the members of your family?

   _____

   _____

   _____

   _____

Speaking Skill Development: Using Transition Words to Help Listeners Understand What You Say

TIME REQUIRED

Teacher Directed Exploration (Activity 4-7): 30–45 minutes

Student Discovery Page (Activity 4-8): 30–45 minutes

TEACHING STRATEGIES

The students will use a creative problem-solving strategy followed in business (the "force fit") to develop a new speaking skill.

ACTIVITY 4-7 _____

SPACE WORDS AND TRANSITION WORDS

[OBJECTIVE]   YOU WILL LEARN TO USE TRANSITION WORDS WHEN YOU SPEAK SO PEOPLE BETTER UNDERSTAND WHAT YOU SAY. YOU WILL KNOW YOU HAVE LEARNED WHEN YOU USE THREE NEW TRANSITION WORDS FROM ACTIVITY 4-8 IN YOUR CONVERSATIONS REGULARLY.

The Apollo astronauts made the first radio broadcast from space in December. When the astronauts spoke, they used many transition words in their speeches. They used these words because people have trouble understanding something they have never seen. Transition words guided their listeners from one description of space to the next.

Today we will use transition words when we speak.

[Hand out Activity 4-8.] Transition words help take the listener or reader from one idea to the next. Without them our speech and writing would be jerky and hard to follow. There are six categories of transition words shown on Activity 4-8. As I read a list of transition words or phrases, write each one where it belongs on the chart. [Dictate the list of transition words in numerical order. The numbers are not important to say aloud; they will ensure that you dictate the words in random order and that you can help the students check the accuracy of their charts.]

(Comparison)

12. as	**9.** similarly	**16.** at the same time
21. like	**27.** as well as	**31.** likewise
38. in comparison	**41.** both	**48.** all
55. by the same token	**60.** furthermore	

(Contrast)

1. but	**8.** on the other hand	**10.** in spite of
15. conversely	**22.** despite	**23.** however
28. nonetheless	**32.** nevertheless	**37.** on the contrary
34. instead	**40.** rather	**42.** notwithstanding
45. though	**49.** yet	**50.** regardless
53. whereas	**61.** although	**63.** in contrast
65. unlike	**67.** for all that	**70.** even though

(Simple Listing)

13. and	**11.** too	**24.** I, III, III . . .
43. finally	**56.** furthermore	**72.** first, second
75. 1, 2, 3 . . .		

(Cause/Effect)

5. because	**14.** accordingly	**17.** since
25. thus	**33.** for this reason	**44.** consequently
52. hence	**57.** resulting	**62.** therefore
66. as a result	**68.** so	**71.** then

(Conclusions)

4. in brief	**13.** in the end	**18.** in summary
26. to reiterate	**36.** in conclusion	**47.** to sum up
58. finally	**74.** therefore	**76.** thus
77. as already stated		

(Time/Order)

6. before	**7.** after	**12.** now
19. previously	**20.** last	**29.** next
30. then	**35.** when	**39.** immediately
46. formerly	**51.** later	**54.** subsequently
59. meanwhile	**64.** presently	**69.** initially
73. ultimately		

[This activity is not a test situation; you may want to help students categorize the words as you read the list, especially for duplications.]

[Help the students check their categorizations.] Now you have many possible transition words to include in your writing and speaking. You will have a chance to use them when you make a radio broadcast or speech about going into space.

You will write a speech which will be words you would say if you were the first person to live on Mars. Your speech tells the people on earth about these aspects of your first three months on Mars:

1. What you have found that we don't have

2. What Martian food is available

3. What you do for pleasure

4. What you miss most about the world

[Students will present their radio broadcast speeches while standing behind the class so no one can see them.]

GRADING CRITERIA: _____

MODIFICATIONS FOR GRADE LEVELS AND STUDENT ABILITY LEVELS

For Kindergarten through Third Grades and Slower Learning Students, introduce only two words, "and" and "but." In addition, you can specify several different topics, related to current issues or content areas, and require only a few transition words in the speeches. *For Fourth through Eighth Grades and Gifted Learners,* challenge them to give longer speeches and to use at least one word from each set as they construct their speech. When they write their speeches, they can use additional moon facts as well. Gifted students may wish to prepare their speeches as radio broadcasts from outer space, tape record them, and deliver them to the class as if they were astronauts.

ADDITIONAL MOON FACTS

The following facts can be used in the speeches of gifted students.

Airlock: The airlock is a small chamber located between the space shuttle's mid-deck and cargo bay. It can be sealed off and slowly emptied of air until the pressure in the chamber is as low as that in space.

Escape Harnesses: These are vests that astronauts wear over their flight suits during launch and landing. The vests have a ring they can use to hook to a rope in case of an emergency.

G's: A term used to describe the amount of gravitational force, as in "3 G's." "1 G" means a gravitational force equal to that of the Earth.

Mission Control: The room at Houston's Lyndon B. Johnson Space Center where NASA engineers monitor each space flight and issue instructions to the crew.

Space Sickness: Uncomfortable sensations experienced by some astronauts during their first two days in space, caused by the body's adjustment to weightlessness.

Spacesuits: The spacesuits are pressurized and control temperature as well as oxygen for the astronauts. These suits allow them to survive in space outside the space shuttle.

ADDITIONAL MOON WORDS FOR YOUNGER GRADES

_____ crater	_____ volcano
_____ spaceship	_____ spacesuit
_____ space station	_____ oxygen tank
_____ face mask	_____ control board
_____ fire	_____ darkness

ADDITIONAL REFERENCES

Ride, Sally. *To Space and Back.* Lothrop, Lee and Shepherd, New York, 1986.
Vogt, Gregory. *The Twenty-Fifth Anniversary Album of NASA.* Franklin Watts Publishing, New York, 1983.

STUDENTS WHO ARE WORKING ON OTHER PROJECTS OR LESSONS: _____

_____

NOTES FOR FUTURE USE: _____

_____

TRANSITION WORDS TO HELP LISTENERS UNDERSTAND WHAT YOU SAY

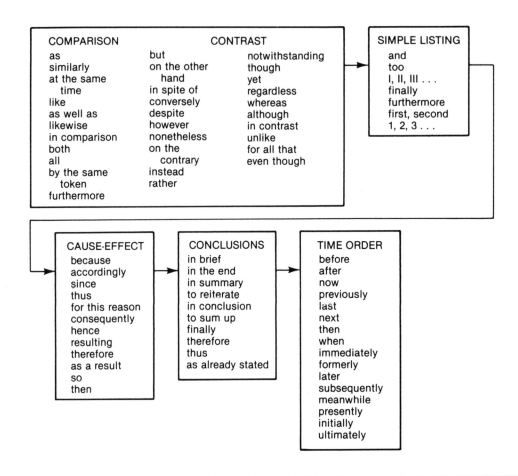

COMPARISON
- as
- similarly
- at the same time
- like
- as well as
- likewise
- in comparison
- both
- all
- by the same token
- furthermore

CONTRAST
- but
- on the other hand
- in spite of
- conversely
- despite
- however
- nonetheless
- on the contrary
- instead
- rather
- notwithstanding
- though
- yet
- regardless
- whereas
- although
- in contrast
- unlike
- for all that
- even though

SIMPLE LISTING
- and
- too
- I, II, III . . .
- finally
- furthermore
- first, second
- 1, 2, 3 . . .

CAUSE-EFFECT
- because
- accordingly
- since
- thus
- for this reason
- consequently
- hence
- resulting
- therefore
- as a result
- so
- then

CONCLUSIONS
- in brief
- in the end
- in summary
- to reiterate
- in conclusion
- to sum up
- finally
- therefore
- thus
- as already stated

TIME ORDER
- before
- after
- now
- previously
- last
- next
- then
- when
- immediately
- formerly
- later
- subsequently
- meanwhile
- presently
- initially
- ultimately

Listening Skill Development: Learning to Make Correct Inferences

TIME REQUIRED

Teacher Directed Exploration (Activity 4-9): 10 minutes

Student Discovery Page (Activity 4-10): 20 minutes

TEACHING STRATEGIES

Students will repeat mini-practice sessions to learn a skill.

ACTIVITY 4-9 _____

MAKING INFERENCES

[OBJECTIVE] YOU WILL LEARN TO PUT INFORMATION IN TWO OR MORE SENTENCES TOGETHER TO BETTER UNDERSTAND WHAT YOU HEAR AND READ.

December has a special holiday. This day is called "Tell Someone They Are Doing a Good Job Day." The purpose of this day is to tell others that you appreciate them.

In a moment I want you to think of someone who is doing a good job. We are going to use what you tell us to try to decide who the person is. To do so, we will make an inference.

To make an inference we will:

—Put clues together to see how all pieces of information are related

—Put pieces of information in order as to how they normally occur in real life as an attempt to build a complete understanding of the full situation

—Think of different possibilities and select the best

—Take a leap in thinking from what is written to a more general and greater meaning by tying individual facts to experiences you've had in your life

—Draw a conclusion based on the facts that were given and the direction similar facts have taken in other experiences you've had

Let's practice.

Suppose I say that I want you to turn in your assignment (work) Tuesday; then I say that you must turn it in Tuesday to receive the highest grade.

Put together the facts I gave you and draw a conclusion about something that I didn't say but meant. **[Students should say that you will count off for papers turned in late.]**

[Pass out Activity 4-10a for younger students; Activity 4-10b for older students. Read the directions on the activity page and then the items from either Figure 4-5a or 4-5b as appropriate.]

[A modification of this activity is to pause after each sentence in the descriptions. The first student to infer the title, with the least number of clues, raises his or her hand and tells classmates how the inference was made.]

ANSWER KEY FOR ACTIVITY 4-10a

2. *The Midnight Moon*

2. *We Hide You Seek*

2. *Cock-a-Doodle-Doo*

2. *Snow White And the Seven Dwarfs*

ANSWER KEY FOR ACTIVITY 4-10b

2. *Johnny Tremain*

3. *Tell Me That You Love Me Junie Moon*

1. *Walk When the Moon Is Full*

4. *The Crazy Iris and Other Stories of the Atomic Aftermath*

5. *Man-Eaters of Kumaon*

GRADING CRITERIA: _____

_____

MODIFICATIONS FOR GRADE LEVELS AND STUDENT ABILITY LEVELS

Suggestions for modifications are given within the activity.

NOTES FOR FUTURE USE: _____

_____

MAKING INFERENCES

We Hide You Seek by Julio Arugo and Ariane Dewey

All that Sunlight by Charlotte Zolotow

The Midnight Moon by Clyde Watson

Cock-A-Doodle-Doo by Berta and Elmer Hadren

The Speckled Hen by Harve Zemuch

Snow White and the Seven Dwarfs by Wanda Gag

DIRECTIONS

Use the above titles to identify which books I am describing. I will read facts about the book and you infer which book I am describing. Put the number of the sentence that I read in a space before the book title from which you infer the sentence came.

MAKING INFERENCES

Johnny Tremain by Esther Forbes

Tell Me That You Love Me Junie Moon by Marjove Kellogg

Walk When the Moon Is Full by Frances Hamerstrom

The Crazy Iris and Other Stories of the Atomic Aftermath by Kenzabro O

Man-Eaters of Kumaon by Jim Corbett

Werewolves by Nancy Garden

DIRECTIONS

Use the above titles to identify which books I am describing. I will read facts about the book and you infer which book I am describing. Put the number of the sentence that I read before the book title from which you infer the sentence came.

FIGURE 4-5a
Clues to the Titles (for Activity 4-10a)

1. Many books have been written about this subject. Some people believe that the subject of this book has its own light. The truth is that the subject of this book depends upon the sun for light. The book that I am talking about is about things that happen at night.

2. At night things are dark. The book I am talking about talks about an activity. This activity can be done at night or during the day. This book is about people who are playing a game. The game they are playing involves one person who is doing something that is different from the other people playing the game.

3. The book I am thinking about now is about an animal. The title of the book gives the clue to the animal because it describes something about the animal. It does not describe what the animal looks like, however.

4. The book I am thinking about describes a story about a woman and several other people. The reason this book is different is because the name of the woman is in the title of the book, and her name is unusual. None of your friends will have her name.

FIGURE 4-5b
Clues to the Titles (for Activity 4-10b)

1. This book is a true story about two youth who lived on a 240-acre farm in Wisconsin. They liked to go exploring, but they explored at a time when most people did not go exploring. Each time they explored they saw things and found surprises that other people did not see.

2. Boston slowly opened its eyes as a glass-eyed Indian watched the pioneers cut wood while the bells in the steeple rang. In 1773, a young apprentice went from a silversmith's shop to become a fighter in the American Revolution. This person will become as famous as Benjamin Franklin and Paul Revere.

3. This book is about young women. In the course of pursuing a career they meet handsome young bosses. They find out too late that these men did not always tell them everything. The women became disillusioned. Their lives end differently than predicted.

4. Four of the chapter titles in this book are "Fireflies," "Summer Flowers," "The Land of Heart's Desire," and "Human Ashes." A quote from page 21 is, "In fact I did not hear of the remains of the mushroom cloud until about 30 or 40 hours after the event. From one moment to another the city of Hiroshima had ceased to exist."

5. This book illustrates that the qualities of physical strength, infinite patience, and great power are present in small actions as well as in larger changes in nature, and in animal behavior. The book is a true story. It concerns danger and rural life. The animals in the story help to maintain the balance in nature.

Grammar Skill Development: Recognizing Proper Agreement between Nouns and Verbs

TIME REQUIRED

Teacher Directed Exploration (Activity 4-11): 10–15 minutes

Student Discovery Page (Activity 4-12): 30 minutes

TEACHING STRATEGIES

Students identify why a skill is important and create their own application of the skill. Students will understand the importance of noun and verb agreement by writing in past and present tenses.

ACTIVITY 4-11

LANDING WITH THE RIGHT TENSE

[OBJECTIVE]   YOU WILL LEARN THE DIFFERENCE BETWEEN AND IM-PORTANCE OF PRESENT, FUTURE, AND PAST TENSE BY PRETENDING YOU WERE A REPORTER WHEN THE PILGRIM'S LANDED. YOU WILL KNOW YOU HAVE USED VERBS PROPERLY WHEN ACTIVITY 4-12 IS COMPLETED IN PRESENT TENSE VERBS.

Today we will learn to use correct noun and verb agreement. The Pilgrims left Plymouth, England on September 16, 1620 and did not land at Plymouth Rock until December 21. It took them 96 days to cross the ocean.

[Discuss what it might have been like to have been a Pilgrim. Discuss some of the emotions they might have felt.]

[Ask students why it is important to have noun and verb agreement. Then discuss the importance of agreement between nouns and verbs. Show and complete the following sample by having it on the overhead projector or on the chalkboard.]

Noun/Verb Tense Samples

Agreement with the word "create"

The boy _____ a new toy for you tomorrow. (will create)

The other boy _____ already _____ another sentence. (has created)

We _____ a new paragraph together yesterday. (created)

[Students complete Landing on Plymouth Rock (Figure 4-6) with you. Then younger students move directly to Activity 4-12, in which they create a story in present or past tense but write as if they were a Pilgrim who landed. Youngest students can dictate the story as you write it on the overhead projector (having made an transparency of Activity 4-12). As the sentences are given, write what they say and tell the class, in advance, to catch any verb tense that is inconsistent.]

[Older students complete Activity 4-11 and Activity 4-12. They can complete 4-11 alone or with you.]

FIGURE 4-6
Landing on Plymouth Rock

Name_____

LANDING ON PLYMOUTH ROCK

DIRECTIONS: Fill in the blanks in the story with the appropriate
verbs. Make sure the verb tenses agree with the rest
of the sentences.

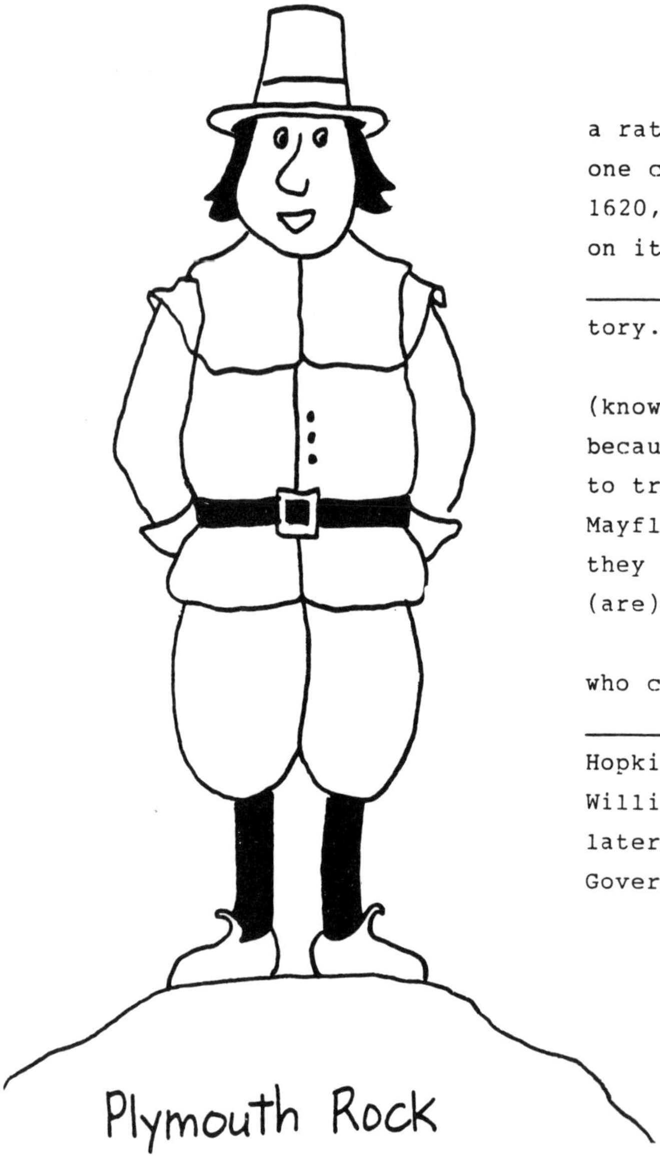

On the bay named Plymouth sat
a rather large rock all alone. Then
one cold December day in the year
1620, the Pilgrims (land)_____
on it and that same rock (become)
_____ a part of American history.

At first, the Pilgrams were
(know)_____ as First Comers,
because they (are)_____ the first
to travel there. Their journey on the
Mayflower (is)_____ very long and
they were all very tired; some of them
(are)_____ very sick.

Some of the names of the Pilgrams
who came over on the Mayflower (are)
_____ : John Carver, Oceanus
Hopkins, Captain Miles Standish, and
William Bradford. William Bradford
later (become)_____ the elected
Governor of the new Plymouth Colony.

Plymouth Rock

GRADING CRITERIA: _____

_____

MODIFICATIONS FOR GRADE LEVELS AND STUDENT ABILITY LEVELS

For Kindergarten through Third Grades and Slower Learning Students, work on noun and verb pairs only; do not use whole writing samples. _For Third through Sixth Grades,_ students should concentrate on tense agreement. _For Seventh and Eighth Grades and Gifted Students,_ students can obtain additional information about Pilgrims and Plymouth Rock. _For Early Finishers,_ students can write a story on Activity 4-12b about being with the Pilgrims on December 21, 1620.

Students who wish can read the following books in the library, for homework, and tell the class more about the Pilgrims.

> Fritz, Jean. _Who's That Stepping on Plymouth Rock?_ Coward McCann Publishing, New York, 1975.
>
> Hall, Olga. _How the Pilgrims Came to Plymouth Rock._ E.P. Dutton and Co., New York, 1961.
>
> Sewall, Marcia. _The Pilgrims of Plymouth._ Atheneum Publishers, New York, 1986.

STUDENTS WHO WILL BE WORKING ON OTHER PROJECTS OR LESSONS: _____

_____

NOTES FOR FUTURE USE: _____

_____

"I WAS THERE": LEARNING TO USE CORRECT VERB TENSES

DIRECTIONS: This is a story about the Pilgrims when they landed
on Plymouth Rock. Read the story very carefully and then after
you have finished, go back through it and circle the verbs. Below
the story, write your own paragraph using correct verb tenses.
"Pretend you were there. Write what happened next."

After much serious discussion between the Pilgrims and Miles
Standish, their captain, on the night of December the twenty-first
the men left the Mayflower and started to settle Plymouth Colony.
They chose a site at the far end of the river, at the place where
an Indian cornfield had been. The exploring men (there were about
twenty) did not return to the Mayflower that night, they built
rough shelters and made plans for their future in America.

_____

_____

_____

_____

_____

_____

_____

ACTIVITY 4-12b

CELEBRATING OUR LANDING IN AMERICA, DECEMBER 21, 1620

Handwriting Skill Development: Learning to Recognize Mistakes in Letters

TIME REQUIRED

Teacher Directed Exploration (Activity 4-13): 30 minutes

Student Discovery Page (Activity 4-14): as long as desired

TEACHING STRATEGIES

Students will use self-evaluation and peer grading.

ACTIVITY 4-13

CELEBRATING IN DECEMBER

[OBJECTIVE] YOU WILL RECOGNIZE MISTAKES IN THE SHAPE OF YOUR HANDWRITTEN LETTERS. YOU WILL ALSO WRITE A STORY ABOUT HOLIDAY TRADITIONS IN A FOREIGN COUNTRY.

[Tell students that in this lesson they will learn about Christmas, Hanukkah, and Kwanzaa celebrations in other countries. Encourage students who know people from different cultures to find out something about their Christmas celebrations to share these facts with the class. For younger students, you may wish to read a story about a holiday celebration in another culture.]

[Begin the lesson by presenting a brief overview of Christmas and Hanukah traditions.]

CHRISTMAS, HANUKKAH, AND KWANZAA TRADITIONS

Each year Christmas is celebrated on December 25th. Festivities include such activities as gift giving, family dinners, and a (on Christmas Eve midnight) visit from Santa Claus.

People who celebrate Christmas in other countries have many special traditions. Perhaps your family follows some of these traditions, too. [Share with the students the information on Figure 4-7 about Christmas traditions around the world. Note that the figure also includes suggestions for classroom party activities related to the traditions. These activities, of course, are optional.]

Hanukkah is celebrated eight days in December. It is a Jewish holiday commemorating the rededication of the Temple of Jerusalem after three years of war with the Syrians. Each day a candle is lit to commemorate the lamp that miraculously burned for eight days with only enough oil for less than one day's burning. This lamp symbolized the return of Jewish people to their Temple.

Kwanzaa was founded in 1966 by Dr. Maulana Karenga. Kwanzaa starts December 26 and goes until January the 1. It is a seven day celebration of Black Pride. It is celebrated as an American Black Family Observance, in recognition of Traditional African Harvest Festivals. This holiday stresses the unity of the black family with a community-wide harvest feast known as Karamu. Kwanzaa means first fruit in Swahili.

Books about Kwanzaa that you may want to read include: (As an information source)ʿ *Kwanzaa: Origin, Concepts, and Practice.* Written by Dr. Maulana Karenga (the founder of Kwanzaa), published in Los Angeles by Kawaida Publications in 1977.

FIGURE 4-7
Christmas around the World Party Suggestions

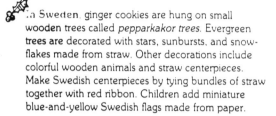

Christmas Around The World

Planning a classroom holiday party? Instead of the usual classroom Christmas party, include a few customs from different lands in your festivities. Decorate a class tree with ornaments representing different countries. Your students will be celebrating *and* learning about different cultures!

 In Mexico, children celebrate by breaking a suspended *piñata*. Set aside several class sessions for children to make a papier-mâché piñata. Fill it with individual sandwich bags filled with wrapped candies, sugarless gum, and balloons. Position children at a safe distance from the child swinging the stick. When the piñata is broken, each child retrieves one bag of goodies.

 In Africa, Christmas festivities include native African dances around bonfires. In South Africa, there are parades and fireworks. Africans of European descent celebrate Christmas as their English, French, and Dutch relatives do. In Ghana, Father Christmas comes from the jungles rather than the North Pole. Together, create a story about "Santa on Safari."

 In France, children place their shoes by the fireplace for *Père Nöel* to fill with gifts on December 24. Play a relay game in which each child runs to a line, removes his shoes, and runs back to tag the next player on his team. Have an older child dressed as Father Christmas put wrapped treats in all of the empty shoes when the relay is over.

 In England, Father Christmas brings gifts to children. Other gifts are given on Boxing Day, December 26. On Christmas Eve, carolers gather in town squares. Provide the words for students to sing along to recorded Christmas carols. Offer a taste of fruitcake or plum pudding to classroom carolers.

 In Japan and China, pine trees are decorated with red paper lanterns, paper fans, and wind chimes. On Christmas Eve in China, there is a lantern parade. Make red, paper lanterns or paper fans for the classroom tree.

 In Denmark, the national colors are red and white. Christmas trees are decorated with red-and-white paper chains and heart-shaped, woven baskets. Make a long, red-and-white paper chain for the class tree.

 In India, Christians decorate banana or coconut trees. Serve banana slices dipped in chocolate syrup and rolled in coconut.

 In Sweden, ginger cookies are hung on small wooden trees called *pepparkakor* trees. Evergreen trees are decorated with stars, sunbursts, and snowflakes made from straw. Other decorations include colorful wooden animals and straw centerpieces. Make Swedish centerpieces by tying bundles of straw together with red ribbon. Children add miniature blue-and-yellow Swedish flags made from paper.

 In Germany, children hang decorated gingerbread cookies, or *lebkuchens*, on their Christmas trees. Help children make gingerbread cookies to decorate and hang on a tree. Make some extras to eat at the party!

In Canada, French-speaking families end the holiday season with a feast on January 6. A special fruitcake is baked with a bean and pea in it. The boy and girl who find these surprises in their pieces of cake are named the King and Queen of the Twelfth Night. Serve cupcakes with a dried bean baked in one and a pea in another. Crown the girl and boy who find the hidden prizes. Give the King and Queen for the Day special privileges.

 In Spain, Puerto Rico, Mexico, and throughout Central and South America, families display manger scenes called *nacimientos*. The figure of the baby Jesus is not added until Christmas Eve. The Three Kings are said to bring gifts to children on January 6. The children leave their shoes filled with carrots, barley, or straw for the camels of the Three Kings. Play a party game in which each team passes a carrot along a line of children. The first team to "feed the camel" at the end of the line wins!

 In Italy, gifts are brought by *Gesù-Bambino*, not Santa Claus. Children write notes to their parents promising to be good. The notes are hidden in the father's napkin or under his plate. After the meal, he reads them aloud. Surprise students with little notes or awards tucked into their Christmas party napkins. Have children write and decorate notes for their parents.

The Mall Bag, Brooks Bird Club, Inc. Used with permission.

The(Juvenile Book dealing with Kwanzaa): *Have a Happy... A Novel.* Written by Mildred Pitts Walter. Story deals with a black boy getting ready for Kwanzaa and the happiness that it brings. Book is suggested for fourth graders to high school students.

(More information about the holiday could also be found in): *Chases Annual Events for 1991.*

[Hand out Activity 4-14.] Some of the December holidays involve gift giving, and after you do this activity you will have a chance to give a gift of handwriting help to a classmate. First, choose a holiday and a country. Write a story describing how the holiday is celebrated in that country. You don't have to write about holiday traditions that you already know about—you can use the encyclopedia or other sources to find information.

When you write your story on the lines on Activity 4-14, practice forming the letters carefully. **[Refer the students to the handwriting model used in conjunction with November's handwriting activity or the model you prefer.]**

[Give the students time to complete their descriptions of December celebrations. Then have students exchange papers and find ten or more mistakes—as well as good points—in the handwriting. Have the students rewrite their stories entirely or correct miswritten words, paying close attention to letter shapes.] If you are careful in the future about the letters your classmate has pointed out, your stories will be easy for people to read and you won't need to rewrite. So you will have received a handwriting gift today!

[Pick up papers and randomly choose two or three to read aloud to allow everyone to hear about some different countries. Students then share what they learned about how to make their handwriting better on a first writing so as to minimize rewriting in the future.]

GRADING CRITERIA: _____

MODIFICATIONS FOR GRADE LEVELS AND STUDENT ABILITY LEVELS

For Kindergarten and First Grade, let the students trace (or copy) different holiday words. They can draw or cut out pictures illustrating them or draw a picture of their family and a tradition they have. *For First through Third Grades and Slower Learning Students,* dictate a story for Activity 4-14 instead of students writing their own. They copy it and then try to find their errors in handwriting. *For Fourth through Eighth Grades,* let students switch papers with a partner and find at least ten (depending on grade level and length of the story) mistakes to correct and rewrite the whole story.

Have partners suggest improvements not only in handwriting but also in punctuation and grammar. *For Gifted Students,* change the misspelled or miswritten word with the same meaning. Students read stories to a partner.

STUDENTS WHO WILL BE WORKING ON OTHER PROJECTS OR LESSONS: _____

NOTES FOR FUTURE USE: _____

ACTIVITY 4-14

CELEBRATING GOOD HANDWRITING

_____ Celebrating: _____

Christmas		America
Hanukkah	IN	China
Kwanzaa		England
		France
		Germany
		Ghana
		Italy
		Mexico
		Sweden
		South Africa

Directions: Circle two of the above words to make the title of your story. After reading about the holiday and country's traditions in the two words you selected, write a story about your reading. You may write fiction or nonfiction.

_____

_____

_____

_____

_____

_____

_____

_____

_____

_____

_____

_____

_____

_____

Weekly Reading and Activities Form

The Weekly Reading and Activities form can be used to keep track of pages read in free reading and to record teacher feedback on classroom activities. The bottom line can be used to record goals or as a reminder of long-term assignment due dates. The form can be sent home at the end of the week to help keep parents informed of student activities. Copies can be kept for long-term progress comparison if desired.

My Weekly Reading and Activities

My Weekly Reading

Name: _____

Date	Book Name	# of Pages Read	Activities	Evaluation of Work
Monday				
Tuesday				
Wednesday				
Thursday				
Friday				
Next Week				

5 *January*

Activities 5-1 through 5-14 center around National Hobby Week, National Pizza Week, National Propaganda Month, National Clean Your Desk Day, National Handwriting Day, and Martin Luther King, Jr.'s birthday.

Scope and Sequence of Language Arts Skills Taught in January

Spelling (Activities 5-1 and 5-2): Students will learn to spell words by using the visual images of word features and configuration.

Reading (Activities 5-3 and 5-4): Students will learn to recognize and overcome propaganda.

Speaking (Activities 5-5 and 5-6): Students will learn to use inflections to make proper distinctions when speaking and will learn speaking mannerisms that are pleasing to others.

Composition (Activities 5-7 and 5-8): Students will learn to use self-evaluation and a composition reaction guide to compose letters.

Listening (Activities 5-9 and 5-10): Students will learn four types of details they can use in discussions, listening, and reading to point toward main ideas and to increase their retention of material heard and read.

Grammar (Activities 5-11 and 5-12): Students will learn four parts of speech.

Handwriting (Activities 5-13 and 5-14): Students will make their own "Declaration of Good Handwriting" stating the values of legible handwriting.

Supplemental Activities

The following activities can be used in a wide variety of ways to enhance January's activities.

1. Students can write to the following addresses for additional information about this month's themes.

National Hobby Month
Hobby Industries of America
Susan Brandt, Director of Comm.
319 E. 54th St.
Elmwood, NJ 07407

National Soup Month
Campbell Soup Company
Communications Center
Campbell Place
Camden, NJ 08101

British Toy and Hobby Manufactures
 Assoc. Lt.
80 Camberwell Road
London, England SES0EG
[International postage rates should
be used.]

National Association of Doll
 Manufacturers, Inc.
605 Third Ave.
New York, NY 10022

Mid-American Craft Hobby Assn.,
 Inc.
P.O. Box 1288
Zanesville, OH 43701

Hat Day Education Committee
Peter Rawitch, Chairperson
Glenmount Elementary
Route 9
Glenmount, NY 12077

National Pizza Week
Pizza Hut
Judy Kelly
P.O. Box 110108
Pittsburgh, PA 15232

National Clean Off Your Desk Day
A. C. Moeller
Box 71
Cleo, MI 48420

"Weeks" Week
Richard R. Falk Assoc.
147 W. 42nd St.
New York, NY 10605

March of Dimes Birth Defects
 Prevention Month
March of Dimes Foundation
Robert Goldberg
125 Mamoroneck Ave.
White Plains, NY 10601

2. The following notable people were born in January. Students can contact or read about those of interest. Students who were born in January can compare themselves to people born on their birthday.

1. Betsy Ross, Paul Revere, Ernest Hemmingway, Barry Goldwater
2. Isaac Asimov, Sally Rand, Roger Miller
3. Ray Miland, Zasu Pitts, Mel Gibson
4. Floyd Patterson, Grace Bumbry
5. Walter Mondale, Pamela Sue Martin, Diane Keaton
6. Carl Sandberg, Loretta Young
7. Saint Bernadette, Millard Filmore, Kenny Loggins
8. Yvette Mimieux, Elvis Presley, David Bowie, Crystal Gayle
9. Gypsy Rose Lee, Richard M. Nixon
10. Ethan Allen, Barbra Hepworth, Pat Benetar
11. Eva Le Gallienne, Alexander Hamilton
12. Patsy Kelly, Jack London, Ray Price
13. Horatio Alger, Gwen Verdon
14. Faye Dunaway, Albert Schweitzer, Andy Rooney
15. Chuck Berry, Martin Luther King, Jr.
16. Dizzy Dean, Ethel Merman, Debbie Allen, Ronnie Milsap
17. Benjamin Franklin, Moria Shearer

18. Mohammad Ali, Cary Grant

19. Shelly Fabares, Edgar Allen Poe, Dolly Parton

20. George Burns, Patricia Neal, Lorenzo Lamas

21. Christian Dior, Jinx Falkenburg, Benny Hill, Robby Benson

22. Lord Byron, Wrong-Way Corrigan, Linda Blair, Bill Bixby

23. John Hancock, Jeanne Moreau, Gil Gerard, Richard Anderson

24. Neil Diamond, Edith Wharton, Natassia Kinski

25. Robert Burns, Virginia Woolf

26. Eartha Kitt, Paul Newman

27. Wolfgang Amadeus Mozart, Donna Reed

28. Artur Rubinstein, Alan Alda

29. Germaine Greer, Tom Selleck, Judy Norton

30. Franklin Delano Roosevelt, Barbara Tuchman, Victoria Principal

31. Norman Mailer, Tallulah Bankhead, Suzanne Pleshette

3. January's activities focus on methods of helping students remember, summarize, and communicate with a variety of audiences and purposes, and the following project will build new skills while helping students integrate Activities 5-1 through 5-14. Students work in cooperative groups to make a model billboard. This billboard centers around a slogan, image, and carefully selected words that remind, persuade, and/or convince people to take action on an important issue. Topics can be as specific as an issue concerning a school or community problem or as global as increasing awareness and advancing global truths and humanistic values, such as helping others or improving a condition in life. You may require that students coin a new word to describe an aspect of their goal. Penny Torres, elementary teacher in Benbrook, Texas, originated this idea.

4. The calendar can be used in many ways, as described earlier.

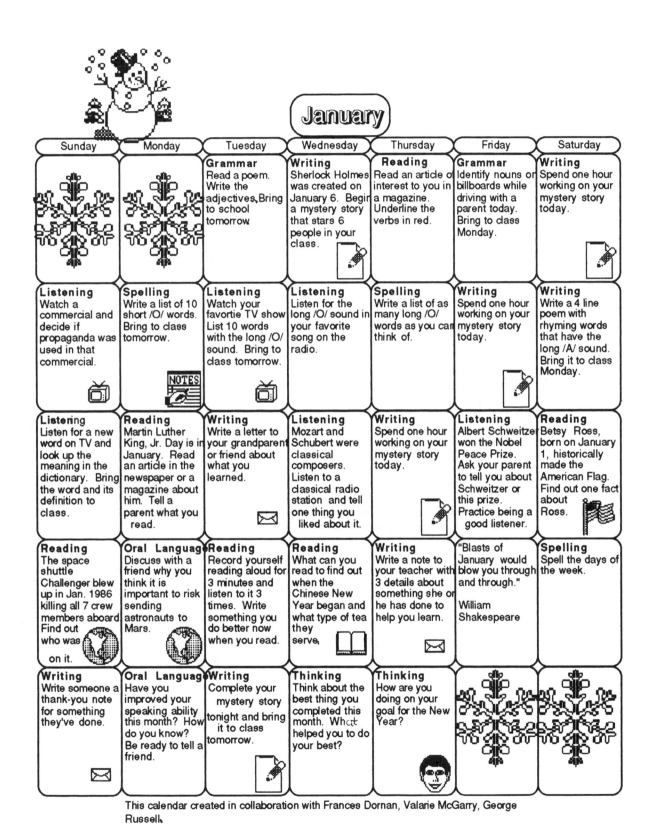

January

Sunday	Monday	Tuesday	Wednesday	Thursday	Friday	Saturday
		Grammar Read a poem. Write the adjectives. Bring to school tomorrow.	**Writing** Sherlock Holmes was created on January 6. Begin a mystery story that stars 6 people in your class.	**Reading** Read an article of interest to you in a magazine. Underline the verbs in red.	**Grammar** Identify nouns on billboards while driving with a parent today. Bring to class Monday.	**Writing** Spend one hour working on your mystery story today.
Listening Watch a commercial and decide if propaganda was used in that commercial.	**Spelling** Write a list of 10 short /O/ words. Bring to class tomorrow.	**Listening** Watch your favortie TV show. List 10 words with the long /O/ sound. Bring to class tomorrow.	**Listening** Listen for the long /O/ sound in your favorite song on the radio.	**Spelling** Write a list of as many long /O/ words as you can think of.	**Writing** Spend one hour working on your mystery story today.	**Writing** Write a 4 line poem with rhyming words that have the long /A/ sound. Bring it to class Monday.
Listening Listen for a new word on TV and look up the meaning in the dictionary. Bring the word and its definition to class.	**Reading** Martin Luther King, Jr. Day is in January. Read an article in the newspaper or a magazine about him. Tell a parent what you read.	**Writing** Write a letter to your grandparent or friend about what you learned.	**Listening** Mozart and Schubert were classical composers. Listen to a classical radio station and tell one thing you liked about it.	**Writing** Spend one hour working on your mystery story today.	**Listening** Albert Schweitzer won the Nobel Peace Prize. Ask your parent to tell you about Schweitzer or this prize. Practice being a good listener.	**Reading** Betsy Ross, born on January 1, historically made the American Flag. Find out one fact about Ross.
Reading The space shuttle Challenger blew up in Jan. 1986 killing all 7 crew members aboard Find out who was on it.	**Oral Language** Discuss with a friend why you think it is important to risk sending astronauts to Mars.	**Reading** Record yourself reading aloud for 3 minutes and listen to it 3 times. Write something you do better now when you read.	**Reading** What can you read to find out when the Chinese New Year began and what type of tea they serve.	**Writing** Write a note to your teacher with 3 details about something she or he has done to help you learn.	"Blasts of January would blow you through and through." William Shakespeare	**Spelling** Spell the days of the week.
Writing Write someone a thank-you note for something they've done.	**Oral Language** Have you improved your speaking ability this month? How do you know? Be ready to tell a friend.	**Writing** Complete your mystery story tonight and bring it to class tomorrow.	**Thinking** Think about the best thing you completed this month. What helped you to do your best?	**Thinking** How are you doing on your goal for the New Year?		

This calendar created in collaboration with Frances Dornan, Valarie McGarry, George Russell.

Spelling Skill Development: Using Visual Imaging and Word Configuration

TIME REQUIRED

Teacher Directed Exploration (Activity 5-1): 7–10 minutes

Student Discovery Page (Activity 5-2): 10–15 minutes with a 30-minute follow-up

TEACHING STRATEGIES

Students will use visual images and configurations.

ACTIVITY 5-1 _____

SPELLING AIDS: MNEMONIC SNOW CLOUDS

[OBJECTIVE] YOU WILL LEARN TO USE THE VISUAL IMAGE OF A WORD AND ITS CONFIGURATION TO IMPROVE YOUR SPELLING ABILITY.

[For younger students, have the words "mittens," "snowman," "tree," "hot chocolate," and "soup," on the board before you start the lesson. Ask what the first sound of each word is. Sound out the rest of the word.]

By paying close attention to a word's first sound and the special shape of a word, you can improve spelling skills. When you pay attention to the length of words and where tall letters are, you see the shape of that word, which can improve your spelling ability. Thus, by combining the sound of the first letter of a word with the word's unique shape, you can learn to spell it correctly.

Today we will learn a way to begin to pay closer attention to a word's shape. Just as each snowflake in winter is unique, so is each word we spell.

We will build a cloud around each word that emphasizes the shape of the word. The way we draw these clouds can help to convey the meaning. For example, as I draw a cloud around the word "flame," I make the cloud look like a flame like this. **[See Figure 5-1.]**

FIGURE 5-1 Word Cloud Samples

When I draw a cloud around the word "pizza" I try to make it look like a pizza, like this. **[Use Figure 5-1.]** These drawings will help us remember the order of the letters and how the word is spelled.

[Pass out Figure 5-2.] You can practice making clouds that look like a part of the meaning for the words in your spelling lists. [Students should draw these clouds with crayons, markers, or pencils/pens. Using different colors for different words can add to students' retention of each word's spelling.]

[Activity 5-2 can now be used as a practice exercise, a pretest, or a post-test over several sets of spelling words. To complete Activity 5-2, students will write their spelling words in the first column, draw each word with a cloud for meaning in the second column, and then, at a later date fold Activity 5-2 to the third column for the final test. Folding the paper will remove the first and second columns from sight.]

[Alternatively, students use 5-2 as a practice exercise. In this case they work in pairs, and cut column 3 out and give columns 1 and 2 to their partner. The partner calls out each word in the column, in random order. Students write the word from memory. The pair then checks column 3 against column 1. They discuss why errors were made and how they can make a better cloud to remember that word before the next test over these words is given.]

[If Activity 5-2 is used as a test, words can come from the spelling unit or from the words individual students have misspelled in their own writing. If the latter approach is used, students divide into pairs and give each other a test over the words they missed in their writings.]

GRADING CRITERIA: _____

MODIFICATIONS FOR GRADE LEVELS AND STUDENT ABILITY LEVELS

For Kindergarten through Third Grades and Slower Learning Groups, use fewer words during Activity 5-2.

INDIVIDUAL STUDENTS' NEEDS: _____

NOTES FOR FUTURE USE: _____

FIGURE 5-2 Mnemonic "Snow Clouds"

Name: _____

ACTIVITY 5-2

MY SPELLING AIDS

<u>Word with drawing of Meaning</u>

<u>Word</u>   <u>Test of Word</u>

Learning to Identify Propaganda Devices

TIME REQUIRED

Teacher Directed Exploration (Activity 5-3): 10–30 minutes of sustained silent reading

Student Discovery Page (Activity 5-4): 20 minutes of directed discussion

TEACHING STRATEGIES

Students will learn by participating in an interclass contest. They will also use TV, newspapers, magazines, and textbooks to find examples of the concepts they have learned.

ACTIVITY 5-3 _____

RECOGNIZING PROPAGANDA

[OBJECTIVE] TODAY YOU WILL LEARN WAYS IN WHICH PROPA-
GANDA CAN BE WRITTEN AND WHY IT IS IMPORTANT TO RECOGNIZE
THESE DEVICES IN ORAL AND WRITTEN COMMUNICATION.

It is important for you to recognize when someone is trying to convince you that something is true. The way people most frequently try to persuade others is through the use of propaganda statements. As a matter of fact, TV advertisements and public speakers use at least ten different propaganda statement types that you can learn to recognize. **[Share Figure 5-3 with the class, either as an overhead transparency or a handout. Once students have discussed these devices, tell them as much of the following information as you desire.]**

Propaganda is a way of trying to change people's ideas and behavior by twisting the truth. It can involve the spread of ideas and information deliberately slanted to further one's cause or damage an opposing cause. This usually occurs subtly, by the propagandist's choice of single words that have good or bad connotations. *Connotations* are subtle emotional meanings commonly attached to words. These emotional meanings may not be clear from the dictionary meaning of the word. For example, "conversationalist" and "chatter-box" have the same dictionary meaning, but the first has a more positive interpretation than the second.

A second example of choosing words according to a point of view is to call the same group of people either "an enthusiastic group of young adults" or "a noisy mob of unruly teenagers."

A *fact* is something you personally experience or something that has been or can be tested. A fact is something with demonstrated reliability (occurs each time the conditions are right for it) and replicability (occurs to other people in other places under the same conditions). A test of a fact can be a sensual test (available to be noticed by human senses) or can be an experimental test (occurring only under certain experimental conditions, such as a scientist might perform in a laboratory).

The reasons people choose to use propaganda can be personal, to gain an advantage for themselves; or the reasons can be idealistic, to gain others' support for certain ideas. When the reason for using persuasive strategies is to gain personal advantage, the techniques employed are often illogical and are usually used deliberately. On the other hand, idealists who attempt to persuade others

FIGURE 5-3   Propaganda Devices That Can Mislead You

1. *Name Calling:*   Using labels instead of discussing the available information. Calling a politician a "crook" and a person whose ideas are unpopular a "fascist" are two examples of unfair labeling.

2. *Glittering Generalities:*   Vague phrases that promise much. "That act will benefit all Americans . . ." or "Everyone should . . ." or "Our way is the American way."

3. *Transfer:*   Applying a set of symbols to a purpose for which they are not intended. An anti-government group might display the American flag and pictures of Washington and Lincoln at a meeting. These positive symbols help conceal the basic purposes of the group and help gain public support. A second example occurs when an incongruous image is coupled with an idea, such as a picture of a mother and child accompanying the idea of buying a particular vehicle so readers or viewers will transfer the feelings of tenderness (evoked by the picture) to the second concept.

4. *Testimonials:*   Getting some prominent person to endorse the idea or product, like Linda Evans endorsing Crystal Light or L'Oreal Hair Color, or a sports figure being pictured on a box of cereal.

5. *Plain Folks:*   Pretending to be "one of the folks," to win the regard of the general public, such as a folksy way of talking, kissing babies, posing for pictures with fishing poles and so forth. For example, some people might try to persuade you by saying, "Howdy, neighbors, y'all remind me of the friendly folks in my home town."

6. *Bandwagon:*   Claiming that "everyone is doing it." A second type of bandwagoning is to claim that something is "common knowledge" (so everybody should believe it).

7. *Card Stacking:*   Presenting only the parts of the facts that favor one side. This occurs when someone uses a quotation out of context, omits a key word from a quotation, uses favorable statistics and omits the unfavorable ones, and/or uses half-truths that cannot be denied or whole truths that sound good but do not really support an argument.

8. *Snob Appeal:*   Trying to convince you that if you agree with them or purchase a certain product, you will be better than other people or that the product will help you gain status. Examples include designer clothes (especially those with a label or identifying mark plainly displayed) that manufacturers market to suggest that the wearer will be better liked and admired by his or her peers because of wearing these garments.

9. *Slanted Words and Phrases:*   Using phrases or words to make you think that the position is objective. For example, many people use phrases like "It's been scientifically proven" or "laboratory-tested," without having seen the actual data or having the ability to interpret it themselves.

10. *Emotional Appeal:*   Using emotionally laden pictures or words to influence your opinion. For example, some greeting card manufacturers try to attach great sentimentality and meaning to printed cards by producing commercials that bring tears to the eye of the viewer by reminding the viewer of a loved one or someone far away.

of their beliefs may not realize that they are employing propaganda. They may feel they are only sharing the truth or "the word."

Since freedom of speech in America ensures equal rights to both honest and dishonest speakers, it is important that you become an effective critical thinker.

Remember, there are many styles of persuasion used in propaganda and advertising. Some styles were not on the list we studied. Propagandists can also use repetition to try to convince you, for the more times you hear or see something, the more familiar it becomes and the more acceptable it seems. Humor is another powerful persuasive tool, for humor relaxes you, and makes you less critical of ideas. This relaxation may also reduce the vigilance against persuasion or cause you to feel that the speaker is "okay" and can be trusted.

[Then hand out Activity 5-4 to older students. You may want them to work in groups and allow the first group to score 100 to earn the pizza party in celebration of National Pizza Week, which occurs each January.]

[For younger students, begin Activity 5-4 by having students tell you claims they have heard that they believe might be propaganda. List these and explain to students why they need to be careful not to be persuaded by propaganda. Then work Activity 5-4 together as a whole class activity.]

[To conclude this lesson, create a National Pizza Week Party Contest if possible. The winner(s) can be the student (for younger groups) or the group (for older students) who by the end of the week: (1) highlights the most examples of propaganda in newspapers and magazines, (2) lists the most examples of propaganda from TV, and/or (3) lists the most page numbers of propaganda phrases in their textbooks. They can win the opportunity to plan a 15-minute, end-of-the-week party in celebration of National Pizza Week.]

_____

GRADING CRITERIA: _____

_____

MODIFICATIONS FOR GRADE LEVELS AND STUDENT ABILITY LEVELS

For Kindergarten through Third Grades and Slower Learning Groups, the length of silent reading and the vocabulary should be adjusted to match ability. *For Fourth through Eighth Grade Levels and Gifted/Able Learners,* students will need a less structured class discussion.

INDIVIDUAL STUDENT NEEDS: _____

_____

STUDENTS WHO ARE WORKING ON OTHER PROJECTS OR LESSONS: _____

_____

NOTES FOR FUTURE USE: _____

_____

RECOGNIZING FACTS, OPINIONS, AND PROPAGANDA

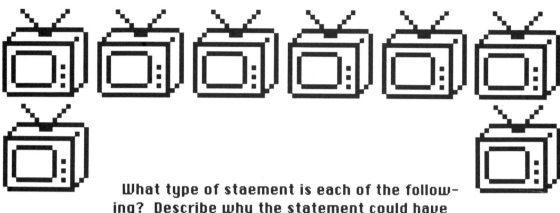

What type of staement is each of the following? Describe why the statement could have been made, such as to convince someone to do something.

1. Our calendar is not perfect because we have leap year every four years. _____
   _____
   _____

2. Chocolate is the best kind of candy. _____
   _____

3. The Empire State Building is a skyscraper. _
   _____

4. The President is the most important person in the United States. _____
   _____

5. You should always say, "Thank you," when someone gives you something. _____
   _____

6. NASA will send astronauts to Pluto next year. _____
   _____

7. This is 100% real cheese. Some aren't. We belive good cooks care. _____
   _____

8. Top Banana Pudding has one-third less calories. Finally, a fruit filling that isn't filling. _____

ACTIVITY 5-4 (Continued)

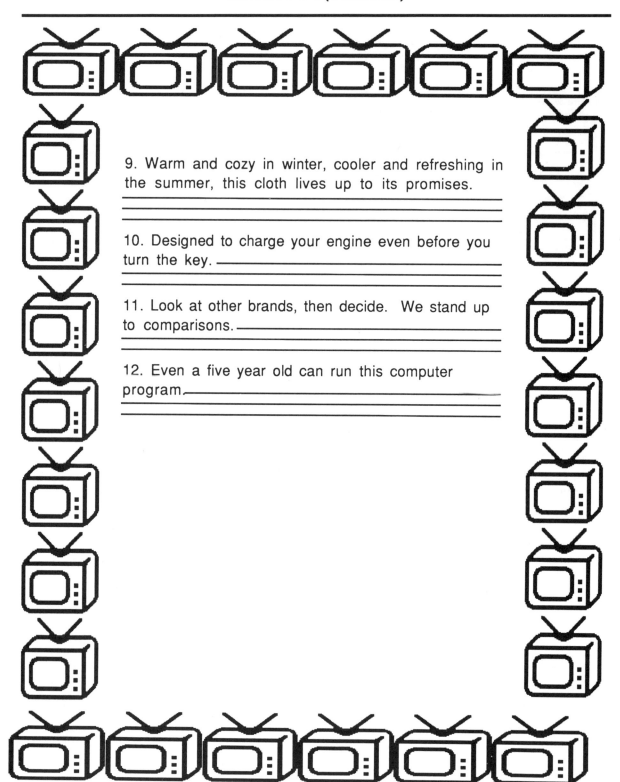

9. Warm and cozy in winter, cooler and refreshing in the summer, this cloth lives up to its promises.

_____

10. Designed to charge your engine even before you turn the key. _____

_____

11. Look at other brands, then decide. We stand up to comparisons. _____

_____

12. Even a five year old can run this computer program. _____

_____

Oral Speaking Skill Development: Learning to Use Proper Inflection When Speaking

TIME REQUIRED

Teacher Directed Exploration (Activity 5-5): 20 minutes

Student Discovery Page (Activity 5-6): as long as you desire, from one 20-minute reading to a week-long play production

TEACHING STRATEGIES

Students will role play and perform a play.

ACTIVITY 5-5 _____

CORRECTING SPEAKING WEAKNESSES

[OBJECTIVE] YOU WILL LEARN HOW TO MAKE YOUR VOICE AND SPEAKING MANNERISMS MORE PLEASING TO OTHERS. YOU WILL KNOW YOU HAVE LEARNED WHEN ONE OF YOUR SPEAKING WEAKNESSES HAS BEEN OVERCOME.

Many people's voices are too high or too low in their pitch. Some people speak too fast or slow. It is important that your voice does not irritate others.

[Younger students now discuss who they most like to listen to and why. Older students are told to ask one of their friends or their parents to help them identify if their voices are too high, too low, too soft, too whiny, too fast, or too slow. They are to ask some time before the next class. Begin the second class by discussing the following information.]

[Distribute copies of Figure 5-4 or project a transparency of it.]

The famous American Martin Luther King, Jr. was born January 15, 1929. One of the ways Dr. King was an effective leader of the Civil Rights movement was by making speeches. In his speeches he inspired his audience to work toward a time when people of all races can live together peacefully and with equal rights.

In this figure is a small part of King's "I Have a Dream" speech. Perhaps you have seen videotapes of King delivering these words. His voice was powerful, and he used it in a way that caught the audience up in the rhythm, the feeling, and the importance of his words. If he had not been such an effective speaker, perhaps his words would not have been remembered as they have been.

Let's make our voices less effective and speak Dr. King's words in ways that would be difficult to understand. Then we'll talk about ways to correct problems in voice or speaking, so we can improve our ability to communicate with others. **[Read the speech excerpt—or have student volunteers read it—in the following five ineffective ways. After each "silly" reading, discuss how to correct such voice or speaking problems.]**

1. *Nasal tone:* Open mouth more.

2. *Voice raised to a high pitch at the end of statements:* Reduce the number of questions asked and practice talking with more confidence when speaking. Other people raise their voices to seek agreement from others.

3. *Words misunderstood or not heard:* If people often ask you to repeat what you said, raise your head, look people in the eye, and use a louder tone.

4. *Monotone or all words spoken slowly:* Practice emphasizing every verb and making the first half of each sentence faster than the last half. Smile as you speak. Often people speak very slowly because they are afraid people are not going to listen to them. Say the first half of every sentence faster and practice speaking more rapidly, increasing the number of gestures you use.

5. *Whiney tone:* Practice thinking of what you want to say before you begin to speak. Reduce the number of questions you ask at first, until your "whiny" tone becomes a stronger, more assertive tone.

One way to improve speaking habits is to practice your voice in new ways. One way is to become an actor in a play. The role you play should be of a person who has a voice like you would like to have. In this way you can practice speaking in a better way.

[Hand out Activity 5-6. For young students, you now read each part of the play and the students repeat the lines, mimicking how you vary your pitch and inflection to match the characters and the words. For older students, divide the class into groups of six. Within each group, assign all 5 parts of narrator to the student who needs the most help in voice modulation. The students can then distribute the rest of the parts among themselves. Those playing Martin Luther King, Jr. meet together to discuss what their character's voice might have sounded like. They practice imitating this voice pattern. Those playing the part of Harriet Tubman meet together and do likewise, as do those who play the teacher, Nat Turner, and Frederick Douglass.]

[Meanwhile, meet with all the narrators, discussing how their parts call for a normal, pleasant voice. Work on each student's speaking problem, anonymously; that is, without calling out a student's name, demonstrate how people overcome tone or inflection problems. Have the students practice with you.]

GRADING CRITERIA: _____

MODIFICATIONS FOR GRADE LEVELS AND STUDENT ABILITY LEVELS

The different approaches to Activity 5-6 for younger and older students were outlined in the previous text.

For Activity 5-5, make sure that younger children understand the meaning of King's words. If you do not want to treat King's speech with brevity add other sentences that he spoke. Students can also read one of the books on pages 178–179 before the play, to learn more about their character.

STUDENTS WHO WILL BE WORKING ON OTHER PROJECTS OR LESSONS: _____

NOTES FOR FUTURE USE: _____

FIGURE 5-4 I Have a Dream

_____ I Have A Dream _____

Martin Luther King, Jr., was a great speaker.
He gave a famous speech on August 28, 1963, in Washington, D.C.
He told about his dream for America.
He wanted all people to live and work together in peace.

"I have a dream.
that my four little children
will one day live in a nation
where they will not be judged
by the color of their skin
but by the content of their character."

ACTIVITY 5-6

THE SOUND OF GREAT VOICES BY D. R. ANDERSON

CHARACTERS

Narrators 1, 2, 3, 4, and 5

Martin Luther King, Jr.

Teacher

Harriet Tubman

Nat Turner

Frederick Douglass

Narrator 1: On January 15, we celebrate the birthday of civil rights leader Martin Luther King, Jr.

Narrator 2: This great man worked his whole life to ensure equality of opportunity for every African-American.

Narrator 3: To help African-Americans gain their rights, Martin Luther King had to overcome many obstacles and hardships.

Narrator 4: Where did he find the wisdom and strength to face these challenges?

Narrator 5: He listened to the sound of great voices—the voices of other men and women who in their own lifetimes worked for the rights of oppressed people.

Narrator 1: When did Martin Luther King first "hear" those great voices?

Narrator 2: You may be surprised to discover that it was when he was very young. Let's go back to his first day in seventh grade to find out.

Narrator 3: On the way to school, many thoughts passed through Martin's mind.

Narrator 4: He wondered why black children and white children had to go to separate schools.

Narrator 5: He wondered why blacks had to sit at the back of public busses and were refused service at many restaurants.

Narrator 1: He wondered why blacks were not allowed to vote.

Narrator 2: Most of all—he wondered if things would ever change.

Narrator 3: Before he knew it, Martin was already at school and sitting in his classroom. It was first period. He was in his history class.

Narrator 4: Martin's teacher handed him a history textbook. Martin opened his.

Narrator 5: He gasped! His teacher looked at him with surprise.

Teacher: Martin, why are you so startled?

Martin: There are black people in this history book!

Teacher: Well, of course there are.

Martin: But none of the other books I've read said a word about famous black people.

Teacher: Then I think it's time you started learning about some right now!

Narrator 1: All the students in Martin's class began to read.

Narrator 2: They learned about important African-American people. Most they had never heard of before.

Narrator 3: Martin couldn't take his eyes off the pages. He couldn't stop reading.

Narrator 4: He really felt as if he were in the same room with these African-American heroes of history.

Narrator 5: Their voices seemed to fill his ears.

Harriet Tubman: I am Harriet Tubman. I was born a slave, but escaped from slavery in 1849. Later I worked for the Underground Railroad, making nineteen long and dangerous trips to help other slaves escape. I even led my mother and father out of slavery and north to freedom.
I always knew in my heart that slavery was an evil thing, and during my lifetime I did all I could to help my people.

Nat Turner: I am Nat Turner. I was born a slave and died a slave. But in spite of that, I learned to read and write and became a preacher.
In 1831 I led a revolt. I knew slavery was wrong and I had to fight against it. I died in the revolt—but in my short life I did all I could to help my people.

Frederick Douglass: I am Frederick Douglass. I was a slave until I ran away. After many hard times, I began to speak out against slavery. I fought against unequal treatment of blacks on trains and struggled to have black children and white children go to school together. I started an anti-slavery newspaper. I consulted with President Abraham Lincoln on the slavery problem. And I served as U.S. minister to Haiti.
I worked hard all my life at many things and did all I could to help my people.

Narrator 1: Martin left school that day and felt as if he were walking on a cloud. He had wondered for so long how he could help his people. And in his history book, he found part of the answer. He learned how some great African-American men and women had helped to bring about change.

Martin Luther King, Jr.
(1929-1968)
Minister, speaker,
and civil rights leader

Bill Cosby
(1937-)
Comedian and TV star

Althea Gibson
(1927-)
World-famous tennis star

Langston Hughes
(1902-1967)
Poet of Harlem

Marian Anderson
(1902-)
Singer

Jackie Robinson
(1919-1972)
Dodgers baseball star

Jesse Owens
(1913-1980)
Winner of Olympic
medals in track

Carter G. Woodson
(1875-1950)
Wrote black history

Thurgood Marshall
(1908-)
First black U.S.
Supreme Court judge

Wilma Rudolph
(1940-)
Olympic runner

Michael Jackson
(1958-)
Rock music star,
songwriter

Charles Richard Drew
(1904-1950)
Set up blood banks

Narrator 2: In years to come, Martin was influenced by other great voices—like those of Henry David Thoreau and Mahatma Gandhi, who believed in using peaceful resistance only, never violence. In 1964, Martin Luther King won the Nobel Peace Prize for leading nonviolent demonstrations. Religious teachings also had a major impact on Martin's life. Just before graduating from college, he was ordained a Baptist minister.

Narrator 3: Although he was killed when he was only 39 years old, Martin Luther King, Jr. largely succeeded in attaining his goal: equal treatment of blacks in stores, on buses, in restaurants, and at the voting polls.

Shirley Chisholm
(1924-)

First black woman
in Congress

Paul Laurence Dunbar
(1872-1906)

Poet, author

Sojourner Truth
(1797-1883)

Traveled and
spoke against slavery

George Washington Carver
(1864-1943)

Scientist who found
ways to help farmers

Frederick Douglass
(1817-1895)

Escaped slave who spoke
and wrote against slavery

Matthew Henson
(1867-1955)

Explorer who reached
the North Pole

Jesse Jackson
(1941-)

Minister, civil rights leader,
candidate for president

Louis Armstrong
(1898-1971)

Jazz trumpet player

Ronald McNair
(1950-1986)

First black astronaut

Harriet Tubman
(1821-1913)

Helped slaves
escape to freedom

Booker T. Washington
(1856-1915)

Began college for blacks

Mary McLeod Bethune
(1875-1955)

Teacher and advisor
to presidents

Narrator 4: Today this great man's history and words are in the history books alongside the heroes he once read about as a boy. Listen to some of his most famous words.

Martin: ". . . I have a dream that my four little children will one day be judged, not by the color of their skin, but by the content of their character. I have a dream today. I have a dream that one day, little black boys and black girls will be able to join hands with little white boys and white girls and walk together as sisters and brothers . . . ."

Narrator 5: Through his deeds and words, Martin Luther King, Jr. will be remembered as one of the great voices in the history of civil rights.

RESOURCES

Theodore Taylor has written a book dedicated to Martin Luther King, and his dream that students may enjoy having you read or reading themselves. The book is entitled *The Cay*. Other resources to help you and your students learn more about King's life and works by other characters in the play are:

The Assassination of Martin Luther King, Jr. by Doris and Harold Faber (Franklin Watts, 1978).

In Search of Peace: The Story of Four Americans Who Won the Nobel Peace Prize by Roberta Strauss Feuerlicht (Julian Messner, 1970).

Martin Luther King: The Peaceful Warrior by Ed Clayton, illustrated by David Hughes (Prentice-Hall, 1968).

The Picture Life of Martin Luther King, Jr. by Margaret B. Young (Franklin Watts, 1968).

BOOKS REFERRED TO IN THE PLAY

Books About Harriett Tubman

Freedom Train; The Story of Harriett Tubman by Dorothy Sterling (Doubleday, Garden City, NY, 1954).

Harriett Tubman Black Liberation by Matthew G. Grant (Mankato, MN, Creative Education, 1974).

Runaway Slave: The Story of Harriet Tubman by Anne McGovern (NY: Four Winds Press, 1965).

Harriett and the Promised Land by Jacob Lawerence (NY: Simon and Schuster, 1968).

When the Rattlesnake Sounds: A Play by Alice Childress (NY: Howard McCann and Goeghegan, 1975).

Harriett Tubman the Road to Freedom by Ray Bains (Mattwah, NY: Troll Associates, 1982).

Harriett Died to Freedom by Sam Epstein (Champaign, IL: Garrarad Publishing Company, 1968).

Books About Frederick Douglass

Frederick Douglass: Slave Fighter Free Man by Anna Wendell (Bontemts, NY: Knops, 1959).

Frederick Douglass Fights for Freedom by Margaret Davison (NY: Four Winds Press, 1968).

Life and Times of Frederick Douglass edited by Genevie S. Grey (NY: Grosset and Dunlap).

Frederick Douglass by Mildred Barger (Chicago: Follet, 1969).

Books About Henry David Thoreau

Conquered Rebel; A Life of Henry D. Thoreau by August William Derleth (Philadelphia, Chilton Company, 1962).

Down to Earth at Walden by Marrilynne K. Roach (Boston: Houghton Mifflin, 1980).

A Man Named Thoreau by Robert Burleigh (NY: Atheneum, 1985).

Books About Mahatma Gandhi

Mohandas Gandhi by Glenn Allen Cheney (New York: Franklin Watts, 1983).

Gandhi by Olivia E. Coolidge (Boston: Houghton Mifflin, 1971).

Mahatma Gandhi: A Biography for Young People by Catherine Owens (Peare, NY: Holt, 1950).

Gandhi and the Struggle for India's Independence by S.W. Rawding (Lerner Publications, Minneapolis, 1982).

The True Story of Gandhi Man of Peace by Reginald Reynolds (Chicago: Children's Press, 1964).

Gandhi: Soldier of Nonviolence by Calvin Kytle (NY: Grosset and Dunlap, 1969).

The Story of Gandhi by Taya Zinkin (NY: Criterion Books, 1966).

Mahatma Gandhi by Doris Faver (NY: J. Messener, 1986).

Gandhi by Kathryn Spink (London: Hamish Hamilton, 1984).

FOLLOW-UP WRITING ACTIVITIES

1. *My Dream:* Ask students to think about what changes in policies or in people's attitudes might help make your school, your community, or the United States a better place. Then ask them to write their own speeches, which might begin with King's words "I have a dream . . . ."

2. *Moment of Greatness:* Martin Luther King, Jr.'s life was filled with accomplishments. Ask students to choose what they feel is his most important achievement and to write a paragraph explaining why that achievement was key. Students can select one or more of the reference books of this activity to document their claims.

3. *Great Models:* Martin Luther King, Jr. was inspired by great people in history who worked for freedom. Ask students to write about someone they admire—such as a relative, a current national figure, or a noted personality from history—and explain why they think this person is admirable.

4. *Special Birthdays:* Our nation officially observes the birthdays of a few leaders every year, such as Martin Luther King's birthday celebrated on the Monday nearest January 15. Ask students if the birthdays of other great Americans should be honored. Encourage them to consider the effect of new national holidays. If they decide someone new should be honored, ask them to describe their position, or write a letter to their congressional representative, lobbying for a holiday honoring that individual.

STUDENTS WHO ARE WORKING ON OTHER PROJECTS OR LESSONS: _____

_____

NOTES FOR FUTURE USE: _____

_____

Creative Writing Skill Development: Improve Writing Skills through Self-Evaluation and Peer Editing

PREREQUISITE

Have a copy of *Winnie-the-Pooh* so you can read an episode from it in your introduction of the lesson.

TIME REQUIRED

49–90 minutes

TEACHING STRATEGIES

Student self-evaluation and the peer editing process are used.

ACTIVITY 5-7

TELLING A STORY ABOUT A PROBLEM

[OBJECTIVE]   YOU WILL LEARN HOW TO IMPROVE YOUR WRITING BY USING A SELF-ASSESSMENT GUIDE AND THE FEEDBACK OF OTHER STUDENTS IN A PEER REVIEW PROCESS. YOU WILL KNOW YOU'VE IMPROVED WHEN THE ANSWERS TO QUESTIONS 1–5 OF THE GUIDE, IN ACTIVITY 5-8 ARE POSITIVE.

A. A. Milne was one of the most creative writers in history. He created a series of books about a lovable, courageous bear named Winnie-the-Pooh. Milne was born on January 18. I want to tell you one thing he did to become a famous author. You will learn to do what he did, and it will improve your writing ability.

Mr. Milne wanted to help people. He decided that if he could learn to write well enough, he could help people solve their problems. He decided to create an animal that people could read about. This animal would solve problems that people have and as the animal solved each problem, people could do as the animal did and solve their own problems. By choosing to use animal models, Mr. Milne could help people learn to solve problems faster because the animals would not appear to be preaching or judging people. Some people do not like others to tell them what to do about their problems. Mr. Milne could also use the bear, Winnie-the-Pooh, to suggest more than one way to solve a problem, and people could choose which way they wanted to use. Without Winnie and the other animals in 100 Acre Wood, Mr. Milne would have had to write about only one way to solve problems, and that way may not have worked for some people.

When you write you should ask yourself the six questions on Activity 5-8. These questions will help you evaluate your writing. You can also ask your friends to suggest ways in which your writing can be improved.

I want you to think of a problem you have solved, or a book or topic about which you desire to tell others. Now write clearly enough that it can help someone else in the class solve that problem if they ever face it or to understand your purpose for writing.

You can write in one of three different ways. You can write using animal characters, as Milne did. (Read an excerpt from his book here and discuss how his animals gave solutions to problems, e.g., through dialogue between characters.) Secondly, you can pretend you are a story teller and write as if you are telling about how another person solved a problem. Lastly, you can decide to be yourself and describe everything just as it occurred.

[As a class exercise, choose a problem on which to base a short story, such as quarreling over use of playground equipment.] What solution to the problem do we want to suggest in our story? What is our purpose **[such as "Show that sharing is better than fighting"]?** What kind of characters do we want to use? **[Reach a class consensus.]**

Our story will be clearer and show our purpose better if we include the 5 "W"s and "H." The 5 "W"s are Why? What? When? Where? and Why? Can anyone tell what "H" stands for in a story?

[List the six story elements on the chalkboard or on an overhead transparency and by each write the suggestions for the class story.] Now we have all the parts of our story. Our story will be most interesting if we use vivid descriptions for each part. **[Solicit details and descriptive words for each element. Add them to the list. Then orally pull the story together, including the suggested elements and descriptive details. A tape recorder could be used for later transcription if desired.]**

[Hand out Activity 5-8. Students write a story illustrating a problem solution.] When you've finished writing, use Activity 5-7, The Bear's Reaction Guide. Without writing any comments on the form, evaluate your writing by answering each question in your mind. Then, make any changes you need.

Then bring your paper and your Reaction Guide sheet to me. I will pair you with another person. You both will evaluate each other's papers. Then you will meet with a third person. The three of you will have read three papers. You will decide how you could combine all three as separate episodes of one long story. You can create or select one main character (for example, an animal, extraterrestrial, or make-believe person) who all three of you agree would be a convincing character to tell others about all three of your problem solutions. Decide the best order for the three episodes. Then each of you write one of the revised episodes.

Share your revised episodes, and edit each others', until you feel they are the best they can be, and that they meet each of the questions on the Reaction Guide. **[You may next want people in the class to read the episodes, with a group of students evaluating the oral sharing using the Reaction Guide.]**

GRADING CRITERIA

1. Ignore errors, grade on effort.

2. Circle errors and count them.

3. Use Activity 5-10.

4. Allow students to revise.

MODIFICATIONS FOR GRADE LEVELS AND STUDENT ABILITY LEVELS

For Kindergarten through Third Grades and Slower Learning Groups, the time for each day's segment can be reduced. *For Younger Grades,* students may need more help to begin writing than do older students.

STUDENTS WHO WILL BE WORKING ON OTHER PROJECTS OR LESSONS: _____

_____

NOTES FOR FUTURE USE: _____

_____

ACTIVITY 5-8

WINNIE THE BEAR'S REACTION GUIDE

Author _____

Title of Writnig _____

1. What do you like about it?

2. What does not make sense?

3. What questions do you have?

4. How can it be revised and improved?

5. Check the things that are clear:

_____ purpose
_____ grammar
_____ spelling
_____ precise wording
_____ organization
_____ punctuation
_____ legibility
_____ descriptions using the 5 W's and H
       (who, what, when, where, why, and how)

Listening Skill Development: Listening for Main Ideas to Help Retention

PREREQUISITE

Ask students a day or two in advance to think about their hobbies and how they could describe them to the class without actually saying what the hobby is.

TIME REQUIRED

Teacher Directed Exploration (Activity 5-9): 10–15 minutes

Student Discovery Page (Activity 5-10): 30–35 minutes

TEACHING STRATEGIES

Cooperative learning groups are used.

ACTIVITY 5-9 _____

HOBBY DETAILS

[OBJECTIVE] YOU WILL LEARN FOUR TYPES OF DETAILS TO LISTEN FOR WHEN OTHERS SPEAK, AND TO NOTE WHEN YOU READ. DETAILS GIVE CLUES TO DISCOVER AUTHORS' MAIN IDEAS. YOU WILL KNOW YOU ARE SUCCESSFUL WHEN YOU COMPLETE ACTIVITY 5-10 CORRECTLY.

Because it is National Hobby Month, you may want to begin a new hobby. Before you select a new hobby you need a basic description of special hobbies. Not only do we need to understand important points and details so we can make a thoughtful choice as to a hobby that will be just right.

You should listen for details when someone is speaking. Details will help you in understanding the main idea not only when dealing with a different hobby, but also when you are listening to someone speak about subjects other than hobbies.

There are four detail types you should attend to when listening:

1. Styles and mannerisms in dialects. These give us clues about who the speaker is and where she or he is from.

2. Nonverbal communication. This includes body movements, gestures, eye contact, loudness, and rate of speaking. This tells us how the speaker really feels about the topic or main idea.

3. Information. This includes any general ideas that give clues as to the main idea.

4. Descriptions. These include any words, such as adjectives or adverbs, or groups of words that describe the main idea without actually saying it.

[Have each student write four or more details about a hobby. When all have written about their hobby, students receive a chance to speak about the hobby without disclosing what it is. Others guess what the hobby might be. Once they feel they have guessed, they fill out Activity 5-10, the Hobby Hunt Sheet, on at least three hobbies that interest them. In cooperative

working groups, students then discuss the hobbies they believe to be most interesting and why.]

MODIFICATIONS FOR GRADE LEVELS AND STUDENT ABILITY LEVELS

For Younger and Slower Students, decrease the difficulty and abstractness of details used in hobby descriptions, making the hobbies more obvious. Students concentrate more on recognizing the value of descriptive details. Students work in small groups, writing only one hobby description, and a parent volunteer or older student writes the description on chart paper to be read to the entire class. This eliminates younger students' need to write. *For Older and Gifted Students,* have them increase the difficulty of descriptions, making details less obvious. Do not create as many examples of descriptions, having them do more descriptions creatively, on their own.

Students may check out a book from the library concerning a hobby and read it at school for a few days.

Time may be given for students exploring the same or similar hobbies to discuss what they have learned. In cooperative learning groups they list details that conflict and details that are similar about their hobbies. The groups share their detail charts. Some students may want to form hobby clubs and work together after school.

Students can use propaganda techniques in speeches designed to convince classmates to "buy" into their hobby. Listeners identify the propaganda devices used. (See Activity 5-3.) Books that can be used for this activity include:

BOOKS ABOUT HOBBIES

Primary Level

1. *Sports Cards* by McLoone and Basta
2. *Jar and Bottle Craft* by Helen Roney Sattler
3. *Potato Printing* by Helen Haddad
4. *Splodges* by Malcolm Carrick
5. *Exciting Things to do with Color* by Janee Allen
6. *Create-a-Kite* by editors of Consumer Guide
7. *Insect Pets: Catching and Caring for Them* by Carla Stevens
8. *The Little Pigs First Cookbook* by Watson
9. *Coins You Can Collect* by Buiton Hobson
10. *Easy Origami* by Dokuohtei Nakano

Intermediate Level

1. *Paint a Rainbow* by John Hawkinson
2. *Collage* by Mickey Klar Marks
3. *Introducing Needlepoint* by Donna Lightbody

4. *Drawing and Painting with the Computer* by Don Bolognese and Robert Thornton

5. *Cookie Craft* by Williams and Williams

6. *Easy Weaving* by Lightbody

7. *Getting Started in Stamp Collecting* by Hobson

8. *How to Paint with Water Colors* by Zaidenberg

9. *Jewelry from Junk* by Helen Roney Sattler

10. *Creating with Burlap* by Fressard

Middle School Level

1. *Mosaics with Natural Stones* by Walter Lauppi

2. *Indian Beadwork* by Hofsinde

3. *More to Collect and Paint from Nature* by John Hawkinson

4. *Batik and Tie Dyeing* by Cameron and Margarte Yuian

5. *Decorate Your Own Room* by Ellen Liman and Carol Panter

6. *Knitting* by Mary Walker Phillips

7. *Beginner's Guide to Photography* by George Laycock

8. *Printing* by Hilary Devonshire

9. *Quilting as a Hobby* by Dorothy Brightbell

10. *Getting Started in Calligraphy* by Nancy Baron

Hobby Books Related to Holidays for All Ages

1. *Christmas Crafts* by Meyer Lobel

2. *Easter Fun* by Judith Hoffman Corwin

3. *Halloween Fun* by Judith Hoffman Corwin

4. *Thanksgiving Fun* by Judith Hoffman Corwin

5. *Christmas Fun* by Judith Hoffman Corwin

ACTIVITY 5-10

HOBBY HUNT WORKSHEET

----

1. Which details gave you information about the hobby?_____

    _____

    What were some descriptive words that gave you clues about the
    hobby?_____

    Did the speaker/author have a certain style of talking/writing
    that gave you a clue? What was it?_____

    _____

    Were there any nonverbal clues? What were they, and what did
    they tell you?_____

    Did the speaker/author use any propaganda devices? Were they
    effective?_____

    What is the hobby?_____

----

2. Which details gave you information about the hobby?_____

    _____

    What were some descriptive words that gave you clues about the
    hobby?_____

    Did the speaker have a certain style of talking that gave you
    a clue? What was it?_____

    _____

    Were there any non verbal clues? What were they, and what did
    they tell you?_____

    Did the speaker/author use any propaganda devices? Were they
    effective?_____

    What is the hobby?_____

----

3. Which details gave you information about the hobby?_____

    _____

    What were some descriptive words that gave you clues about the
    hobby?_____

    Did the speaker/author have a certain style of talking/writing
    that gave you a clue? What was it?_____

    _____

    Were there any nonverbal clues: What were they, and what did
    they tell you?_____

    Did the speaker/author use any propaganda devices? Were they
    effective?_____

    What is the hobby?_____

Grammar Skill Development: Flying High with the Parts of Speech

PREREQUISITE

Students should already understand nouns, verbs, conjunctions, and adjectives.

TIME REQUIRED

Teacher Directed Exploration (Activity 5-11): 20–30 minutes

Student Discovery Page (Activity 5-12): 20–30 minutes, preferably on a second day

TEACHING STRATEGIES

A game, and teacher-modeled "think-alouds." Will be used to stimulate recognition of learned concepts.

ACTIVITY 5-11

FOUR MORE PARTS OF SPEECH

[OBJECTIVE]   YOU WILL LEARN FOUR NEW PARTS OF SPEECH. YOU WILL KNOW YOU ARE SUCCESSFUL WHEN YOUR BALLOON RISES TO THE TOP OF THE PAGE IN THE BALLOON GAME.

In this month we mark the birthday of aviation in America. What do you think of when you hear the word "aviation." Aviation includes all the activities involved in building and flying aircraft – including balloons. On January 9, 1793, a Frenchman named Jean Pierre Blanchard made the first manned free-balloon flight in America. It occurred in Philadelphia, and George Washington was part of the crowd. The hydrogen-filled balloon rose to a height of about 5,800 feet, traveled some 15 miles, and landed 6 minutes later. Reportedly, Blanchard had one passenger on the flight – a little black dog.

A free-floating balloon travels in whatever direction the wind blows. A pilot can control the balloon by rising or descending to find a wind blowing in the desired direction. You will make a flight of your own by successfully learning four of the eight parts of speech. **[Remember, the other four were taught in September.]** You will learn about adverbs, pronouns, interjections, and prepositions. When you learn these, you will be able to complete the bulletin board game.

[Discuss the following characteristics and correct usage of each part of speech. Write key words on the chalkboard or an overhead transparency.]

Adverb: A word used to describe a verb, telling where, when, how, or to what extent. It can also modify an adjective, another adverb, or the whole sentence. Many end in *-ly*. It can have various positions in the sentence.

Pronoun: A word used in place of a noun. It does not follow "a," "an," "the," or an adjective. It functions as a noun and names a specific person, place, or thing.

Preposition: A word that shows the relationship between a noun or pronoun and another word. It introduces a prepositional phrase. (It is sometimes remembered as "anything a rabbit can do to a barrel"—for example, it can be *in* a barrel, *under* a barrel, *between* barrels.)

Interjection: A word or short group of words used to express strong feeling. It may be a word or just a sound. It may express surprise, joy, longing, anger, or sorrow. It is usually followed by an exclamation point. It may stand alone or be inserted into the sentence.

[Write sentence 1 (below) on the board. First, talk aloud, as if to yourself, as you find the nouns, adjectives, conjunctions, and verbs, thus reviewing with the students the parts of speech they should already know as they were studied in a previous activity. Then look at each unidentified word, asking what it does in the sentence. Do two or three sample sentences on the board as a class, going through the same process as you did in sentence 1.]

1. *Hooray, many bright and shiny balloons are flying slowly over us!* Hooray, interjection; *slowly,* adverb; *over,* preposition; *us,* pronoun.

2. *Oh no! The purple balloon crashed into some very tall trees.* Oh no, interjection; *into,* preposition; *very,* adverb.

3. *I often go into a large, open field and watch the balloons fly above me.* I, pronoun; *often,* adverb; *to,* preposition; *above,* preposition; *me,* pronoun.

4. *Did anyone tell you about the balloon race yesterday?* anyone, pronoun; *you,* pronoun; *about,* preposition.

5. *One of the most colorful balloons almost beat them.* One, pronoun; *of,* preposition; *most,* adverb; *them,* pronoun.

[Distribute Activity 5-12 and the "Parts of Speech Grading Game." Have each child work through the sentences independently. In the spaces of the game board, students write the word (either a pronoun, preposition, adverb, or interjection) found in the sentence that corresponds to the number of the game space. In the second they will write its part of speech. Check their work. When finished students can create five sentences correctly. (You check their sentences as they finish. They can be placed on the bulletin board, with a sample shown in Figure 5-4.) Let them glue their sentences and place it on the bulletin board.]

ANSWER KEY

1. it—pronoun

2. Oh—interjection

3. with—preposition

4. I—pronoun

5. tomorrow—adverb

6. over—preposition

7. in—preposition

    8. wow – interjection

    9. both – pronoun

  10. loudly – adverb

  11. below – preposition

  12. very – adverb

  13. us – pronoun

  14. by – preposition

  15. rats – interjection

  16. someone – pronoun

  17. extremely – adverb

GRADING CRITERIA: _____

_____

EARLY FINISHERS

Have books on balloons and aviation available from which students can choose sentences to identify parts of speech or can just read. They can also decorate their balloon tags.

MODIFICATIONS FOR GRADE LEVELS AND STUDENT ABILITY LEVELS

For Younger and Slower Students, teach only one part of speech a day. Have four grading sheets—one for each part of speech. Dictate sentences you create and/or have students work together. *For Older and Gifted Students,* increase the amount and depth of material taught. (For example, discuss personal pronouns, agreement of pronoun and antecedent, pronoun cases, and so forth.) Increase the difficulty of the sentences. Increase the number of sentences that must be created before they can be placed on the bulletin board.

STUDENTS WHO WILL BE WORKING ON OTHER PROJECTS OR LESSONS: _____

_____

NOTES FOR FUTURE USE: _____

_____

FLYING HIGH WITH THE PARTS OF SPEECH

1. It flew.

2. Oh, the balloon is pretty!

3. The balloon is covered with big, red stars.

4. I like watching giant hot-air balloons work.

5. Tomorrow, the man will show how hot-air balloons work.

6. That balloon is going over some high mountains.

7. There is a little girl in the balloon!

8. Wow, the girl is holding a little black dog!

9. Both are waving.

10. The crowd is cheering loudly.

11. The things below the balloon look tiny.

12. Many balloons are very colorful.

13. My granddad gave us a yellow and green hot-air balloon.

14. A large bird flew by our balloon.

15. Rats, the balloon has a hole!

16. Someone might get hurt!

17. Hot-air balloons can be extremely dangerous.

PARTS OF SPEECH GRADING GAME

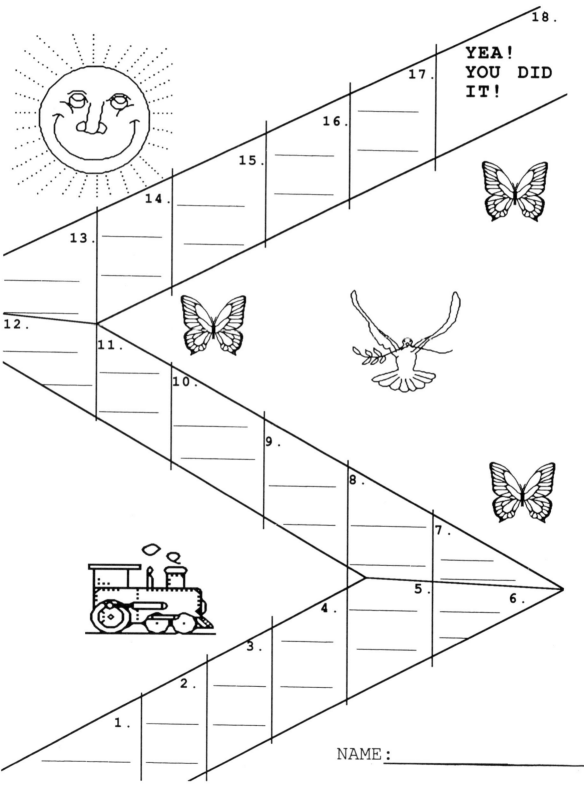

YEA!
YOU DID
IT!

18.

17.

16.

15.

14.

13.

12.

11.

10.

9.

8.

7.

6.

5.

4.

3.

2.

1.

NAME: _____

FIGURE 5-4   Sample Balloon Bulletin Board

FLYING HIGH WITH THE PARTS OF SPEECH

Handwriting Skill Development: Learning the Correct Steps to Form Letters

TIME REQUIRED

Approximately 50 minutes—20 minutes of teacher instruction and class discussion and 30 minutes of individual practice

TEACHING STRATEGIES

Students develop their own goals and practice skills.

ACTIVITY 5-13

DECLARATION OF GOOD HANDWRITING

[OBJECTIVE]   YOU WILL IMPROVE YOUR WRITING BY SETTING YOUR OWN GOALS AND MAKING A DECLARATION OF GOOD HANDWRITING OR ANOTHER TYPE OF DECLARATION. YOU WILL EACH SIGN IT USING YOUR BEST LETTER FORMS.

January 23 is National Handwriting Day because it is the birthday of John Hancock, President of the Continental Congress that wrote the Declaration of Independence. **[Show an overhead transparency of a copy of Figure 5-5. Read excerpts from the Declaration of Independence (Figure 5-6). Discuss the values of legible handwriting by showing the contrasts of Thomas Jefferson's first draft and the final copy.]**

Thomas Jefferson's final copy of the Declaration of Independence is very impressive today, even though we may find it difficult to read because our handwriting style has changed. What differences can you see in the way letters were formed then?

[Students may remark on the decorativeness of the uppercase letters and the different form of the lowercase "s." If they do not notice, point these differences out yourself. Students may also comment on the unusual paragraphing—to save space?]

The people in the 1700s could easily read well-formed letters of the style they were taught; we have a certain style for good handwriting also. We can use it to make sure our special messages are easy to understand. **[Show or distribute copies of the letter-formation charts in Figure 5-7 or the system in your curriculum. Draw attention to letters that seem to be troublesome for your class. Have students copy the following, filling in their own individual goals (example, "I will make the long strokes of lowercase letters all the same height") and sign them.**

WHEREAS good handwriting is very important,

BE IT RESOLVED I will:

(1) _____

(2) _____

[Hand out Activity 5-14. Tell the students they are going to write their declarations in their best handwriting so they can be kept and appreciated. A Declaration of Good Handwriting can be made to include individual goals set in Activity 5-13.]

FIGURE 5-5 Jefferson's First Draft and Final Declaration

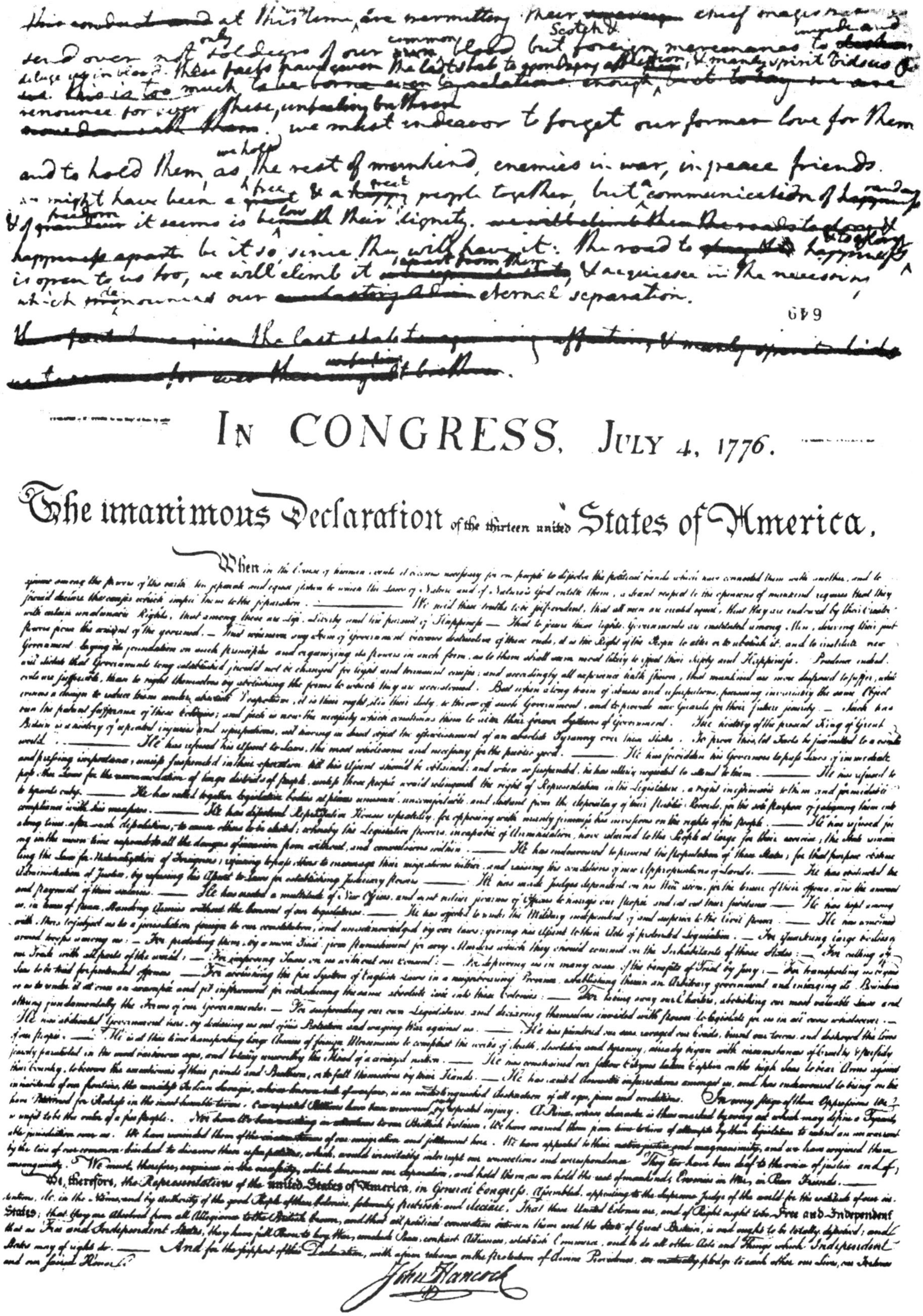

FIGURE 5-6   The Declaration of Independence

THE DECLARATION OF INDEPENDENCE

When in the Course of human events it becomes necessary for one people to dissolve the political bands which have connected them with another, and to assume among the powers of the earth, the separate and equal station to which the Laws of Nature and of Nature's God entitle them, a decent respect to the opinions of mankind requires that they should declare the causes which impel them to the separation.

We hold these truths to be self-evident, that all men are created equal, that they are endowed by their Creator with certain unalienable Rights, that among these are Life, Liberty and the pursuit of Happiness. That to secure these rights, Governments are instituted among Men, deriving their just powers from the consent of the governed. That whenever any Form of Government becomes destructive of these ends, it is the Right of the People to alter or to abolish it, and to institute new Government, laying its foundation on such principles, and organizing its powers in such form, as to them shall seem most likely to effect their Safety and Happiness. Prudence, indeed, will dictate that Governments long established should not be changed for light and transient causes; and accordingly all experience hath shewn, that mankind are more disposed to suffer, while evils are sufferable, than to right themselves by abolishing the forms to which they are accustomed. But when a long train of abuses and usurpations, pursuing invariably the same Object, evinces a design to reduce them under absolute Despotism, it is their right, it is their duty, to throw off such Government, and to provide new Guards for their future security. Such has been the patient sufferance of these Colonies; and such is now the necessity which constrains them to alter their former Systems of Government. The history of the present King of Great Britain is a history of repeated injuries and usurpations, all having in direct object the establishment of an absolute Tyranny over these States. To prove this, let Facts be submitted to a candid world.

He has refused his Assent to Laws, the most wholesome and necessary for the public good.

He has forbidden his Governors to pass Laws of immediate and pressing importance, unless suspended in their operation till his Assent should be obtained; and when so suspended, he has utterly neglected to attend to them.

He has refused to pass other Laws for the accommodation of large districts of people, unless those people would relinquish the right of Representation in the Legislature, a right inestimable to them and formidable to tyrants only.

He has called together legislative bodies at places unusual, uncomfortable, and distant from the depository of their public Records, for the sole purpose of fatiguing them into compliance with his measures.

He has dissolved Representative Houses repeatedly, for opposing with manly firmness his invasions on the rights of the people.

He has refused for a long time after such dissolutions, to cause others to be elected; whereby the Legislative powers, incapable of Annihilation, have returned to the People at large for their exercise; the State remaining in the meantime exposed to all the dangers of invasion from without, and convulsions within.

He has endeavoured to prevent the population of these States, for that purpose obstructing the Laws of Naturalization of Foreigners, refusing to pass others to encourage their migrations hither, and raising the conditions of new Appropriations of Lands.

He has obstructed the Administration of Justice, by refusing his Assent to Laws for establishing Judiciary powers.

He has made Judges dependent on his Will alone, for the tenure of their offices, and the amount and payment of their salaries.

He has erected a multitude of New Offices, and sent hither swarms of Officers to harass our people, and eat out their substance.

He has kept among us, in times of peace Standing Armies, without the Consent of our legislatures.

He has affected to render the Military independent of and superior to the Civil power.

He has combined with others to subject us to a jurisdiction foreign to our constitution, and unacknowledged by our laws; giving his Assent to their Acts of pretended Legislation: For quartering large bodies of armed troops among us: For protecting them by a mock Trial from punishment for any Murders which they should commit on the Inhabitants of these States: For cutting off our Trade with all parts of the world: For imposing Taxes on us without our Consent: For depriving us in many cases of the benefits of Trial by Jury: For transporting us beyond Seas to be tried for pretended offenses: For abolishing the free System of English Laws in a neighbouring Province, establishing therein an Arbitrary government, and enlarging its Boundaries so as to render it at once an example and fit instrument for introducing the same absolute rule into these Colonies: For taking away our Charters, abolishing our most valuable Laws and altering fundamentally the Forms of our Governments: For suspending our own Legislatures, and declaring themselves invested with power to legislate for us in all cases whatsoever.

He has abdicated Government here by declaring us out of his Protection and waging War against us.

He has plundered our seas, ravaged our Coasts, burnt our towns, and destroyed the lives of our people.

He is at this time transporting large Armies of foreign Mercenaries to complete the works of death, desolation and tyranny, already begun with circumstances of Cruelty and perfidy scarcely paralleled in the most barbarous ages, and totally unworthy the Head of a civilized nation.

He has constrained our fellow Citizens taken Captive on the high Seas to bear Arms against their Country, to become the executioners of their friends and Brethren, or to fall themselves by their Hands.

He has excited domestic insurrections amongst us, and has endeavoured to bring on the inhabitants of our frontiers, the merciless Indian Savages, whose known rule of warfare is an undistinguished destruction of all ages, sexes and conditions. In every stage of these Oppressions We have Petitioned for Redress in the most humble terms. Our repeated Petitions have been answered by repeated injury: A Prince, whose character is thus marked by every act which may define a Tyrant, is unfit to be the ruler of a free people. Nor have We been wanting in attentions to our British brethren. We have warned them from time to time of attempts by their legislature to extend an unwarrantable jurisdiction over us. We have reminded them of the circumstances of our emigration and settlement here. We have appealed to their native justice and magnanimity, and we have conjured them by the ties of our common kindred to disavow these usurpations, which would inevitably interrupt our connections and correspondence. They too have been deaf to the voice of justice and of consanguinity. We must, therefore, acquiesce in the necessity, which denounces our Separation, and hold them, as we hold the rest of mankind, Enemies in War, in Peace Friends.

WE, THEREFORE, the Representatives of the UNITED STATES OF AMERICA, in General Congress, Assembled, appealing to the Supreme Judge of the world for the rectitude of our intentions, do, in the Name and by authority of the good People of these Colonies solemnly publish and declare That these United Colonies are and of Right ought to be FREE AND INDEPENDENT STATES; that they are Absolved from all Allegiance to the British Crown, and that all political connection between them and the State of Great Britain, is and ought to be totally dissolved; and that as Free and Independent States, they have full Power to levy War, conclude Peace, contract Alliances, establish Commerce, and to do all other Acts and Things which Independent States may of right do. And for the support of this Declaration, with a firm reliance on the protection of divine Providence, we mutually pledge to each other our Lives, our Fortunes, and our sacred Honor.

[Alternatively, they can make their Declaration from a topic you give, a content area topic from current events, or a concern to them. They may work individually or in small groups. Students sign their declarations in their best handwriting; they will be displayed in the classroom.]

GRADING CRITERIA: _____

EARLY FINISHERS

The first of the final activities at the end of this chapter provides for more handwriting practice in an interesting context. It and the room-designing work sheet could be used at any time for early finishers.

MODIFICATIONS FOR GRADE LEVELS AND STUDENT ABILITY LEVELS

For Kindergarten through Third Grades and Slower Learning Groups, this activity could be done about a week before National Handwriting Day, January 23. The classes could give copies of their handwriting declarations to other classes as part of a schoolwide effort to improve handwriting.

FIGURE 5-7   Forming Correct Letters

FIGURE 5-7   Forming Correct Letters (continued)

INDIVIDUAL STUDENTS NEEDS: _____

_____

STUDENTS WHO WILL BE WORKING ON OTHER PROJECTS OR
LESSONS: _____

_____

NOTES FOR FUTURE USE: _____

_____

Declaration

DESIGNING OUR CLASSROOM

Measure the size of the room on the grid at the bottom. Cut the pieces that are models of things in our room. Arrange the room as you'd like it.

Chairs

desk desk desk

desk desk desk

desk desk desk

Chalkboard

Bookshelves

Bulletin board

Rug

Project table

Art

DESIGNING OUR CLASSROOM GRID

6 *February*

In February our lessons are built on the themes of Black History Month, Groundhog's Day, Student Volunteer Day, Health Education Week, International Friendship Week, Valentine's Day, Weatherman's Day, National Inventor's Day, and the opening of the first public school in America.

Scope and Sequence of Language Arts Skills Taught in February

Reading (Activity 6-1 and 6-2): The students will learn the importance of using context clues to increase comprehension.

Listening (Activities 6-3 and 6-4): The students will improve their listening skills by learning to clarify misunderstandings and summarize (as they listen) for increased retention.

Handwriting (Activities 6-5 and 6-6): Students will improve handwriting ability by learning to grade their own slant and by using a Handwriting Self-Evaluation Form.

Grammar (Activite 6-7 and 6-8): Students will learn the importance of using synonyms, antonyms, and homonyms correctly.

Spelling (Activities 6-9 and 6-10): Students will learn the most common spelling patterns for short and long vowel sounds.

Composition (Activities 6-11 and 6-12): Students will learn how to organize ideas in different ways to write for different audiences and different end products.

Speaking (Activities 6-13 and 6-14): Students will learn to use more specific adjectives as they speak.

Additional Activities for February

The following information can be used in a wide variety of ways to extend Activities 6-1 through 6-14.

1. Students can work alone or in small groups to learn more about famous African Americans throughout the month. A list of such famous people appears below.

A Partial Listing of Famous African Americans

Shirley Chisholm (1924-) First Black Women in Congress.

Paul Laurence Dunbar (1872–1906) Poet, Author

Sojourner Truth (1797–1883) Traveled and spoke against slavery

George Washington Carver (1864–1943) Scientist who found ways to help farmers

Frederick Douglass (1817–1895) Escaped slave who spoke and wrote against slavery

Matthew Henson (1867–1955) Explorer who reached the North Pole

Jesse Jackson (1941-) Minister, civil rights leader, candidate for President

Louis Armstrong (1898–1971) Jazz trumpet player

Ronald McNair (1950–1986) Astronaut

Harriet Tubman (1821–1913) Helped slaves escape to freedom

Booker T. Washington (1856–1915) Began college for blacks

Mary McLeod Bethune (1875–1955) Teacher and advisor to presidents

Martin Luther King, Jr. (1929–1968) Minister, speaker, and civil rights leader

Bill Cosby (1937-) Comedian and TV star

Althea Gibson (1927-) World-famous tennis star

Langston Hughes (1902–1967) poet of Harlem

Marian Anderson (1902-) Singer

Jackie Robinson (1919–1972) Dodgers baseball star

Jesse Owens (1913–1980) Winner of Olympic medals in track

Carter G. Woodson (1875–1950) Wrote black history

Thurgood Marshall (1908-) First black U.S. Supreme Court Judge

Wilma Rudolph (1958-) Olympic runner

Michael Jackson (1958-) Rock music star, songwriter

Charles Richard Drew (1904–1950) Set up blood banks

2. Students can write to the following addresses to receive more information about the themes studied in February.

National Chocolate Lovers Month
The Promotion Group Inc.
Daniel J. Gorman
145 E. 49th St.
New York, NY 10017

International Friendship Month
Franklin D. Roosevelt Philatelic
  Society
154 Laguna Ct.
St. Augustine Shores, FL 32086

Health Education Week
NY State Health Department
Health Education Promotion
  Services
Corning Tower Bldg. Rm. 1084
Empire State Plaza
Albany, NY 12237

Student Volunteer Day
Susquehanna University
Public Information
Selinsgrove, PA 17870

Chinese New Year
Chinese Chamber of Commerce
Bill Hong, VP
425 Ginling Way
Los Angeles, CA 90012

National Inventors Day
Oscar Mastin, Asst. Dir. of
  Information
Patent and Trademark Office
Washington, D.C. 20203

Abraham Lincoln's Birthday
U.S. Department of the Interior
National Park Service Rt. 1
Hogenville, KY 42748

3. Students can create questions and interview sheets for classmates. Students would ask classmates questions and prepare bulletin boards or posters that list answers classmates gave. Topics of interest include Valentine's Day, Abraham Lincoln, Groundhog's Day, and George Washington. Questions should be creative—for example, "If you could go back in time and meet President Lincoln, what is the first thing you'd ask him?"

4. The following notable people were born in February. Students can contact or read about those of interest. Students who were born in February can compare themselves to people born on their birthday.

1. Clark Gable, Charles Joseph Fax, Don Everly, Sherman Hemsley

2. James Joyce, Farrah Fawcett, Martina Arroyo, Nash Graham, Bonita Granville, Jascha Heifetz, Gale Gordon

3. Gertude Stein, Norman Rockwell, Blythe Danner, Morgan Fairchild, Melane, Shelley Berman, Joey Bishop

4. Charles Lindbergh, David Brenner, Lisa Eichhorn, Ida Lupino, Betty Friedan, Erich Leinsdorf

5. Hank Aaron, Bob Marley, Jane Bryant Guinn, Arthur Sulzberger, Val Dufour, Barbara Hershey

6. Ronald Reagan, Babe Ruth, Tom Brokaw, Louis Nizer, Fabian Forte, Mike Farrell, John Lund

7. Eddie Barclen, Charles Dickens, Laura Ingalls Wilder

8. Jules Verne, Jack Lemmon, Nick Nolte, Ted Koppel, Robert Klein

9. Mia Farrow, Carole King, Judith Light, Ronald Coleman, Kathryn Grayson

10. Jimmy Durante, Leontyne Price, Judith Anderson, Peter Alan, Roberta Flack

11. Thomas Edison, Eva Gabor, Leslie Nielsen, Sergio Mendes, Rudolf Firkusny, Conrad Janis

12. Simon MacCorkindale, Abraham Lincoln, Charles Darwin, Joe Garagiola, Maud Adams, Lorne Greene, Todd Duncan

13. Bess Truman, Chuck Yeager, Carol Lynley, Eileen Farrell, Erne (Tennessee) Ford

14. Jack Benny, Florence Henderson, Alan Parker, Gregory Hines, Hugh Downs, Mel Allen

15. John Barrymore, Susan B. Anthony, Kevin McCarthy, Melissa Manchester, Harvey Korman, Keene Curtis, Leonard Woodcox, Claire Bloom

16. Jeffrey Lynn, Edgar Bergen, Patty Andrews, Sonny Bono, William Katt

17. Arthur Kennedy, Hall Holbrook, Margaret Truman, Marian Anderson, Red Berber

18. Bill Cullen, Matt Dillon, George Kennedy, Helen Brown

19. Copernicus, Smokey Robinson, Justine Bateman, Lee Marvin, Margeaux Hemingway, Carlin Glynn, John Frankenheimer

20. Sidney Poitier, Gloria Vanderbilt, Robert Altman, Edward Albert, Amanda Blake, Jennifer O'Neil, John Daly, Sandy Duncan

21. Barbara Jordan, Erma Bombeck, Christopher Akins, Tyne Daly, Jill Eikenberry, Rue McClanahan

22. John Mills, Sheldon Leonard, George Washington, Julius Irving, Edward Kennedy

23. George Frederick Handel, Ed "Too Tall" Jones, Peter Fonda, William S. Shirer

24. Wilhelm Grimm, Renata Scotto, Michel Legrand, James Farentino

25. Jim Backus, George Harrison, Pierre-Auguste Renoir, Enrico Caruso

26. Buffalo Bill Cody, Betty Hutton, Fats Domino, Robert Taft, Jr., Lazar Berman, Priscilla Lopez

27. Ralph Nader, Henry Wadsworth Longfellow, Pascale Petit, Howard Hesseman

28. Zero Mostel, Mario Andretti, Linus Pauling, Bernadette Peters, Gavin MacLeod, Charles Durning

29. Jimmy Dorsey, James Mitchell

5. The February calendar can be used in the many ways described in Chapter 1.

Reading Skill Development: Learning to Improve Reading Comprehension

TIME REQUIRED

Teacher Directed Exploration (Activity 6-2): 25–30 minutes

Student Discovery Page (Activity 6-2): 20 minutes

TEACHING STRATEGIES

Students create examples of a concept to demonstrate they understand it.

ACTIVITY 6-1
_____

LEARNING TO USE CONTEXT CLUES

[OBJECTIVE] TODAY YOU WILL LEARN HOW TO USE CONTEXT CLUES TO FIND THE MEANINGS OF NEW WORDS. YOU WILL KNOW YOU HAVE LEARNED WHEN YOU SUCCESSFULLY DEDUCE THE MEANING OF AT LEAST FIVE UNKNOWN WORDS FROM YOUR READING.

Many times when you read, you come across a word you don't know. One way to learn what it means is to look to see how the other words in the sentence relate to it. You also look at the other sentence in the paragraph to see if they give you a clue to its meaning. This skill is using the meaning around a word as a clue to the meaning of an unknown word. It is called using context clues.

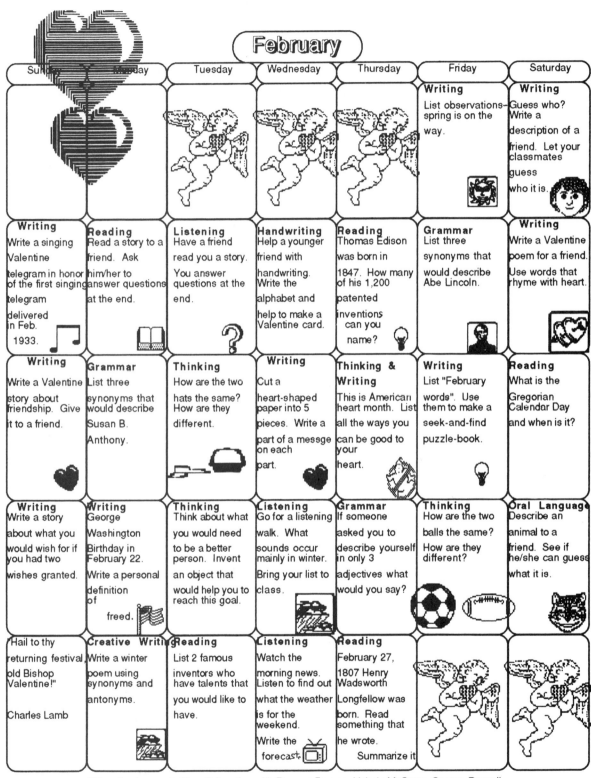

February

Sunday	Monday	Tuesday	Wednesday	Thursday	Friday	Saturday
					Writing List observations– spring is on the way.	**Writing** Guess who? Write a description of a friend. Let your classmates guess who it is.
Writing Write a singing Valentine telegram in honor of the first singing telegram delivered in Feb. 1933.	**Reading** Read a story to a friend. Ask him/her to answer questions at the end.	**Listening** Have a friend read you a story. You answer questions at the end.	**Handwriting** Help a younger friend with handwriting. Write the alphabet and help to make a Valentine card.	**Reading** Thomas Edison was born in 1847. How many of his 1,200 patented inventions can you name?	**Grammar** List three synonyms that would describe Abe Lincoln.	**Writing** Write a Valentine poem for a friend. Use words that rhyme with heart.
Writing Write a Valentine story about friendship. Give it to a friend.	**Grammar** List three synonyms that would describe Susan B. Anthony.	**Thinking** How are the two hats the same? How are they different.	**Writing** Cut a heart-shaped paper into 5 pieces. Write a part of a messge on each part.	**Thinking & Writing** This is American heart month. List all the ways you can be good to your heart.	**Writing** List "February words". Use them to make a seek-and-find puzzle-book.	**Reading** What is the Gregorian Calendar Day and when is it?
Writing Write a story about what you would wish for if you had two wishes granted.	**Writing** George Washington Birthday in February 22. Write a personal definition of freed.	**Thinking** Think about what you would need to be a better person. Invent an object that would help you to reach this goal.	**Listening** Go for a listening walk. What sounds occur mainly in winter. Bring your list to class.	**Grammar** If someone asked you to describe yourself in only 3 adjectives what would you say?	**Thinking** How are the two balls the same? How are they different?	**Oral Language** Describe an animal to a friend. See if he/she can guess what it is.
"Hail to thy returning festival old Bishop Valentine!" Charles Lamb	**Creative Writing** Write a winter poem using synonyms and antonyms.	**Reading** List 2 famous inventors who have talents that you would like to have.	**Listening** Watch the morning news. Listen to find out what the weather is for the weekend. Write the forecast.	**Reading** February 27, 1807 Henry Wadsworth Longfellow was born. Read something that he wrote. Summarize it		

This calendar created in collaboration with Frances Dornan, Valerie McGarry, George Russell.

This is the same skill you use when you look at a picture and try to figure out how all the parts relate.

Let me show you what I mean. **[Show the class an overhead transparency of Figure 6-1.]** In the original picture the boy was holding something in his hand. Use the meaning of all the other things in the picture to tell me what the boy was holding in his hand. **[Correct answer—paint brush.]** This is the same thing you do when you read. Let's try it and let me show you what I mean.

[Read a passage from the story in the basal reader or in a context area. Pretend you don't know a word while you read, and demonstrate using context clues of the passage to figure out the meaning in a "think aloud" manner. Then assign silent reading of a story from the basic reader or a passage from a content book. Students are to complete Activity 6-2 as described in the Modifications section.]

GRADING CRITERIA: _____

MODIFICATIONS FOR GRADE LEVELS AND STUDENT ABILITY LEVELS

For Kindergarten through Third Grades and Slower Learning Groups, do Activity 6-2 as a whole class, orally. *For Fourth through Eighth Grades and Gifted/Most Able Learners,* allow those who finish early to pick words from the dictionary that classmates won't know. These students then write context clues to share with the class. They write the word and the context clues in a sentence on sentence strip paper or on the chalkboard.

FIGURE 6-1   A Context Puzzle

<u>LEARNING TO USE CONTEXT CLUES</u>

What was the boy holding in his right hand, and how do you know?

ACTIVITY 6-2

USING CONTEXT TO COMPREHEND MORE

Directions: Write in a word you did not know
as you read. Write the meaning you gave to the word
after using context clues. Write the context clue
you used.

WORD	MEANING	CONTEXT CLUE
1.		
2.		
3.		
4.		
5.		
6.		
7.		

Listening Skill Development: Learning to Raise Questions and to Summarize as You Listen

TIME REQUIRED

10 minutes plus 10 minutes of introduction; 2 minutes oral speaking per student

Teacher Directed Exploration (Activity 6-3): 10 minutes

Student Discovery Page (Activity 6-4): 10 minutes

TEACHING STRATEGIES

Students will use several mini-practice sessions to learn a new skill.

ACTIVITY 6-3

UNDERSTANDING THE WEATHER BY ASKING QUESTIONS

[OBJECTIVE] YOU WILL LEARN TO RAISE QUESTIONS IN YOUR MIND AS YOU LISTEN, TO CLARIFY MISUNDERSTANDINGS AND TO SUMMARIZE FOR INCREASED RETENTION. YOU WILL KNOW YOU HAVE LEARNED WHEN YOU USE QUESTIONS TO HELP YOU UNDERSTAND AND REMEMBER WHAT YOUR CLASSMATES SAY.

In February we celebrate Weather Forecaster's Day. The special event was established as a way to show our appreciation for the ways weathermen protect us from bad weather.

We can learn to protect ourselves from misunderstandings. We must learn to question what we hear. We will learn to do that now.

[Have students listen to the weather broadcast (on television at school that you have pre-recorded or at home) for home work. Model how you ask questions as you listen. Students write a three-paragraph description of it and the questions they had as they listened that were not answered on the broadcast. Students can also prepare a short talk on a special interest they have or on a current event they read about or saw on TV.]

[Students then present their descriptions and/or short talks to the class. At the end of each presentation, students ask questions that they thought about as they listened. If students do not readily ask questions, ask one student to summarize.]

[After several or all the students have presented, ask the class why it is important to question while they listen. Students should fill in examples on Activity 6-4 as they listen.]

GRADING CRITERIA: _____

MODIFICATIONS FOR GRADE LEVELS AND STUDENT ABILITY LEVELS

For Kindergarten through Third Grades and Slower Learning Groups, students will listen to only a few classmates instead of the entire class, as you may decide that only the most able prepare speeches. *For Fourth through Eighth Grades and Gifted/Most Able Learners,* you may allow students to present a 2-minute presentation on a current news event as well.

STUDENTS WHO WILL BE WORKING ON OTHER PROJECTS OR LESSONS: _____

_____

NOTES FOR FUTURE USE: _____

_____

WEATHER FORECASTER'S DAY LISTENING CLUES

North

West ➤➤➤ 🍎 ⬅️⬅️ East

South

North

West ➤➤➤ 🍎 ⬅️⬅️ East

South

Directions: In the blanks below, write examples of when you used the clues to help you listen better.

1. WORD IS UNKNOWN TO ME:
   Ask myself if it is possibly similar to any other word said: _____
   _____

2. MY MIND WANDERED AND I'M CONFUSED NOW:
   Ask myself if the sentence the speaker is saying now is a detail or
   main point: _____
   _____

3. I'M CONFUSED BECAUSE I EXPECTED THE SPEAKER TO SAY SOMETHING
   DIFFERENT FROM WHAT WAS SAID:
   Ask myself if I did not hear the word "Not," "But," or "Yet": _____
   _____

4. I'M HEARING SO MANY NEW POINTS THAT I'M FORGETTING SOME OF THEM:
   Ask myself what are three main points I'll remember: _____
   _____

5. HOW CAN I REMEMBER WHAT THE SPEAKER SAID:
   Tell myself to remember the most important thing I want to tell others
   from this speech: _____
   _____

Handwriting Skill Development: Learning to Make Letters Slant Correctly

TIME REQUIRED

Teacher Directed Exploration (Activity 6-5): 10 minutes

Student Discovery Page (Activity 6-6): 30 minutes

TEACHING STRATEGIES

Students will practice skills by creating a message that can be used by another class in the school.

ACTIVITY 6-5 _____

LIKE CUPID'S ARROW: SLANTING LETTERS CORRECTLY

[OBJECTIVE] YOU WILL IMPROVE YOUR HANDWRITING BY LEARNING TO GRADE THE CORRECT SIZE, SHAPE, SLANT, AND SPACING OF YOUR OWN WRITING ON UNLINED PAPER. YOU WILL KNOW YOU HAVE LEARNED TO WRITE BETTER LETTERS BY COMPARING YOUR LETTERS TO THE ONES MODELED BY THE OLDER STUDENTS AND BY LEARNING TO ANALYZE YOUR OWN HANDWRITING IMPROVEMENT AND NEEDS THROUGH THE USE OF A "SELF-ANALYSIS OF MY HANDWRITING" CHART.

[Read the following brief history of Valentine's Day.]
Valentine's Day is February 14. The way it began is hard to understand. In Rome, some believe that a Christian priest named Valentine is responsible. He would send an unsigned note that said "From Your Valentine," the day someone was to be killed. Another legend holds that the holiday evolved as a Christian replacement for the pagan feast of Lupercabia. It was celebrated by the Romans on February 15. The feast featured the random pairing of young men and women accomplished through a lottery-style drawing.

Historians have dredged up as many as eight possible St. Valentines who could have inspired the customs that developed around February 14. It is also fairly well accepted that two Christians martyrs, named Valentine, who lived and perished in the third century could be connected to the holiday. One was a priest and physician who was beheaded by the Romans on February 14, 269 A.D. The second, possibly the Bishop of Terni, may have been beheaded on February 14 a year later.

Another tale maintains that a Valentine martyr became a love symbol because of a doomed romance with his jailer's daughter. None of these Valentines had any special relationship with cupids, arrows, matchmaking or greeting cards. Yet, somehow, Valentine's Day, February 14, became the premier romantic holiday in America.

Even though there are ways to tell people that you love them, a special handwritten note is appreciated. We will practice improving our handwriting by learning to make letters slant at the same angle (the same way). **[Display an overhead transparency of Figure 6-2, using one or both of the slant sections depending on the age and level of your students. Demonstrate using the correct slant by writing:]**

FIGURE 6-2 Slant Sheet

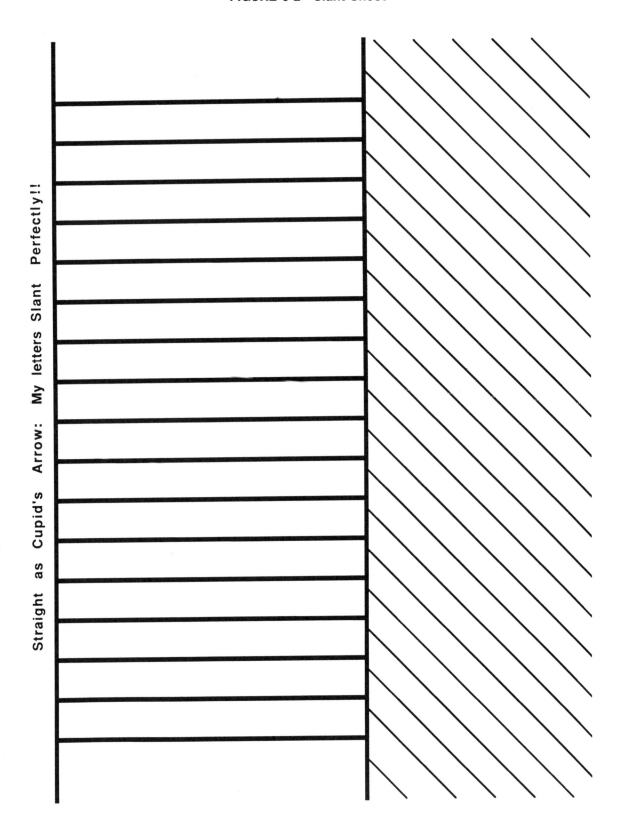

**ON VALENTINE'S DAY
I WANT TO SAY
MY LOVE IS HERE TO STAY**

[Have students practice writing this message on unlined paper without the slant sheet. When finished, they place the slant sheet under the unlined paper. They circle any letter that does not slant appropriately. Depending on your class, students can then either place a new sheet over the slant sheet and practice again, or practice writing letters directly on the slant sheet to check their finished work. When older students have finished their Valentine message, they work Activity 6-6, completing the self-evaluation. Save the students practice pages from this activity for comparison to writing they create in May.]

_____

GRADING CRITERIA: _____

_____

MODIFICATIONS FOR GRADE LEVELS AND STUDENT ABILITY LEVELS

For Kindergarten through Second Grades and Slower Learners, the time allowed for letter modeling can be broken into two days' work. *For Grades Three through Eight,* students will work on improving their cursive writing skills. *For Faster Learners,* calligraphy could be introduced by inviting someone who specializes in calligraphy to class to teach it. Valentine messages can then be written in calligraphy.

INDIVIDUAL STUDENT NEEDS: _____

_____

STUDENTS WHO WILL BE WORKING ON OTHER PROJECTS OR LESSONS: _____

_____

NOTES FOR FUTURE USE: _____

_____

ACTIVITY 6-6

USING CUPID'S ARROW TO MAKE MY VALENTINE MESSAGE FIRST RATE

My Handwriting Self-Analysis Sheet

A. Here is how I write when in a hurry: Is my slant as straight as an arrow in flight? (Write your Valentine message here.)

_____

_____

B. Here is how I write when I do my best writing: What did I do to improve my slant? (Write your Valentine message here.) _____

_____

_____

C. Here is my analysis of my handwriting:

	Excellent	Good	Fair	Poor
1. SLANT................ Do all my letters lean the same way? If not which one doesn't?	___	___	___	___
2. SPACING........... Are spaces between my letters and words even?	___	___	___	___
3. SIZE.................... Are all my letters evenly tall? ?	___	___	___	___
4. ALIGNMENT........ Do all my letters touch the bottom line?	___	___	___	___

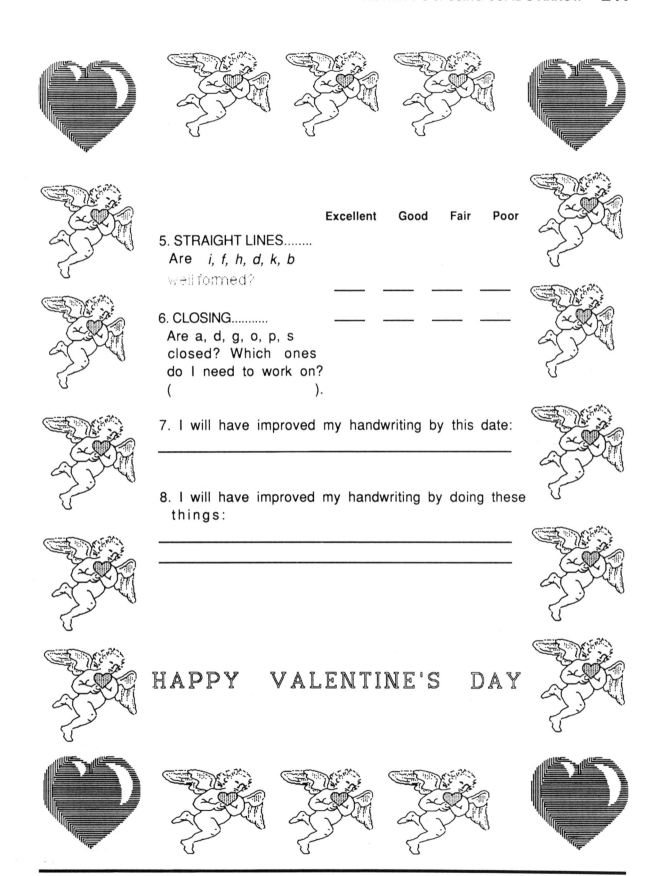

	Excellent	Good	Fair	Poor
5. STRAIGHT LINES........ Are *i, f, h, d, k, b* well formed?	___	___	___	___
6. CLOSING.......... Are a, d, g, o, p, s closed? Which ones do I need to work on? ( ).	___	___	___	___

7. I will have improved my handwriting by this date:

_____

8. I will have improved my handwriting by doing these things:

_____

_____

HAPPY   VALENTINE'S   DAY

Grammar Skill Development: Skillful Use of Synonyms, Antonyms, and Homonyms

TIME REQUIRED

Teacher Directed Exploration (Activity 6-6): 10 minutes for a brief history as to how reading and grammar were taught before and after the opening of the first public school in America and 20 minutes to describe what synonyms are

Student Discovery Page (Activity 6-8): 20 minutes

TEACHING STRATEGIES

Students will learn about synonyms and antonyms by completing a written activity. Students will then create new synonyms and antonyms and peers will check their work.

ACTIVITY 6-7

CELEBRATING THE FIRST PUBLIC SCHOOL IN AMERICA WITH SPECIAL WORDS

[OBJECTIVE] YOU WILL LEARN SYNONYMS, HOMONYMS, AND ANTONYMS. YOU WILL KNOW YOU HAVE BEEN SUCCESSFUL WHEN YOU WORK 80% OF ACTIVITY 6-8 CORRECTLY.

Some of our earliest records indicate that it was in February, in the early 1500s that the first schools opened in America. We are going to use this event to learn to speak with better words. It is important that we speak with clarity because people can more easily picture what we mean.

Life would be pretty dull if we ate the same foods at every meal or played the same game each day. Life would be equally dull if we said and heard the same words all the time. We can give the words we use most often a rest by using synonyms. Synonyms are words that have similar meanings, like "little," "small," and "tiny."

It is also important that we learn to tell people the exact opposites of words. Telling them the opposite can sometimes help them more clearly understand the true meaning. These types of words are called antonyms.

Another type of word that can confuse understanding is a homonym. This is a word that sounds the same but has a different meaning and spelling than the word it sounds like. **[Hand out copies of Figure 6-3 or use an overhead transparency.]** Follow along as I read the article in Figure 6-3 and underline any words you don't know.

[If the students have underlined unfamiliar words, have them write out the words in a list.] Now you have a list of words that are new to you. Try to figure out what each word means by looking for context clues around it; as you practiced before. Any word that you can figure out that way will be a synonym for the other word (such as "try" for "strive" in the first paragraph). Another way to learn a synonym (or antonym) for a word is to look up the word in a dictionary or thesaurus.

[Introduce how to use a thesaurus. Also show that some dictionary entries include synonyms and antonyms.]

FIGURE 6-3 History of Reading Instruction

Throughout history, how reading has been taught has changed. This is because teachers and administrators constantly strive to find better ways to teach. They also try to make their teaching match their ideals of what a good school should be.

Early teaching of reading occurred in the home. As a matter of fact, teaching reading at home still occurs in some families. Teaching reading at home came to be considered a problem with the development of democratic forms of government and the desire for public schools to give all children an equal opportunity to learn.

Teaching children to spell and sound out words was the method used to teach reading to children for hundreds of years. Drill on the alphabet and letter sounds was emphasized after the students entered first grade. Nothing was considered as important as teaching students these word elements.

To the child, reading meant memorizing elements that had no meaning. The work was uninteresting and boring. In 1831, Lyman Cobb stated in his book *Juvenile Reader No. 1* that no one should make an attempt to read until he or she is able to recognize the words at sight that are most common in the composition. He believed this could be done by using words in a spelling book. Later, the philosophy developed that school subjects should stir interest in students and become more meaningful. It wasn't until the first quarter of our present century, about 1925, that reading was recognized as having meaningful outcomes and that it should be taught with an emphasis upon comprehension, decoding words, and stimulating student interest in reading.

Today, reading instruction helps students comprehend the thoughts of an author. This current method of instruction shows how much education has changed in the last two hundred years.

GRADING CRITERIA: _____

MODIFICATIONS FOR GRADE LEVELS AND STUDENT ABILITY LEVELS

For Kindergarten through Third Grades and Slower Learning Groups, this skill development can be broken down into two or three days. You can develop the skill of synonyms on day 1 and the skill of antonyms on day 2. *For Younger Students,* the brief history could consist of methods used for reading and grammar lessons before and after the opening of the first public school in America. *For Older Students* the lesson could be expanded to include research on characteristics of early American students. *For Advanced Students* the lesson could contrast today's methods of teaching reading and grammar to those in the 1700s and 1800s. More able students may not find any unfamiliar words in the article. Be prepared with a list of at least five challenging words appropriate for their level to use in Activity 6-7.

STUDENTS WHO WILL BE WORKING ON OTHER PROJECTS OR LESSONS: _____

_____

NOTES FOR FUTURE USE: _____

_____

ACTIVITY 6-8

PRACTICE WITH SYNONYMS, ANTONYMS, AND HOMONYMS

WE'VE USED THEM FOR CENTURIES

Synonyms & Antonyms

1. Do you know an antonym to use in place of small? _____
2. Do you know another word that is a synonym for big? _____
3. Do you know an antonym for bad? _____
4. Do you know a synonym for nice? _____

Write two synonyms and two antonyms for each of the above words. By using synonyms and antonyms you will become a more interesting speaker and writer.

5. _____
   _____

6. _____
   _____

7. _____
   _____

8. _____
   _____

Which Homonyms are described?

9. Water from the sky: _____
   Guide strap for a horse: _____
   To rule: _____
10. An interjection of surprise: _____
    To need to repay: _____
11. Antonym for day: _____
    Medieval soldier: _____
12. To use needle and thread: _____
    To plant seeds: _____
    Thus, very, as a result: _____
13. Trash: _____
    Belt line: _____

Spelling Skill Development: Common Spelling Patterns of Vowel Sounds in Celebration of February Birthdays

TIME REQUIRED

Teacher Directed Exploration (Activity 6-9): 40 minutes

Student Discovery Page (Activity 6-10): 20 minutes. *Note: Activity 6-10 is optional and designed for older students.*

TEACHING STRATEGIES

Students will develop skills through paired learning and rule learning.

ACTIVITY 6-9

SPELLING LONG AND SHORT VOWEL SOUNDS

[OBJECTIVE] YOU WILL LEARN THE MOST COMMON SPELLING PATTERNS OF LONG AND SHORT VOWEL SOUNDS. YOU WILL KNOW YOU HAVE IMPROVED YOUR SPELLING ABILITY WHEN YOU CAN MAKE CORRECT DECISIONS ABOUT THE WAY TEN WORDS (CONTAINING SHORT OR LONG VOWEL SOUNDS) ARE SPELLED.

In September you learned several spelling patterns in the words "Happy Birthday." Today in celebration of famous people born in February, you will learn to improve your spelling by learning the way long and short vowel sounds are usually spelled. **[Place the following eleven spelling generalizations on the board or overhead projector and ask the class to give other words that fit each generalization. Also, ask them to pay special attention to how long and short vowel sounds are usually spelled, because they will take a test in a few minutes to see how well they have learned these rules.]**

1. A word that ends in silent *e* usually drops the *e* when a suffix beginning with a vowel is added: breeze, breezing, two other words:

   _____, _____.

2. A one-syllable word that ends in one consonant, preceded by a short vowel, usually doubles the consonant before a suffix that begins with

   a vowel: fat, fattest, two other words: _____, _____.

3. A word ending in *y* that follows a consonant usually changes the *y* to *i* before a suffix is added unless the suffix begins with *i*: cry, crying,

   two other words: _____, _____.

4. A word ending in *y* that follows a vowel usually keeps the *y* when a

   suffix is added: buy, buys, buying, two other words: _____,

   _____.

5. If the only vowel letter is at the end of a word, the letter usually stands

   for the long sound: so, be, two other words: _____, _____.

6. The *r* gives the preceding vowel a sound that is neither long nor short;

   horn, two other words: _____, _____.

7. When a vowel is in the middle of a one-syllable word, the vowel is usually short: rest, two other words: _____ , _____ .

8. The first vowel is usually long and the second is usually silent in the diagraphs *ai, ea,* and *oa*; nail, two other words: _____ , _____ .

9. Words having double *e* usually have the long *e* sound: tree, two other words: _____ , _____ . In *ay* the *y* is silent and gives the vowel its long sound; play, say, day.

10. When *y* is the final letter in a word, it usually has a vowel sound: dry: two other words: _____ , _____ .

11. When there are two vowels, one of which is final *e,* the first vowel is usually long and the *e* is silent: bone, two other words: _____ , _____ .

[Once you've covered the rules, go over the spelling of vowel sounds as listed in Figure 4-4, using the chalkboard or an overhead transparency. Then give the following list of words as a test, having the students spell the words correctly and test the generalization governing the spelling. Younger students can complete the test as a whole-class, oral activity. For older students, you give the test to the class, and each student writes the spelling and the rule. Then you grade them.]

1. moving
2. biggest
3. trying
4. lays
5. me
6. worn
7. grass
8. boat
9. seem
10. fly
11. home

[Once the older students have completed Activity 6-9, distribute Activity 6-10, which contains a list of words that are incorrectly spelled. Each student will secretly be assigned a word from this list by you. One by one, students come to the front of the room to act out their assigned word, like the game of Charades. The student then chooses a class member to tell what word they were acting out and to spell it. (Students must know the correct spelling for their Charade words.) This activity will be complete once all irregularly spelled words are spelled correctly. Students can later use Activity 6-4 to write stories about President Washington & Lincoln.]

ANSWER KEY FOR ACTIVITY 6-9 TEST

1. moving—a word that ends in a silent "e" drops the "e" when a suffix is added

2. biggest—a one-syllable word that ends in one consonant and has a short vowel before it will double the last consonant before adding a suffix of "-ing," "-er," "-est," "-able," or "-ed"

3. trying—to add a suffix to a word that ends in "y" you change "y" to "i" unless the suffix is "-ing." Then the "y" does not change.

4. lays—a word that ends in "y" and has a vowel before it keeps the "y" when a suffix is added

5. me—if the only vowel sound in a word is long and comes at the end of the word, the vowel will usually be the last letter in the word

6. worn—if an "r" comes after a vowel, the vowel sound will be neither long nor short

7. grass—if a one-syllable word has a short vowel sound, the vowel is in the middle of the word

8. boat—if a one-syllable word has a long vowel sound in the middle of the word, the spelling is usually either "ai," "ea," "oa" or "ee"

9. seem—same rule as above

10. fly—when "y" ends a word, it has a vowel sound

11. home—when a word has a long vowel sound in the middle of a word (and the word doesn't look correct if you spell it with "ai," "ea," or, "ee." it has a single vowel, whose sound is long, in the middle of the word, and a silent "e" will appear at the end of the word

ANSWER KEY FOR ACTIVITY 6-10

breathing	stories
bobbing	digging
pays	wet
boys	hoe
making	boat
flu	playing
horn	net
popping	toys
plain	trying
loving	lays
warning	train
pass	cry

GRADING CRITERIA: _____

FIGURE 6-4 Spelling of Vowels Sounds

Symbols	Spellings	Examples
a	a,ai,al,au	at,plaid,half,laugh
ā	a,ai,ao,au,ay, e,ea,eigh,et, ei,ey	age,aid,gaol,gauge,say suede,break,eight,bouquet, vein,they
a	a,ae,ai,ay, e,ea,ei,hei	care,aerial,air,prayer where,pear,their,heir
a	a,ah,al,e, ea	father,ah,calm,sergeant heart
e	a,ai,ay,e,ea, ei,eo,ie,u	any,said,says,end,bread, heifer,leopard,friend,bury
ē	ay,e,ea,ee,ei, eo,ey,i,ie, is,oe,y	quay,equal,eat,eel,receive, people,key,machine,believe, debris,phoebe,city
er	ea,er,err,ir, irr,olo,our, or,ur,urr,yr	earth,stern,err,first, whirr,colonel,journey, word,urge,purr,myrtle
i	e,ea,ee,ei, i,ie,o,u, ui,y	England,near,been,weird, it,sieve,women,busy, build,myth
ī	ai,ais,ay,ei, eigh,eye,i,ie,igh, is,uy,y,ye	Hawaii,aisle,bayou,eider, height,eye,ice,lie,high, island,buy,sky,rye
o	a,ach,ho,o	watch,yacht,honest,odd
ō	au,eau,eo,ew, o,oa,oe,oh,ol, oo,ou,ough,ow	chauffeur,beau,yeoman,sew, open,oak,toe,oh,folk, brooch,soul,though,own
o	a,ah,al,au	all,Utah,walk,author
o	augh,aw,o,oa, ou,ough	taught,awful,order,broad, cough,bought
oi	oi,oy	oil,boy
ou	hou,ou,ough,ow	hour,out,owl
ū	eau,eu,eue, ew,iew,u,ue, yew,you,yu	beauty,feud,queue, few,view,use,cue, yew,you,yule
u	o,oo,oul,u	wolf,good,should,full
u	eu,ew,ieu, o,oe,oo,ou, ough,u,ue	maneuer,threw,lieutenant, move,shoe,food,soup, through,rule,blue
u	o,oe,oo	son,does,flood

*Modified from a list originally compiled by Carl R. Peronke and Dale D. Johnson, in *Language Arts Instruction and the Beginning Teacher: A Practical Guide.* Englewood Cliffs, Prentice-Hall, 1987

MODIFICATIONS FOR GRADE LEVELS AND STUDENT ABILITY LEVELS

For *Kindergarten through Third Grades and Slower Learning Groups,* omit Activity 6-10. Also, do not use Activity 6-9 or Activity 6-10 for grades Kindergarten and First. *For Fourth through Eighth Grades and Gifted/Most Able Learners,* allow them to find examples in their books of words spelled like the words in Activity 6-10 and test each other, in pairs, as to correct spelling.

INDIVIDUAL STUDENT NEEDS: _____

_____

STUDENTS WHO WILL BE WORKING ON OTHER PROJECTS OR LESSONS: _____

_____

NOTES FOR FUTURE USE: _____

_____

ACTIVITY 6-10

CHARADE LIST

Directions: Students are divided into two teams. Each student is given one word from this list. No other student sees the word any other student receives. Each student learns the correct spelling of his/her word. Each student "acts out" his/her word in a game of charades before his/her team. If the word is guessed correctly, the team must spell it correctly, and write it on the board. The team with the most words spelled correctly wins.

After the game is over, students write a fictional story about Lincoln or Washington, using as many words from the following list as possible.

Word List:

breatheing
bobing
paies
boies
makeing
flue
harn
poping
plan
loveing
warn
passe
storys
diging
weat
ho
bot
plaiing
nete
toies
triing
layies
tran
cri

Creative Writing Skill Development: Organizing Ideas

PREREQUISITES

Students need to be familiar with transformations. Examples of a cartoon and a diary should be chosen.

TIME REQUIRED

Teacher Directed Exploration (Activity 6-11): 30 minutes

Student Discovery Page (Activity 6-12): 20 minutes

TEACHING STRATEGIES

Students will learn through a small-group composing process.

ACTIVITY 6-11

LEARNING TO ORGANIZE IDEAS TO CELEBRATE STUDENT VOLUNTEER DAY

[OBJECTIVE] YOU WILL LEARN HOW TO ORGANIZE IDEAS IN DIF-FERENT WAYS AND TO WRITE FOR DIFFERENT AUDIENCES AND DIF-FERENT END PRODUCTS AS A FIRST STEP TO EFFECTIVE COMMUNICATION.

In February a special day is set aside as Student Volunteer Day. On this day students have an opportunity to give something to their school or city. Volunteering means that you do something and do not get paid for it. We are going to celebrate this day next week by doing something you would like to do for our school or city.

[Prepare two examples as overhead transparencies to illustrate the differences that exist when writing to different audiences. The first can be a cartoon strip.] Cartoon strips are written for the pleasure of the general public. They usually depict a funny occurrence in our everyday lives. They usually do not include much writing; much of the communication is generated through pictures. **[The second example can be an excerpt from a diary.]** The audience the second example is intended for is one's self. There is much writing in diaries that is considered private and personal. Diaries may include information about everyday occurrences and personal feelings.

[Because younger writers need to feel as if they are accomplishing tasks when writing, instead of struggling through words, transformations will be beneficial in this activity for the younger students. When sentences are transformed, syntax and structure remain the same. The only changes are single words or phrases; thus students feel they are creating the meaning of the sentence. For example, the sentence "I will *play* under *my* bed to escape from *my big brother*" can be changed by a student to a totally different meaningful sentence—for example, "I will *run* under *the tree* to escape from the *rain*." The sentence structure is still present, but meaning is changed.]

For Student Volunteer Day you will write a letter together to the school volunteering your services during recess or another free period.

[Older students can compose all of the letter themselves.] Before writing the transformation letter the class needs to discuss the purpose of their writing as well as the audience to whom the writing is directed.

What kind of services could you volunteer to do? **[Sample student responses follow.]**

picking up trash on school grounds
cleaning the lunchroom
monitoring the halls
delivering notes from the office

[An example of a transformation classroom letter for younger students might look like:]

Dear _____,

Our _____ class is very interested in

_____ on Student Volunteer Day. Please _____

us if there are any activities such as _____

that we could volunteer to do.

Thank you,

_____

[For Activity 6-12, students discuss audiences and purposes of other types of writing, as listed on Activity 6-12. Students write a message to two different audiences they select. They write how their writing was transformed to meet the needs of two different audiences.]

_____

GRADING CRITERIA: _____

_____

MODIFICATIONS FOR GRADE LEVELS AND STUDENT ABILITY LEVELS

For Kindergarten through Third Grades and Slower Learning Groups, the entire class will write one letter and select one other type of writing from Activity 6-12. After both are written, the class discusses differences in writing styles. *For Fourth through Eighth Grades and Gifted/Most Able Learners,* students may complete Activity 6-12 alone, in pairs, or in small groups.

STUDENTS WHO WILL BE WORKING ON OTHER PROJECTS OR LESSONS: _____

_____

NOTES FOR FUTURE USE: _____

_____

USING DIFFERENT TYPES OF WRITING TO COMMUNICATE AND HELP OTHERS

STUDENT VOLUNTEER DAY AND
USING DIFFERENT TYPES OF
WRITING TO COMMUNICATE AND
HELP OTHERS

1. Advertisements
2. announcements
3. autobiographies
4. awards
5. brochures
6. bulletins
7. bumper stickers
8. campaign speeches
9. directions, essays
10. laboratory notes
11. letters
12. lists
13. logs
14. observational notes
15. pamphlets
16. persuasive letters
17. posters
18. questionnaires
19. reports
20. slogans
21. autobiographies
22. bedtime stories
23. book jackets
24. book reviews
25. captions
26. cartoons
27. certificates
28. character sketches
29. comic strips

30. contracts
31. critiques
32. definitions
33. diaries
34. directories
35. dramas
36. editorials
37. epitaphs
38. encyclopedia entries
39. fables
40. game rules
41. graffitti
42. grocery list
43. headlines
44. interviews
45. job applications
46. journals
47. lyrics
48. magazines
49. menus
50. mysteries
51. newspapers
52. notes
53. obituaries
54. parodies
55. poems

56. plays
57. questions
58. quizzes
59. quotations
60. recipes
61. requests
62. resumes
63. reviews
64. riddles
65. schedules
66. self-description
67. serialized stories
68. TV commercials
69. telegrams
70. vignettes
71. want ads
72. wanted posters

Oral Language Skill Development: Learning to Use More Specific Adjectives

TIME REQUIRED

Teacher Directed Exploration (Activity 6-13): 20 minutes

Student Discovery Page (Activity 6-14): 20 minutes

TEACHING STRATEGIES

Students will learn through creating speeches that have a specific purpose and result in selection of classroom officers.

ACTIVITY 6-13

DESCRIBING WITH MEANING AND INTEREST

[OBJECTIVE] TODAY YOU WILL LEARN HOW IMPORTANT SPECIFIC ADJECTIVES ARE WHEN YOU SPEAK. YOU WILL KNOW YOU HAVE INCREASED YOUR SPEAKING EFFECTIVENESS WHEN YOU INCLUDE TWO NEW ADJECTIVES IN THE SPEECH YOU GIVE.

In February we celebrate International Friendship Month. During this month we take time to appreciate our friends and to make new friends. Many countries give gifts of friendship to other countries, as well.

Today you are going to learn how to become a better speaker. You will learn to use more specific adjectives and to use inflection to add meaning to your conversation. These two skills will enable you to show your joy and emotions to your friends more clearly and to speak so others find it easier to listen to you.

Let me teach you how to change your voice so as to increase the meaning and the interest of your words. What you do is pick adjectives that come as close to describing what you want to say as possible. Then you say the adjective slowly and emphasize it with the feeling you have toward the object the adjective describes. For example, if I want you to know what kind of pet I have (and to tell you that I really love my pet) I could say one word so that you know what I mean without my naming my pet. See if you understand what I mean. **[Say the word "soft" with such emphasis that the students can tell that you are describing a pet cat that you love very much. If students guess that your pet is a cat, ask them how they knew. Describe how you thought about a word that would best describe your cat and how you used your voice to show how you felt about the cat. For example, you can tell them that you slowed down, and you added pride by making your voice a little higher in pitch than normal.]**

[Now give three more examples (below) so that students can see three other ways to change their voices. After saying each word, ask the class how you changed your voice to communicate the feeling and meaning (or animal) you intended.

grizzly (bear)
squeaky (mouse)
slithering (snake)]

Now you will select three things to describe. These things do not have to be animals. Think of one word you want to describe the first thing. Then look up the word you are trying to describe, in a dictionary, and use the definition to think of another word to describe your object or person. Then look up both the adjectives in a dictionary to find a third word you could use to describe your object.

[Divide the class into two teams. Each person, in turn, comes to the front and says the word that best describes his or her object or person. Both teams try to guess the object or person being described. If a team guesses the object with only one word, the team scores two points. (Praise the student for doing such a good job in using the voice to convey meaning. If the object is not guessed on the first word, the person speaking can give the other two adjectives. The team that guesses correctly scores a point. (Praise the student and ask the class to describe what the student did well in speaking that helped identify the word.) Continue in this way until all students have had a chance to describe their object or person.]

[Distribute Activity 6-14. Students are to choose adjectives to describe a classmate whom they want to nominate for one of the awards. Students work in pairs. They prepare a 30-second talk to nominate that person. Once the students have selected at least two adjectives they outline their speech. Each pair stands before the group and speaks with the best voices they can, using adjectives and inflection to promote their candidate.]

GRADING CRITERIA: _____

MODIFICATIONS FOR GRADE LEVELS AND STUDENT ABILITY LEVELS

For Kindergarten through Third Grades and Slower Learning Groups, Activity 6-13 can be completed over several days, with independent oral practice sessions in K–1. *For Grades Four through Six* additional material and in-depth discussion can be added such as to allow students to find library materials for a speech, and an award can be given to the pair with the most descriptive adjectives.

STUDENTS WHO WILL BE WORKING ON OTHER PROJECTS OR LESSONS: _____

NOTES FOR FUTURE USE: _____

ACTIVITY 6-14

TO BE NOMINATED IN SPEECH

Classroom Awards

Record Keeping for Cooperative Groups

This form will make it easier to build cooperative learning teams. You group the class in as many different groups as you wish, and each group works together to learn a body of knowledge. To ensure that each group has a full range of ability, assign students on the basis of a set of test scores from a previous grading period. You then place the student that scored lowest in group 1, second lowest in group 2, and so on until all students have been placed in a group. The groups work together to learn the material, building group work skills and rapport. At the end, you can give a second test and improvement points are computed; you can give prizes for the group that has the largest improvement score.

COOPERATIVE GROUPS RECORD KEEPING SYSTEM

STUDENT	DATE: SUBJECT: 1ST SCORE	2ND SCORE	IMPROV. POINTS	DATE: SUBJECT: 1ST SCORE	2ND SCORE	IMPROV. POINTS	DATE: SUBJECT: 1ST SCORE	2ND SCORE	IMPROV. POINTS

CHAPTER

7 *March*

March is filled with many special activities. It is National Nutrition Month and Mental Retardation Month. Dr. Seuss's birthday occurs during March, as does Johnny Appleseed Day, Fun Mail Week, Appreciation Week, and National Poison Prevention Week.

March 23 is Liberty Day, the day Patrick Henry said, "I know not what course others may take but as for me, give me liberty or give me death." March also has the Festival of Flowers in Baltimore, Saint Patrick's Day, and the first day of spring.

Scope and Sequence of Language Arts Skills Taught in March

The activities in March are designed to continue to strengthen the foundation laid in previous months' work. The skills to be taught are listed below, in the order in which each language arts skill activity appears in this chapter.

Handwriting (Activities 7-1 and 7-2): Students will improve their legibility with increased speed and correct letter formation. Timed tests will be given before and after the lesson to determine improvement.

Composition (Activities 7-3 and 7-4): Students will learn to combine related sentences and eliminate excess words. This will improve their writing skills.

Listening (Activities 7-5 and 7-6): Students will learn to recognize how details fit together to make a point and to ask for clarification when directions are vague.

Speaking (Activities 7-7 and 7-8): Students will learn to conduct a panel discussion and to answer questions briefly but effectively.

Reading (Activities 7-9 and 7-10): Students will learn to recognize, analyze, and distinguish between statements of cause and effect, problems/solution, and summary.

Grammar (Activities 7-11 and 7-12): Students will improve their sentence structure.

Spelling (Activities 7-12 and 7-13): Students will learn to spell most frequently misspelled words by telling what part of the word is irregular and how they will remember the visual image it projects.

Notable March Birthdays

Students who have birthdays in this month can learn more about the other people born on their birthday.

1. David Niven, Dinah Shore, Ron Howard, Pete Rozelle, Harry Belefonte, Dirk Benedick

2. Sam Houston, Dr. Seuss, John Cullum, Jennifer Jones, Robert Michael, Tom Wolfe

3. Alexander Graham Bell, Jean Harlow

4. Knute Rockne, Bobby Fischer, Barbara McNair, Paul Prentiss

5. Rex Harrison, Rocky Bleier, Samantha Eggar, Andy Gibb, James Noble

6. Elizabeth Barrett Browning, Michelangelo, Lorin Maazel, Thomas Foley, Alan Greenspan, William Webster, Ed McMahon, Joanna Miles, Ben Murphy

7. Ivan Lendl, Daniel Travanti

8. Oliver Wendell Holmes, Jr., Cyd Charisse

9. Mickey Spillane, Yuri Gararin, Mickey Gilly, Raul Julia, Emmanuel Lewis

10. Nancy Cunard, Lillian Wald, Pamela Mason

11. Dorothy Gish, Lawrence Welk, Tina Louise, San Donaldson

12. Liza Minnelli, Jack Kerouac, Barbara Feldon, Al Jarreau, Andrew Young

13. Neil Sedaka

14. Albert Einstein, Michael Caine, Billy Crystal, Steve Kanaly, Frank Borman

15. Andrew Jackson, Judd Hirsch

16. James Madison, Jerry Lewis, Erik Estrada, Jerry Lewis, Pat Nixon, Daniel Moynihan, Mike Mansfield, Kate Nelligan

17. Nat "King" Cole, Lesley-Ann Down, Patrick Duffy, Mercedes, Rudolf Nureyev

18. Neville Chamberlain, George Plimpton, Grover Cleveland, Kevin Dobson, Peter Graves, Charlie Pride

19. Wyatt Earp, David Livingston, Ursula Andress, Patrick McGoohan, Phyllis Newman

20. Fred Rogers, Bobby Orr, Larry Elgart, Ray Goulding, William Hurt, Hal Linden, Lenore Hershey

21. Johann Sebastian Bach, James Coco, Al Freeman, Jr., Eugene Leontovich, Mort Lindsey

22. Chico Marx, Marcel Marceau, Werner Klemperer, Karl Malden, George Benson, Orrin Hatch

23. Joan Crawford, Fanny Farmer, Hazel Dawn, Chaka Khan, Amanda Plummer

24. Steve McQueen, Fatty Arbuickle, Norman Fell, Harry Houdini

25. Elton John, Gloria Steinem, Aretha Franklin, Paul Michael Glaser, Mary Gross, Nancy Kelly, Bonnie Bedelia, Howard Cosell, David Lean

26. Diana Ross, Sandra Day O'Connor, Alan Arkin, Robert Woodward, Vicki Lawrence, Bob Elliott, Leonard Nimoy, Teddy Pendergrass

27. Gloria Swanson, Sarah Vaughn, Richard Denning, Cyrus Vance

28. Paul Whiteman, Ken Howard, Reba McEntire, Edmund Muskie, Freddie Bartholomew, Dirk Bogarde

29. Eugene McCarthy, Pearl Bailey, Eileen Heckart

30. Vincent Van Gogh, Warren Beatty, John Astin, Astrud Gilberto, Frankie Laine

31. Franz Joseph Haydn, Shirley Jones, Herb Alpert, Gabe Kaplan, Richard Kiley, William Daniels, Cesar Chavez, Harry Morgan

The following projects can be used with early finishers and in a wide variety of ways this month.

1. To celebrate the Vernal Equinox, on or about March 21st, students can be alerted to write or place objects on the bulletin board that signify the beginning of spring.

2. Harry Houdini's birthday is March 24, and students can construct mini-magic lessons taken from books about magicians.

3. Students may be surprised to learn about Saint Patrick on their March calendar. St. Patrick could be studied by several students because he had an interesting life—even including pirates! Students could create a play about him.

4. While waiting for warmer days, students can create butterflies and a theme of their choice for reading and writing. Colored celophane paper and construction paper could be used for the bodies of the butterflies, and the themes they depict could range from symbolism to realistic descriptions of the insects' life cycle.

5. The March calendar can be used in many ways, as discussed in Chapter 1.

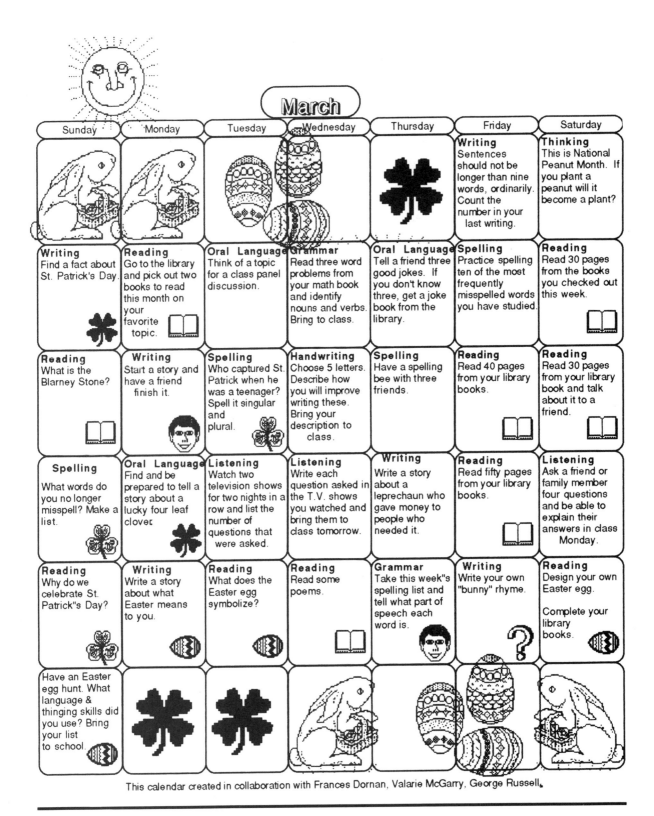

March

Sunday	Monday	Tuesday	Wednesday	Thursday	Friday	Saturday
					Writing Sentences should not be longer than nine words, ordinarily. Count the number in your last writing.	**Thinking** This is National Peanut Month. If you plant a peanut will it become a plant?
Writing Find a fact about St. Patrick's Day.	**Reading** Go to the library and pick out two books to read this month on your favorite topic.	**Oral Language** Think of a topic for a class panel discussion.	**Grammar** Read three word problems from your math book and identify nouns and verbs. Bring to class.	**Oral Language** Tell a friend three good jokes. If you don't know three, get a joke book from the library.	**Spelling** Practice spelling ten of the most frequently misspelled words you have studied.	**Reading** Read 30 pages from the books you checked out this week.
Reading What is the Blarney Stone?	**Writing** Start a story and have a friend finish it.	**Spelling** Who captured St. Patrick when he was a teenager? Spell it singular and plural.	**Handwriting** Choose 5 letters. Describe how you will improve writing these. Bring your description to class.	**Spelling** Have a spelling bee with three friends.	**Reading** Read 40 pages from your library books.	**Reading** Read 30 pages from your library book and talk about it to a friend.
Spelling What words do you no longer misspell? Make a list.	**Oral Language** Find and be prepared to tell a story about a lucky four leaf clover.	**Listening** Watch two television shows for two nights in a row and list the number of questions that were asked.	**Listening** Write each question asked in the T.V. shows you watched and bring them to class tomorrow.	**Writing** Write a story about a leprechaun who gave money to people who needed it.	**Reading** Read fifty pages from your library books.	**Listening** Ask a friend or family member four questions and be able to explain their answers in class Monday.
Reading Why do we celebrate St. Patrick"s Day?	**Writing** Write a story about what Easter means to you.	**Reading** What does the Easter egg symbolize?	**Reading** Read some poems.	**Grammar** Take this week"s spelling list and tell what part of speech each word is.	**Writing** Write your own "bunny" rhyme.	**Reading** Design your own Easter egg. Complete your library books.
Have an Easter egg hunt. What language & thinging skills did you use? Bring your list to school.						

This calendar created in collaboration with Frances Dornan, Valarie McGarry, George Russell.

Handwriting Skill Development: Learning to Improve Legibility with Increased Speed*

TIME REQUIRED

Teacher Directed Exploration (Activity 7-1): 40 minutes

Student Discovery Page (Activity 7-2) (for younger students only): 20 minutes

TEACHING STRATEGIES

Students will increase their handwriting speed through timed writings.

ACTIVITY 7-1

IMPROVING HANDWRITING SPEED AND LEGIBILITY

[OBJECTIVE] YOU WILL IMPROVE YOUR LEGIBILITY WITH IN-CREASED SPEED AND LETTER FORMATION. A TIMED TEST WILL BE GIVEN BEFORE AND AFTER THE LESSON TO DETERMINE IMPROVEMENT.

How many of you like to play games? What would happen if you could not read the directions for the game because the writing was bad? It is important to be able to handwrite clearly so others can read and understand what you write.

[Have students copy the following sentences from the board. Tell them to form letters carefully. Set a timer for 30 seconds. When the timer rings, tell the students to stop writing and count the number of letters they wrote (don't count spaces).]

1. Johnny Appleseed was a hero. (23 letters)

2. He was born in 1774. (15 letters)

3. His real name was John Chapman. (25 letters)

4. He planted apple seeds. (19 letters)

[Demonstrate proper letter formation according to the letter. Explain spacing and slant.]

There are at least seven reasons why your handwriting might not be as neat as it could be. **[Demonstrate each of the following as you teach how to correct them.]**

1. Faulty endings

2. Incorrectly made undercurves

3. Mixed slant

4. Failure to give letters in a group proper slant

5. Incorrect formation of the initial endings in final "h," "m," "n"

7. Failure to make the downstroke of "t" and "d"

[To make children aware of certain legibility difficulties, write the suggested words and ask them to do the following.]

*Adapted by permission from an activity created by Fort Worth teacher Joanne Gabel.

1. In the words "add," "gold," and "dare," analyze the letters "a," "d," and "g." What happens if the letters are not closed at the top?

2. In the words "no," "nail," "make," and "name," analyze the letters "m" and "n." What happens if the top is not rounded?

3. In the words "it," "tin," "nine," and "trip," analyze the letters "t" and "i." What happens if the letters have open loops?

4. In the words "late," "melt," and "lend," analyze the letters "l" and "e." What happens if the loops are not open?

5. In the words "up," "under," and "run," analyze the letter "u." What happens if these letters are not made correctly?

[Have the students write the same sentences as before, but without the timer. Monitor their progress. Teach about most common errors you see while walking around the desks. Have the children compare size, shape, and slant with the first sample.]

[Have children write the same sentences once more, and use a timer for 30 seconds. After the bell rings, have children exchange papers. Compare the correctness and number of letters written with the first sample. Collect papers. Grade size, shape, and slant.]

GRADING CRITERIA

Papers will be checked for improvement. Letter grades may be given based on a scale of how many letters were written on the final timed test and then weighed by the quality of handwriting.

MODIFICATIONS FOR GRADE LEVELS AND STUDENT ABILITY LEVELS

For Kindergarten through Third Grades and Slower Learning Groups, children will use manuscript and concentrate on a few letters. Pass out game grid with a vocabulary list of words from Johnny Appleseed's life (Activity 7-2). Children are instructed to fill out the grid first with words from the list. Then any empty spaces are filled with random letters. Children are to take great care in writing letters as instructed in Activity 7-1. If time permits, children can decorate their grids or swap them with another student and work the puzzle.

For Fourth through Eighth Grades and Gifted Learners, students will practice cursive writing on the most difficult formations. Calligraphy can be used for the most advanced. Gifted may also use both the Spanish and English versions of Activity 7-2.

Upper grades: Cards are distributed along with a suggested vocabulary list from Johnny Appleseed's life. The children will write each word on two cards using their best manuscript writing. The cards may be decorated and used for a game of Concentration with a partner. More advanced students could make a crossword puzzle with the vocabulary list.

Spanish speaking students can use the Spanish version.

INDIVIDUAL STUDENT NEEDS: _____

_____

STUDENTS WHO WILL BE WORKING ON OTHER PROJECTS OR LESSONS: _____

_____

NOTES FOR FUTURE USE: _____

_____

ACTIVITY 7-2

MANUSCRIPT WRITING PRACTICE

My Handwriting Skill Grows High!
El Dia De Johnny Appleseed

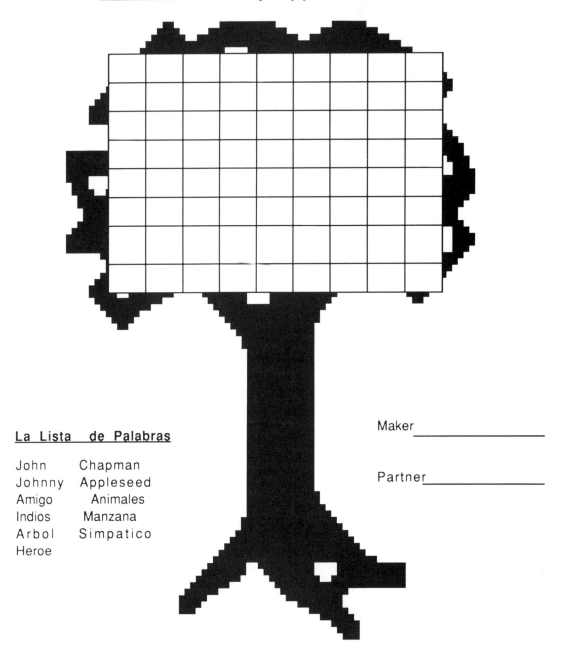

La Lista de Palabras

John	Chapman
Johnny	Appleseed
Amigo	Animales
Indios	Manzana
Arbol	Simpatico
Heroe	

Maker _____

Partner _____

ACTIVITY 7-2

MANUSCRIPT WRITING PRACTICE

My Handwriting Skill Grows High!
<u>Johnny Appleseed Day</u>

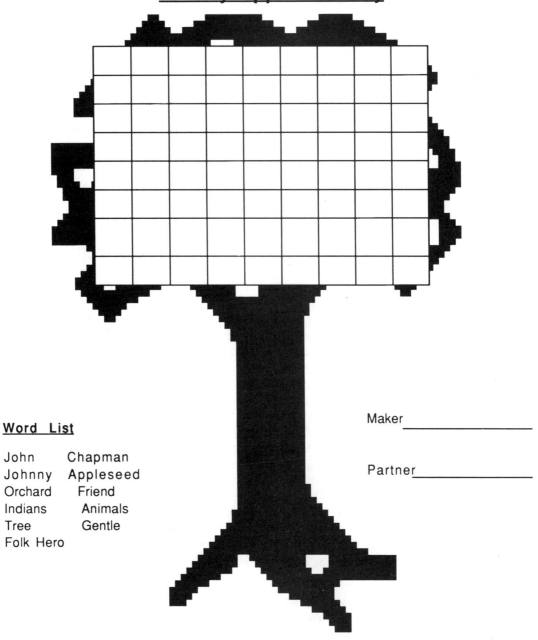

Maker _____

Partner _____

Word List

John	Chapman
Johnny	Appleseed
Orchard	Friend
Indians	Animals
Tree	Gentle
Folk Hero	

Composition Skill Development: Learning to Combine Related Sentences, Vary Sentence Patterns, and Eliminate Excessive Words

TIME REQUIRED

Teacher Directed Exploration (Activity 7-3): 30 minutes

Student Discovery Page (Activity 7-4): 20 minutes

TEACHING STRATEGIES

Students learn through pre- and posttest comparisons and self-evaluation.

ACTIVITY 7-3

WRITING ABOUT A LEPRECHAUN

[OBJECTIVE] YOU WILL LEARN TO INCREASE YOUR WRITING ABILITY AND BECOME A MORE INTERESTING WRITER BY VARYING YOUR SENTENCE PATTERNS, ELIMINATING RUN-ON SENTENCES, AND ELIMINATING EXCESSIVE WORDS. YOU WILL KNOW YOU HAVE BEEN SUCCESSFUL WHEN YOU CAN IDENTIFY AND EDIT PROBLEMS IN YOUR PAST WRITING SAMPLES AND THROUGH A PRE- AND POSTTEST COMPARISON BETWEEN WRITING SAMPLES DONE BEFORE AND AFTER THIS LESSON.

[After discussing the objective for this lesson, ask older students to find and bring to class one of their best writings from the past. The younger students will dictate a story about a recent event in the class. Write the story on the blackboard or overhead projector.]

[Have the class edit the story they composed, or have individual students edit a past story they wrote. Ask students to rewrite the story and compare to their previous one. Then distribute Activity 7-4, which can be completed alone or in pairs.]

[Carry on the following discussion with the class before presenting the following rules to improve writing.]

During March we celebrate Saint Patrick's Day. Some items and ideas sometimes associated with this day are shamrocks and leprechauns. Leprechauns and make-believe characters like elves are supposed to be able to do magic. They wear green to help people have good luck.

In a moment we are going to pretend that you have a leprechaun, and you will describe what it eats. You will try to use the following rules as you write.

Rules That Help You Vary Your Sentence Types, Eliminate Excess Words, and Improve Your Writing

1. Try not to repeat a word in the same paragraph. For example, study the following paragraph you might have written about your leprechaun and apply this rule.

My leprechaun likes ice cream. My leprechaun likes ice cream because it is made from milk. Ice cream is cold. Ice cream comes in many flavors. Chocolate ice cream is brown. Strawberry ice cream is pink and red. Ice cream is frozen milk. **[Discuss why this paragraph is not fun to read and have the class rewrite it.]**

2. Try to change the length of your sentences. You need to be able to convey thoughts and feelings clearly and in short as well as long sentences. When you use both kinds, people have to pay closer attention to what you are saying, and they understand you better. Sentences that are short and to the point are clearer, make points directly and are easier to understand than are longer sentences. Longer sentences, on the other hand, are sometimes necessary to communicate detailed descriptions and feelings.

3. Do not use "and" more than once in a paragraph. You may connect two or more ideas together in a paragraph, but if you need to do so more than once, use words such as "but," "as well as," "yet," or "or" to do so.

4. Try to describe a noun in one sentence instead of using several, as we did in the ice cream example.

[Hand out Activity 7-4 and have students complete it individually.]

EARLY FINISHERS

An early finisher or gifted student can look up the meaning of Saint Patrick's Day and present the results of the investigation when appropriate in the lesson.

MODIFICATIONS FOR GRADE LEVELS AND STUDENT ABILITY LEVELS

For Kindergarten through Third Grades and Slower Learning Groups, students may work in pairs on Activity 7-4 and use only a group-composed story instead of the pre- and posttest suggestions of Activity 7-3. *For Fourth through Eighth Grades and Gifted Learners,* you may wish to see if transfer to their normal writing skills has occurred by grading their next creative writing assignment based on the amount of improvement they have made in their sentence structure.

STUDENTS WHO WILL BE WORKING ON OTHER PROJECTS OR LESSONS: _____

NOTES FOR FUTURE USE: _____

ACTIVITY 7-4

ST. PATRICK'S DAY FUN: WHAT MY LEPRECHAUN LIKES TO EAT

Directions: Rewrite the following paragraphs using rules we
learned for making sentences clearer and more
fun to read.

The Strange St. Patrick's Day Event

1. The little girl leprechaun heard a big noise and she went up
   on the top of her four-leaf clover to see what happened
   while she ate her favorite food and she saw something and
   it looked like a football and then she went to bed and when
   she got up the next morning she listened to the news on her
   tiny radio and then she heard that the big noise was really
   a piece of a giant rocket that had taken off in America.

The Leprechaun Race

2. The leprechaun race is held every year at the pond and every
   leprechaun is invited to bring their fastest leprechaun from
   their village to race and each leprechaun lines up at the start-
   ing line and somebody yells, "Let them go!" and everybody
   watches as the leprechauns go and some start walking very
   fast and everybody starts yelling and finally one leprechaun
   crosses the finish line and everybody cheers some more and
   they give the prize to the winning leprechaun village.

On a separate sheet of paper, answer the following questions about
your leprechaun. Write in the best sentences you can:

3. What is your leprechaun's favorite food and why?

4. Write sentences about how, when, and how often your
   leprechaun eats this favorite food.

5. If your leprechaun could change anything about your school,
   what would the leprechaun change? Tell three reasons why it
   needs to be changed.

Listening Skill Development: Asking for Clarification When Directions or Descriptions Are Vague

TIME REQUIRED

Teacher Directed Exploration (Activity 7-5): 20 minutes

Student Discovery Page (Activity 7-6): 20 minutes

TEACHING STRATEGIES

Students learn by using a criteria checklist.

ACTIVITY 7-5

CLARITY IN GIVING AND RECEIVING DIRECTIONS

[OBJECTIVE] YOU WILL LEARN TO MAKE A POINT AND TO ASK FOR CLARIFICATION WHEN DIRECTIONS OR DESCRIPTIONS ARE VAGUE. YOU WILL LEARN TO USE DETAILS TO MAKE A POINT CLEARLY. YOU WILL KNOW YOU HAVE SUCCEEDED WHEN YOU CAN GIVE DIRECTIONS SO CLEARLY THAT CLASSMATES KNOW WHAT IS BEING DESCRIBED AND YOU CAN ASK FOR, AND UNDERSTAND, DIRECTIONS FROM A CLASSMATE.

Alexander Graham Bell was born on March 3rd almost 100 years ago. When he invented the telephone, he gave us added reason to learn to ask questions of clarification when someone is describing something or giving directions. Developing our listening abilities will help us when we follow all types of directions, when we work. or when we watch television or listen to the radio.

I want each of you to think of a destination to describe in a talk or story. The destination can be nearby, such as the school library, a building in our city, or far away, such as the Gettysburg National Cemetery. Tell us how to get there and what we could do when we arrive. Give details that make us want to go there. **[Give students a few minutes to decide what destination to describe and to jot down details to include.]**

Good speakers make sure their main idea is clear so that you know what they want to say. They give directions in order so you can follow them. And they give details to help you understand what they are saying and be interested in it.

But not all speakers are good speakers. Sometimes you need to work as a good *listener* to understand and remember a speaker's message. **[Hand out Activity 7-6.]** This sheet suggests what you can do to be an active, successful listener. **[Go over Activity 7-6 with the students.]**

I am going to give a destination talk now, and we'll pretend I didn't take any time to organize it or think of details to include. Try to use the suggestions for good listening. When I am finished, you can ask me questions to clarify what I said. **[Deliver a vague, disjointed, boring destination talk for about 3 minutes. (Students enjoy "catching" teachers in mistakes, and it is better to feign ineptitude yourself than to embarrass students by using their talks as examples of poor organization.) Encourage the students to bring order out of your talk's chaos by using the listening tips of Activity 7-6, especially questioning for clarification.]**

You have already planned some details to include in your destination description, so your talks will be much better than mine. But your classmates will ask you questions anyway, for practice in good listening. **[Let student volunteers deliver their destination talks as classmates act as active listeners, using the checklist of Activity 7-6. (Note: Students can also work in pairs.)]**

GRADING CRITERIA: _____

MODIFICATIONS FOR GRADE LEVELS AND STUDENT ABILITY LEVELS

For Kindergarten through Third Grades and Slower Learning Groups, complete the entire activity as a group discussion and use the Activity 7-6 checklist only in special situations. *For Fourth through Eighth Grades and Gifted Learners,* extend the Student Discovery Page by asking the class to give each other directions to places without telling the destination. The person who correctly guesses the place or asks the first question for clarification will give the next set of directions.

STUDENTS WHO WILL BE WORKING ON OTHER PROJECTS OR LESSONS: _____

NOTES FOR FUTURE USE: _____

ALEXANDER GRAHAM BELL'S TELEPHONE CHECKLIST: LEARNING TO ASK FOR CLARIFICATIONS WHEN NEEDED

When the Speaker:	What I can do is:	Examples of when I used it:
1. Is talking about many things at once.	1. Fit details together one at a time.	
2. Rambles	2. Ask speaker to give the main point again.	
3. Doesn't develop ideas well. Speaks with too little detail.	3. Ask speaker to give an example.	
4. Main idea is not carried throughout the talk, but many topics are discussed before the speaker stops.	4. Return to the first point and ask a direct question.	
5. Uses limited vocabulary.	5. Ask the speaker to give you one or more adjectives and verbs that most distinctly describe the topic.	
6. Lacks interest.	6. Picture yourself doing something the speaker said or picture one of the characters on your favorite TV show doing something the speaker described.	
7. Lacks sequence.	7. Paraphrase what you under-stand, and ask the speaker if what you understood was correct.	

Speaking Skill Development: Learning to Participate in Panel Discussions and to Answer Questions Briefly but Effectively

TIME REQUIRED

Teacher Directed Exploration (Activity 7-7): 20 minutes

Student Discovery Page (Activity 7-8): 20 minutes

TEACHING STRATEGIES

Students will learn through simulation, practice sessions, and peer evaluation.

ACTIVITY 7-7

BEING SUCCESSFUL PANELISTS

[OBJECTIVE] YOU WILL LEARN TO CONDUCT A PANEL DISCUSSION AND TO ANSWER QUESTIONS EFFECTIVELY AND CLEARLY. YOU WILL KNOW YOU ARE SUCCESSFUL WHEN YOUR PANEL COVERS THE QUESTIONS POSED AND THE CLASS JUDGES YOUR ANSWERS TO HAVE SUSTAINED THEIR INTEREST.

Many famous authors were born in March, and many of your favorite books were being written during this month. We are going to use the birthdays of Dr. Seuss and Elizabeth Barrett Browning to help us learn to conduct more effective panel discussions and to answer questions more directly and effectively. In a moment, you will get to select a character from a Dr. Seuss book, a book by Elizabeth Barrett or one of your favorite books.

Each of you will be allowed to practice becoming a more effective and interesting speaker by being a member of a panel. You will practice answering questions simply and effectively.

In the process you will learn to speak before a group more effectively. Before we begin we will learn the rules for effective panel discussions. **[Hand out Activity 7-7.]** Then you will break into groups and decide on a topic you want to present to the class. When your selection is made, elect a leader. This leader will post your topic choice on the bulletin board and will collect questions from the class concerning your group's topic. These questions will be written in the last 5 minutes of the day and given to the leader to take home to study. The leader will organize the questions by following the rules we are about to learn.

When they are organized in this way, the panel discussion will be more interesting. More than one person can be the leader, but these people must agree on the way in which the questions will be used during the discussion. Make these decisions over the phone or at one person's house tonight.

Once I have presented the rules for panel discussions and answering questions effectively in groups, fill out Activity 7-8 for your group. **[You may wish to complete Activity 7-8 orally with younger children, using an overhead transparency and having each group answer the questions at the top of the activity page. Then go over the list of rules for effective panel discussions and skills to master to answer questions effectively.]**

GRADING CRITERIA: _____

_____

MODIFICATIONS FOR GRADE LEVELS AND STUDENT ABILITY LEVELS

For Kindergarten through Third Grades and Slower Learning Groups, allow them to become one of the characters in their favorite book when they serve on the panel. _For Fourth through Eighth Grades and Gifted Learners,_ students can follow Activity 7-8 by talking about a concern of theirs in small groups. Their peers in the group will then evaluate their effectiveness.

You may wish to tape record the discussions and do this activity again in May. Tape the second panel discussion and allow the groups to hear their improvements. You might also like to make this a celebrative experience. You could do so by scheduling the event near Spring Break or on a Friday and allowing the students to have snacks. They can also select an author, as a class, to write to and find out more about to judge the accuracy of the panel responses.

STUDENTS WHO WILL BE WORKING ON OTHER PROJECTS OR LESSONS: _____

_____

NOTES FOR FUTURE USE: _____

_____

PANEL DISCUSSION AND HOW TO BETTER ANSWER QUESTIONS IN CONVERSATIONS

Name of Panel: _____   Panel Leader: _____

Topic that will be discussed: _____

_____

Why the group selected this topic and what type of question they would like to receive:

_____

_____

HOW TO HAVE AN EFFECTIVE PANEL DISCUSSION

1. The panel leader introduces each member and his or her area of "expertise" concerning the topic to be discussed.

2. The panel leader then explains to the audience why the topic was judged to be important, such as, the topic is of interest to many people, or the topic is a current issue and more than one opinion exists.

3. The panel leader will move from general questions to more specific ones. When questions are given in advance, the panel leader organizes them so as to accomplish this goal. When questions are not given in advance, panel members will usually respond with general answers and the panel leader will ask for a more specific answer about one aspect concerning the topic.

4. During the discussion, the panel leader will help to ensure that panel members participate equally. To avoid having the audience direct the majority of questions to only one person, the panel leader assigns different aspects of the question to different members of the panel. Panel members can then read and interview community people to gain information about the assignment before the panel discussion is held. The panel leader can also redirect general questions to panel members who need a chance to talk.

ACTIVITY 7-8

BECOMING MORE EFFECTIVE SPEAKERS IN A GROUP DISCUSSION

1. During the group work if you or someone else talked more than others, what can the group do so more people's ideas are heard?

2. If someone tends to give too long or an answer to a question someone asked, what can be done?

3. If someone too often gives an opinion rather than seeking facts, what can be done?

4. What can be done if people do not believe what you say?

5. What skill do you want to develop to become a better speaker in group settings?

SAMPLE ANSWERS FOR ACTIVITY 7-8

1. If students tend to dominate the group, they can be taught how to give shorter answers. Classmates can remind them of what the class learned about speaking in groups. One strategy students can learn is when they feel a need to preface an answer or statement they wish to make, by providing their group with additional information, they should only use two sentences to do so. Then, if students want more information after the two sentence background, they will ask for it. If they don't, the speaker will know that the group is ready for a simple sentence answer or statement of fact or opinion. Then another group member can speak.

2. Students can learn to think about their answer before they talk. They practice doing so until they develop the ability to answer questions in three sentences or less. The first sentence of the answer is the direct answer, and the next two, if necessary, cite two reasons or details concerning that answer. Students can also be taught that in group discussions, if group members do not ask a follow-up question concerning the answer they gave, group members are ready to hear someone else speak, so the first speaker should relinquish the floor.

3. Students should be taught to answer questions by citing facts as much as possible. When this is not possible, students can learn to state "in my opinion", followed by one sentence. Students should also learn that many times they will not need to tell why they hold the opinion they voice; if group members want that information they will ask for it.

4. Students should learn to avoid using superlative words when they talk, as listeners tend to become on guard. Listeners trust statements more when words such as "best, always, never" are not used frequently. Students can learn to listen and value opinions that differ from theirs. By not seeking to persuade others, group members increase their levels of trust.

Reading Skill Development: Learning to Comprehend by Relating Causes and Effects

TIME REQUIRED

Teacher Directed Exploration (Activity 7-9): 20 minutes

Student Discovery Page (Activity 7-10): 30 minutes

TEACHING STRATEGIES

Students learn through self-reflection and concept mapping. The self-reflection involves retelling and giving the reason for one's answer.

ACTIVITY 7-9 _____

STATEMENTS THAT CLARIFY MEANING

[OBJECTIVE] YOU WILL LEARN TO RECOGNIZE, ANALYZE, AND DISTINGUISH BETWEEN STATEMENTS OF CAUSE AND EFFECT, PROBLEM/SOLUTION, AND SUMMARY. YOU WILL KNOW YOU HAVE LEARNED WHEN YOU COMPLETE 80% OF ACTIVITY 7-10 CORRECTLY.

Have you ever read a story and not been able to understand what you read or how the events in the story relate? Today you will discover how much of a story you comprehend. You are going to learn about cause and effect.

Authors present ideas by summarizing and by writing about cause and effects, as well as problems and solutions. Since we have National Inventor's Day this month, we will learn how cause and effect statements and problem and solution statements can be used to convey new information.

At the end I want you to be able to tell someone else three things you have learned from this lesson about cause and effect.

The cause means what happens first. The effect is what happens second. The cause is why. The effect is what.

[On the board write the following.]

The cause means:

1. how come

2. brings about

3. reason

4. gives rise to

5. happens first

The effect means:

1. consequence

2. result

3. outcome

4. conclusion

5. pay off

To see if you understand what cause and effect means, let's look at this sentence: "The cake wasn't done because the oven was accidentally turned off." What was the cause and what was the effect? In your life, tell me something that caused an effect upon you.

Problem and solution statements are a special type of cause and effect. They tell the effect that eliminated the cause. An example is when a germ enters your body (cause) and you become ill (effect = problem), and you take medicine (solution that eliminates the cause) and the germ dies.

Summary statements describe the main points. They show how causes and effects, ideas, and problems and solutions relate together.

[Go over the following sentences with the class. Ask them to identify each statement as cause and effect, problem and solution, or summary.]

Kindergarten through Second Grade Level Sentences:

1. When I am tired, I take a nap.
2. Bill did not go to school today because he is sick.
3. There are many trees Mary likes to climb.
4. Bill missed the bus, but his Father took him to school so he wouldn't be late.
5. The farmer has many, many animals.

(Answer Key for Kindergarten through Second Grade Level Sentences:

1. Problem and Solution Statement
2. Cause and Effect Statement
3. Summary Statement
4. Problem and Solution Statement
5. Summary Statement)

Third through Eighth Grade Sentences:

1. There are many trees in Ava's backyard. The elm trees are taller than the maple trees, by far!
2. Mitzi bought the most Motown records at the garage sale.
3. If more than six inches of rain falls at one time, serious mudslides occur in Cooper Canyon.
4. John took the car to be serviced, but if the bill was to be more than $40.00, he would have to go home to get his mother and the credit card. The bill was $30.00.
5. Stuart worried because if the television network runs a special show tonight, his favorite television show will be cancelled.

(Answer Key for Third through Eighth Grade Sentences:

1. Summary Statements
2. Summary Statement

3. Cause and Effect Statement

4. Problem and Solution Statements

5. Cause and Effect Statement)

[Hand out Activity 7-10. It can be completed in several ways (see Modifications).]

_____

GRADING CRITERIA: _____

_____

MODIFICATIONS FOR GRADE LEVELS AND STUDENT ABILITY LEVELS

For Kindergarten through Third Grades and Slower Learning Groups, both activities may need to be done as whole-class experiences. *For Fourth through Eighth Grades and Gifted/Most Able Learners,* students can transfer this skill by writing their own story using cause and effect, problems and solution, or summaries.

Students can complete the Activity 7-10 orally with you. As a large group, students find sentences from any of their content books that are statements of cause and effect, problem solution, or summary. The student who suggests a sentence tells why he or she judged it to be a certain type. If the class agrees, both the statement and the reason are written on the activity sheet.

Alternatively, you can use Activity 7-10 as one that students complete independently. Students find as many statements as they can in the time available, writing the reason they judge the statement to be what type they say below each statement. If the activity is used in this way, students complete the bottom section in writing, in a specified amount of time. The student with the most correct items on Activity 7-10 can be acknowledged.

You can complete this activity by breaking students into pairs and asking them to discuss and then write together the best answer to the following question: How will what you learned today cause you to be a better reader?

STUDENTS WHO WILL BE WORKING ON OTHER PROJECTS OR LESSONS: _____

_____

NOTES FOR FUTURE USE: _____

_____

UNCOVERING MEANING THROUGH USING CAUSE AND EFFECT, PROBLEM AND SOLUTION, OR SUMMARY STATEMENTS

Sentences in Books	Type of Statement	Reason
1.		
2.		
3.		
4.		
5.		
6.		

Three things I learned from this lesson are:

1.

2.

3.

Grammar Skill Development: Learning to Form Compound Sentences Correctly and to Improve Basic Sentence Structures*

TIME REQUIRED

Teacher Directed Exploration (Activity 7-11): 20 minutes

Student Discovery Page (Activity 7-12): 20 minutes

TEACHING STRATEGIES

Students will learn by improving their own writing samples.

ACTIVITY 7-11

CELEBRATING NATIONAL NUTRITION MONTH WITH COMPOUND SENTENCES

[OBJECTIVE] YOU WILL LEARN TO FORM COMPOUND SENTENCES BY COMBINING RELATED SENTENCE PARTS AND YOU WILL LEARN TO ELIMINATE EXCESS DESCRIPTIVE WORDS. YOU WILL KNOW YOU HAVE LEARNED WHEN YOU BEGIN TO USE THESE SKILLS IN NEW COMPOSITIONS YOU WRITE.

March is National Nutrition Month. During this month many companies advertise ways in which their products can increse our health. In doing so they will use compound sentences often, because they want to tie their products to your health. The words that join compound sentences together are:

> **and**
> **for**
> **so**
> **but**
> **or**
> **yet**

Today we will learn to form compound sentences correctly and to eliminate unnecessary words in your writing. When you learn the meaning and use of connective words you can avoid being misled by advertisements and can make it easier for others to understand your writings.

"And" means that both parts of the sentence happen, perhaps independently of each other. For example, "He read his book, and elsewhere the students played ball." "For" means that the second part of the sentence is the reason for the first part. For example, "I cannot go on, for I am weary and cold."

"So" means that one part of the sentence causes the second part or at least explains the second part. For example, "We ate breakfast, *so* we had energy for class.

"But" means that the thing you might expect to occur did not occur. For example, "I ate a lot of food, *but* I didn't worry about gaining weight because I was about to run a race."

*This activity was developed in collaboration with Monica Moore, a graduate student in the Department of Curriculum and Instruction at Texas Christian University.

"Or" means that one of the parts of a sentence will happen and that one of the parts will not happen. For example, "I will eat lunch at McDonald's *or* Jack-in-the-Box today."

Now I want you each to construct ten pairs of sentences using classmates as subjects. For example, "Maria sits beside me. Maria likes to talk to me." Write one of the connective words, such as "and," "but," "or" beside each pair. Then exchange papers with someone and work each other's pairs of sentences into single, correct compound sentences using the suggested conjunctions. Remember that in a compound sentence a comma comes before the conjunction. **[The two then grade each other's papers.]**

[Give each student two pictures of food cut out of magazines.] Write a sentence for each of your food pictures and then combine the sentences with one of the conjunctions, or connective words, that we have talked about. **[Then the students will take turns revealing their pictures and the compound sentence used to tie the two pictures together. The speaker must also tell reasons for choosing the conjunction used.]**

[After this activity, hand out Activity 7-12. The students should write the six conjunctions studied in the top part of the activity page. Have the students break into four groups. Each group will be assigned a basic food group and should circle it on the activity page. All the students in each group will write a sentence about a different characteristic of their food group. (Some classroom research may be necessary.) The groups will then work to combine sentences and eliminate unnecessary words (see Activities 7-3 and 7-4) before reading their report to the class.]

GRADING CRITERIA: _____

EARLY FINISHERS

Those who finish early can go back to one of their previous writing samples and see if any of their sentences should be combined into compound sentences.

MODIFICATIONS FOR GRADE LEVELS AND STUDENT ABILITY LEVELS

For Kindergarten through Third Grades and Slower Learning Groups, complete both activities as oral, whole-class exercises. *For Fourth through Eighth Grades and Gifted/Most Able Learners,* you can give a posttest by asking students to go back to one of their former writings and edit it in light of what they learned in this lesson.

INDIVIDUAL STUDENT NEEDS: _____

STUDENTS WHO WILL BE WORKING ON OTHER PROJECTS OR LESSONS: _____

NOTES FOR FUTURE USE: _____

ACTIVITY 7-12

COMBINING FOOD INFORMATION

NATIONAL NUTRITION MONTH: THESE WORDS HELP BUILD COMPOUND
SENTENCES AND IMPROVE MY WRITING:

1. _____   3. _____   5. _____

2. _____   4. _____   6. _____

THE FOUR BASIC FOOD GROUPS

Whole Grain or Enriched
Bread/Cereals

cereal
wheat
nutrition

Milk, Milk Products
Cheese

dairy
homogenized

Fruits/Vegetables

carbohydrates
watermelon
banana
pineapple

Poultry,
Fish, Eggs,
Nuts, Beans

poultry
protein
vitamins

Spelling Skill Development: Learning to Spell Common Spelling Demons

TIME REQUIRED

Teacher Directed Exploration (Activity 7-13): Allow as much time as you desire

Student Discovery Page (Activity 7-14): 20–45 minutes, depending upon the modifications of the lesson you implement

TEACHING STRATEGIES

Students will learn in cooperative groups.

ACTIVITY 7-13 _____

CELEBRATING NATIONAL TEENAGERS' DAY WITH "WHEEL OF FORTUNE" SPELLING

[OBJECTIVE] YOU WILL LEARN TO SPELL THE MOST FREQUENTLY OCCURRING IRREGULAR WORDS BY TELLING WHAT PART OF THE WORD IS IRREGULAR AND TELLING HOW YOU WILL REMEMBER THE SPELLING. YOU WILL KNOW YOU ARE SUCCESSFUL IF YOU SCORE 80% OR BETTER ON YOUR TEST OVER THE WORDS.

National Teenager's Day falls in the month of March. Because many teenagers enjoy TV game shows, we'll honor the most frequently watched game show, "The Wheel of Fortune." You will have to use your reasoning and logic skills to sound out or spell words that are most frequently misspelled.

[Use one of the following grade-level spelling demons list or a list of your choice as appropriate for your class.]

Kindergarten and First Grade

buy	nice	they	close
does	name	read	been
fuel	here	tear	first
off	easy	were	among
says	dear	some	forty
skis	come	right	little
too	aunt	none	store
toys	color	many	shoes
two	half	hello	since
you	goes	train	sure
your	every	some	grade
very	hear	soon	could
said	hour	often	along
once			

Second and Third Grade

there	tired	outside	making
their	sugar	wrote	loving
you're	skiing	April	loose
lose	when	whole	know
they're	raise	we're	knew
who's	quit	tonight	house
write	quite	again	having
would	pretty	please	haven't
white	plays	people	getting
where	played	rough	busy
weigh	piece	all right	blue
used	peace	o'clock	early
until	party	mother	didn't
truly			

Fourth and Fifth Grade

accent	fourth	Easter	summer
desert	guess	guard	sometime
accept	choose	heard	school
whose	built	height	teacher
about	friend	instead	writing
address	coming	laid	which
advise	cough	latter	trouble
several	country	letter	together
surely	dairy	maybe	thought
already	cousin	minute	receive
always	doctor	poison	quarter
women	enough	route	morning
because	football	Saturday	lessons
before			

Sixth through Eighth Grade

although	favorite	something	traveling
arithmetic	February	straight	Tuesday
awhile	fierce	studying	vacation
balloon	Friday	Sunday	weather
birthday	Halloween	suppose	surprise
bought	handkerchief	surrounded	practice
children	hospital	swimming	neither
chocolate	principal	terrible	ascent
Christmas	received	Thanksgiving	assent
couldn't	remember	though	dessert
decorate	Santa Claus	through	loss
everybody	schoolhouse	tomorrow	except

[Distribute the word list of your choice. Students will break into groups of four to play a "Wheel of Fortune-type game." One student secretly writes the letters from one of the words on the list on separate notecards and covers each letter with a blank card. The game then begins with that student serving as the moderator. The remaining group members take turns guessing

letters. With each correct letter guessed, the player earns one point and the blank notecard is taken off that letter. After the five words are identified, the student with most points in each group wins. This player becomes the new moderator for the group, and the process is repeated. Students may wish to have tournaments between groups.]

[Give a test on twenty of the spelling demons, using Activity 7-14. Have students grade each other's papers.]

_____

GRADING CRITERIA: _____

_____

MODIFICATIONS FOR GRADE LEVELS AND STUDENT ABILITY LEVELS

For Kindergarten through Third Grades and Slower Learning Groups, select the appropriate word lists. *For Fourth through Eighth Grades and Gifted Learners,* select the most difficult word lists.

INDIVIDUAL STUDENT NEEDS: _____

_____

STUDENTS WHO WILL BE WORKING ON OTHER PROJECTS OR LESSONS: _____

_____

NOTES FOR FUTURE USE: _____

_____

ACTIVITY 7-14

CELEBRATING NATIONAL TEENAGERS DAY
BY CONQUERING SPELLING DEMONS

Now that I've practiced spelling common "demons," I'll show how many I've conquered!

1. _____   11. _____

2. _____   12. _____

3. _____   13. _____

4. _____   14. _____

5. _____   15. _____

6. _____   16. _____

7. _____   17. _____

8. _____   18. _____

9. _____   19. _____

10. _____   20. _____

Number conquered: _____

Corrected by: _____

Student Contract Form

The Individual Student Contract form can be used in many different ways throughout the school year. You can identify specific needs students have. You write these needs on the Student Contract Form for that student, which is completed during individual work times of the language arts period or as homework.

There are two special features of this form. The first is that students evaluate their own work, and then turn it in for your assessment. This self-evaluation builds their abilities to measure their own understandings.

The second special feature is that students can be paired, to work together and help each other learn new language and thinking skills. The pairing can be of students with comparable or varied ability levels. Both types of pairs will attain different benefits and growth. When Student Contract Forms are used in pairs, one contract per pair is turned in. If the Student Contract is used by students individually, the column marked "Name of Partner" can be completed by a student responsible for "monitoring" seat work (the classroom officer) that week. This student makes anecdotal comments to you, in the column "Name of Partner" concerning his or her classmate's good work habits during the week. In this way, the student monitors increase their awareness of good work and study habits. The comments the monitor makes can also build classmates' self-esteem.

INDIVIDUAL STUDENT CONTRACT

Name _____ Grade Level _____ Name of Partner _____ Grade Level _____

SKILL TO BE EMPHASIZED	SELF-EVALUATION	SKILL TO BE EMPHASIZED	SELF-EVALUATION

CHAPTER

8 *April*

In April we commemorate Paul Revere's ride, the Civil War, National Library Week, Pets Are Wonderful Month, Reading Is Fun Week, and Spring Break. We will use each of these events in our activities for the month.

Scope and Sequence of Activities

Handwriting (Activities 8-1 and 8-2): Students will use correct spacing, size, and slant of letters and words to improve handwriting.

Grammar (Activities 8-3 and 8-4): Students will learn how to use past and present tense verbs correctly.

Reading (Activities 8-5 and 8-6): Students will make inferences as they read and will learn the steps in inferential comprehension.

Speaking (Activities 8-7 and 8-8): Students will learn skills of debating.

Listening (Activities 8-9 and 8-10): Students will learn how to identify listening "road blocks" that interfere with how much we understand.

Spelling (Activities 8-11 and 8-12): Students will learn to use suffixes to increase the number of words they can spell.

Composition (Activities 8-13 and 8-14): Students will enhance their debating skills.

Supplemental Activities for April

The following projects can be used in a wide variety of ways to enhance the activities in April.

1. Students can write to the following addresses to obtain more information about the themes of April.

Pets Are Wonderful Council
Ellan Ryan
500 N. Michigan Ave.
Chicago, IL 60611

American Library Association
(Linda Wallace, Dir.)
Public Information Office
50 E. Huron
Chicago, IL 60611

The National Arbor Day Foundation
100 Arbor Ave.
Nebraska City, NE 68410

Dr. Robert E. Collier
Dean of Texas Woman's University
Box 22675
TWU Station
Denton, TX 76204

American Cancer Society
Joann Schellenback
Dir. Press Relations
4 W. 35th St.
New York, NY 10001

Reading Is Fundamental
600 Maryland Ave. SW
Room 500
Washington, DC 20560

Four States Fair Assoc.
AK, TX, LA, OK
Mr. Blair Dean, Director
Box 1915
Texarkana, Ark-TX 75504

National Book Committee
1 Park Ave.
New York, NY 10016

2. April has two important dates for conservationists. April 15 is Bird Day and April 26 marks the birth of John James Audubon. Students can learn about birds, migration, songs of birds, feeding habits, habitats, and preservation of species.

3. A activity for Easter is to read *The Golden Egg Book* by Margaret Brown, published by Western Publishing Company. Place a large paper egg on the bulletin board. While you read the story, have each child draw what he or she imagines might be growing in the egg, and attach the drawings to the bulletin board. Older children will enjoy checking the answer after they read the book by themselves.

4. On April 4, 1818, the present American flag was adopted. Students can find as many books as they can about the American flag and depict their findings in a play or class book.

5. Students could identify a Jewish community leader who could come to class to help them understand the significance of Passover. The students who are in charge of this project prepare questions in advance, research the subject, and give a report to prepare the class before the speaker comes. Students can bring symbolic objects and foods of the Passover time.

6. Have a group of students identify a creative way to celebrate April Fool's Day using a language arts objective they learned during one of last month's activities.

7. Students in grades kindergarten through 2 can make stand-up people and animals. They can glue the trimmings to an egg as a face or body part. Hair, cotton, yarn, paper, for facial features students can use bits of cloth, paper, or draw them on with paint or felt markers. For ears, tails, and whiskers, students can use pipe cleaners, felt scraps, yarn, or straws. To make stands for the egg figures, glue small bottle caps or a cardboard tube cut into circles or roll and glue small strips of cardboard into cylinders for a collar or legs can be used. The girls may make baskets and bonnets if they wish. Baskets are made from containers covered with crepe or contact paper and decorated with flowers, bunnies, and other springtime objects.

8. Students in grades 3–5 can make shadow-box eggs by creating their own miniature world inside an egg. The children can dye the egg. Then cut a window with manicure scissors by putting a small hole in the top of the egg. They then insert small objects with tweezers. A simpler way is to hinge together two egg cartons sections with tape. Paint and fill these cartons with spring flowers, chicks, and bunnies made of paper, gumdrops and marshmellows.

9. Students in grades 6–8 can use the anniversary of Samuel Morse's birthday to experience the coded language of Morse Code. Begin by a reading a story or book to the students about Samuel Morse. Tell them there are many different types of languages codes. you will then let the students solve some coded sentences on the board and also write messages in code on the board. Then the students will trade sentences and decode each others.

MORSE CODE

A .−	M − −	Y −.− −	period .−.−.−
B −...	N −.	Z −−..	comma −−..−−
C −.−.	O −−−	1 .−−−−	interrogation ..−−..
D −..	P .−−.	2 ..−−−	colon −−−...
E .	Q −−.−	3 ...−−	semicolon −.−.−.
F ..−.	R .−.	4 ....−	quotation marks .−..−.
G −−.	S ...	5	−.
H	T −	6 −....	SOS ...−−−...
I ..	U ..−	7 −−...	start −.−
J .−−−	V ...−	8 −−−..	wait .−...
K −.−	W .−−	9 −−−−.	end of message .−.−.
L .−..	X −..−	0 −−−−−	understand .−...
			error ....

Can You Read The Following Message?

−− −−− −.. ... .   −.−. −−− −.. .   .. .− ... −.−. ... − . −−

−−− −.−. .−.. −−− − ... .   −−.−. −.. .− ... .   −−..−−

.− −. −.. .   ... .− −.−. ... .   −−.−. .   − .... . .−

− . −− .−.. .− .− −.−. ... . .−. . .   .. −. .   − ....

..− −. .. − −.. .   ... − .− − . ...   .− −. −.. .   −.−. .− −. .− −.. .− .−

−−− −. −.−. .   ..− ... . −.. .   − −−− .   ... −. −.. .   −− . ...− −−. . ...

−... −.. .   .− .. .−.. . .   .−.−.− .   − .... . .   −.−, −−− −.. −. .− ...

−. .− −− . −.. .   .−−. −−− −.   .− −− . .−. .   −− −−− .−. ... . , ...

− . .−.. . −−. .− −.− . ... −. ..−. .−−−− −−.. .... .−−−−− −.−.−.

− .... .   .−−. .− − . −.   − .... .− −   −−− −.−. −.−. ..− .−.

−− −−− ... − .   −.−. .− − −.−. .− − . ... −. −.   .. −.   −−− ..− .−

.−−. .−− −. −.. ..− .− −−. .   .− .−. .   .−.−.− .−−. .−. . ... . −. − −. . −..

−... −.− .   − ....− −− −.−. .−.. . −

... −.−− −− −... −−− ....−.−.−

ANSWER KEY FOR CODED MESSAGE

Morse code is a system
of dots, dashes,
and spaces, telegraphers in the
United States and Canada
once used to send messages
by wire. The code was
named for Samuel Morse,
who patened the
telegraph in 1840.
The letters that occur
most frequently in our
language are represented
by the simplest
symbols.

10. Students of all ages can make a book of tree records. Use books, encyclopedias, and almanacs to find out about the world's tallest tree, oldest tree, widest tree, hardest tree, most unusual tree, and so forth. Students can also plant a tree in the school yard.

11. The following notable people was born in April. Students can locate the addresses of some of these people in library reference materials. Students whose birthdays occur in April can also read autobiographies or biographies of people born in or near their birth date. Students enjoy comparing themselves to these people.

Notable April Birth Dates

1. Debbie Reynolds, Rusty Staub, Robert Gottlieb, George Grizzard, Jane Powell

2. Buddy Ebsen, Emmylou Harris, Hans Christian Andersen, Alec Guinness

3. Doris Day, Eddie Murphy, Wayne Newton, Tony Orlando, Marlon Brando

4. Cloris Leachman, Bartlett Giamatti, Christine Lohti, Nancy McKeon, Anthony Perkins, Frances Langford, Maya Angelou, Arthur Murray

5. Frank Gershin, Max Gail, Bette Davis, Michael Moriarty, Gregory Peck, Booker T. Washington

6. Ivan Dixen, Merle Haggard, Andre Previn, Michelle Phillips, Billy D. Williams

7. David Frost, James Garner, Janis Ian, John Oates, Billy Holiday

8. Betty Ford, John Gavin, Edward Mulhare, Catfish Hunter

9. W. C. Fields, William J. Fulbright, Billy Graham, Gene Belmondo, Antol Dorati, Michael Learned, Dennis Quaid, Keshia K. Pulliam

10. Gary Morgan, John Madden, Arthur Ashe, Joseph Pulitzer

11. Joel Grey, Louise Lasser, Ethel Kennedy

12. Ann Miller, David Letterman, Lionel Hampton, Herbie Hancock, Herbert Mills

13. Al Green, Howard Keel, Thomas Jefferson, Catherine de Medici

14. John Gielgud, Loretta Lynn, Mary Healy

15. Harold Washington, Leonardo da Vinci, Bessie Smith

16. Kareen Abdul-Jabbar, Charles Chaplin, Barry Nelson, Herbie Mann, Henry Mancini

17. Harry Reasoner, Thornton Wilder, Nikita Khrushchev

18. Leopold Stokowski, Clarence Darrow, Robert Hooks, Barbara Hale, Hayley Mills

19. Jayne Mansfield, Dudley Moore, Hugh O'Brian, Don Adams

20. John Paul Stevens, Ryan O'Neal, Nina Foch, Jessica Lange, Joan Miro

21. Elizabeth II, Charlotte Bronte, Tony Danza, Groebli Frick, Charles Grodin

22. Eddie Albert, Joseph Bottoms, V. I. Lenin

23. Shirley Temple Black, William Shakespeare, Joyce DeWitt, David Birney

24. Jill Ireland, Shirley MacLaine, Robert Penn Warren

25. Al Pacino, Ella Fitzgerald, Melissa Hayden, William Brennan

26. John James Audubon, Carol Burnett

27. Sheena Easton, Sandy Dennis, Jack Klugman, Anouk Aimee, Ulysses Grant, Coretta Scott King

28. James Monroe, Ann-Margaret, Jack Nicholson, James A. Baker

29. Duke Ellington, William Randolph Hearst, Zubin Mehta, Donald Mills, Kate Mulgrew, Tom Ewell, Sandra Dee, Celeste Holm

30. Alice B. Toklas, Eve Arden, Willie Nelson, Perry King

7. The April calendar can be used in many ways, as suggested in Chapter 1.

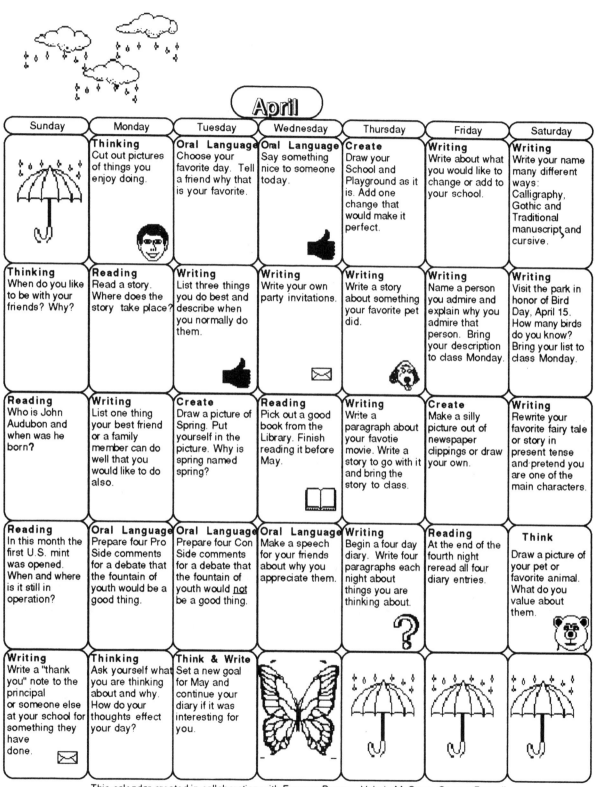

April

Sunday	Monday	Tuesday	Wednesday	Thursday	Friday	Saturday
	Thinking Cut out pictures of things you enjoy doing.	**Oral Language** Choose your favorite day. Tell a friend why that is your favorite.	**Oral Language** Say something nice to someone today.	**Create** Draw your School and Playground as it is. Add one change that would make it perfect.	**Writing** Write about what you would like to change or add to your school.	**Writing** Write your name many different ways: Calligraphy, Gothic and Traditional manuscript and cursive.
Thinking When do you like to be with your friends? Why?	**Reading** Read a story. Where does the story take place?	**Writing** List three things you do best and describe when you normally do them.	**Writing** Write your own party invitations.	**Writing** Write a story about something your favorite pet did.	**Writing** Name a person you admire and explain why you admire that person. Bring your description to class Monday.	**Writing** Visit the park in honor of Bird Day, April 15. How many birds do you know? Bring your list to class Monday.
Reading Who is John Audubon and when was he born?	**Writing** List one thing your best friend or a family member can do well that you would like to do also.	**Create** Draw a picture of Spring. Put yourself in the picture. Why is spring named spring?	**Reading** Pick out a good book from the Library. Finish reading it before May.	**Writing** Write a paragraph about your favotie movie. Write a story to go with it and bring the story to class.	**Create** Make a silly picture out of newspaper clippings or draw your own.	**Writing** Rewrite your favorite fairy tale or story in present tense and pretend you are one of the main characters.
Reading In this month the first U.S. mint was opened. When and where is it still in operation?	**Oral Language** Prepare four Pro Side comments for a debate that the fountain of youth would be a good thing.	**Oral Language** Prepare four Con Side comments for a debate that the fountain of youth would <u>not</u> be a good thing.	**Oral Language** Make a speech for your friends about why you appreciate them.	**Writing** Begin a four day diary. Write four paragraphs each night about things you are thinking about.	**Reading** At the end of the fourth night reread all four diary entries.	**Think** Draw a picture of your pet or favorite animal. What do you value about them.
Writing Write a "thank you" note to the principal or someone else at your school for something they have done.	**Thinking** Ask yourself what you are thinking about and why. How do your thoughts effect your day?	**Think & Write** Set a new goal for May and continue your diary if it was interesting for you.				

This calendar created in collaboration with Frances Dornan, Valarie McGarry, George Russell.

Handwriting Skill Development: Learning to Write for Decorative Purposes

TIME REQUIRED

Teacher Directed Exploration (Activity 8-1): 15–30 minutes each

Student Discovery Page (Activity 8-2): 30 minutes

TEACHING STRATEGIES

Students will learn by discerning the mistakes in bad examples.

ACTIVITY 8-1 _____

WHAT MAKES GOOD POSTERS?

[OBJECTIVE] YOU WILL LEARN TO MAKE POSTERS TO HELP CELEBRATE NATIONAL LIBRARY WEEK. YOU WILL USE YOUR BEST PRINTING SO YOUR CLASSMATES CAN UNDERSTAND THE POSTERS AS THEY WALK DOWN THE HALLWAYS.

Neater, more legible handwriting is valuable because it lets people better understand the message. **[Discuss places where correct, neat handwriting is important and what could happen if it is not readable (e.g., envelopes, phone messages).]**

[Show Figure 8-1.] Here you see two examples of posters, one that is correct and one that is incorrect. What differences do you see between the two? On a poster we need to have correct spacing between letters and words, because if the letters or words are too close together or too far apart, people will not be able to understand the poster's message. Also, correct letter size and slant will make the poster more readable and much prettier.

Now, work together in groups and brainstorm a motto for our National Library Week. **[Once groups agree on a saying, the students design and print the group slogan on the Activity 8-2 mini-poster sheet, working alone or as a group. Each group shows its posters and the class selects the favorite one. Each student then receives a 4″ × 11″ strip of white contact paper like a bumper sticker. Students practice using their best spacing and letter formation to copy the slogan onto their bumper stickers, which they may take them home, put on their lockers, or have displayed in the room or school.]**

_____

GRADING CRITERIA: _____

_____

MODIFICATIONS FOR GRADE LEVELS AND STUDENT ABILITY LEVELS

For Kindergarten through Third Grades and Slower Learning Groups, students may not be able to write letters, so they can work on centering pictures on a poster. For slower learners, allow more time to complete the assignment, up to several days. *For Fourth through Eighth Grade Levels and Gifted/Most Able Learners,* students will use their own individual slogans.

FIGURE 8-1
Examples of Incorrect and Correct Letter Spacing
and Formation for Decorative Writing

"Keep America Beautiful" Month

KeEp amErica

bea u tiful

mOn th

Incorrect

Keep America

Beautiful

Month

Correct

STUDENTS WHO WILL BE WORKING ON OTHER PROJECTS OR LESSONS: _____

_____

NOTES FOR FUTURE USE: _____

_____

ACTIVITY 8-2

NATIONAL LIBRARY MONTH MINI-POSTER

Directions: This is a practice page. Design a scale on this page that will correspond to the size of the poster you will make. To do so, mark the space below to be six inches long by six inches wide. Measure the size of your poster. Use your mathematical skills and determine how much one square inch on this practice page will represent on your poster. Create your saying "to scale" on this page so you can accurately space and size your saying on your poster.

Grammar Skill Development: Recognizing the Correct Tense of Irregular Verbs*

TIME REQUIRED

Teacher Directed Exploration (Activity 8-3): 30 minutes

Student Discovery Page (Activity 8-4): 30 minutes

TEACHING STRATEGIES

Students role play becoming biographers and autobiographers to learn correct verb tenses.

ACTIVITY 8-3

RIDING WITH PAUL REVERE IN PRESENT AND PAST TENSE

[OBJECTIVE] WHEN YOU ARE FINISHED WITH THIS LESSON ON IR-REGULAR VERBS, YOU SHOULD RECOGNIZE IF A VERB IS IN ITS PRESENT TENSE OR PAST TENSE. YOU SHOULD ALSO BE CAPABLE OF CHANGING THE TENSE OF A VERB FROM PRESENT TO PAST TENSE. YOU WILL DEMONSTRATE THAT YOU HAVE LEARNED THIS WHEN YOU SCORE 80% OR MORE ON ACTIVITY 8-4.

For someone to understand if you are talking or writing about something that happened in the past or something that is happening in the present, you need to know how to change verb tenses.

[Choose the appropriate word list from the following and write it on the chalkboard. Pronounce each word, telling which tense is being used. Use some of the irregular verbs from the list in a simple sentence. Then say the same sentence, changing the verb tense. Explain that even though a word has been changed, the meaning is the same, only the tense of the sentence has changed.]

Kindergarten and First Grade

Present	Past	Past Participle
1. am	was	been
2. are	were	been
3. do	did	done
4. is	was	has been
5. let	let	let
6. go	went	gone
7. put	put	put
8. set	set	set
9. wet	wet	wet
10. run	ran	run
11. sit	sat	sat
12. saw	sawed	sawed/sawn
13. say	said	said
14. see	saw	seen

*The activities were created in collaboration with Monica Moore, a graduate student in the Department of Curriculum and Instruction at Texas Christian University.

Kindergarten and First Grade (continued)

15. sell	sold	sold
16. sew	sewed	sewed/sewn
17. lay	laid	laid
18. lie	lay	lain
19. get	got	got/gotten
20. fly	flew	flown
21. has	had	had
22. cut	cut	cut
23. dig	dug	dug
24. bet	bet	bet
25. eat	ate	eaten
26. fall	fell	fallen
27. mow	mowed	mowed/mown
28. sow	sowed	sowed/sown
29. tell	told	told
30. win	won	won

Grades 2–3

Present	*Past*	*Past Participle*
1. beat	beat	beaten
2. begin	began	begun
3. bend	bent/bended	bent/bended
4. bite	bit	bitten
5. catch	caught	caught
6. creep	crept	crept
7. draw	drew	drawn
8. feel	felt	felt
9. freeze	froze	frozen
10. give	gave	given
11. hear	heard	heard
12. hold	held	held
13. know	knew	known
14. light	lit	lit
15. make	made	made
16. read	read	read
17. ride	rode	ridden
18. shine	shined/shone	shined/shone
19. sleep	slept	slept
20. slide	slid	slid
21. spin	spun	spun
22. sing	sang	sung
23. take	took	taken
24. come	came	come
25. think	thought	thought
26. cost	cost	cost
27. write	wrote	written
28. wear	wore	worn
29. wake	woke/waked	woken/waked
30. swim	swam	swum

Grades 4–5

Present	Past	Past Participle
1. understand	understood	understood
2. teach	taught	taught
3. stand	stood	stood
4. sweat	sweat/sweated	sweat/sweated
5. weave	wove	woven
6. spread	spread	spread
7. spring	sprang/sprung	sprung
8. speak	spoke	spoken
9. shrink	shrank/shrunk	shrunk
10. read	read	read
11. hang	hung/hanged	hung
12. break	broke	broken
13. drive	drove	driven
14. drink	drank	drunk
15. feed	fed	fed
16. grow	grew	grown
17. forgive	forgave	forgiven
18. forget	forgot	forgotten
19. dream	dreamed/dreamt	dreamed/dreamt
20. blow	blew	blown
21. fight	fought	fought
22. show	showed	shown/showed
23. split	split	split
24. sink	sank	sunk
25. mean	meant	meant
26. shake	shook	shaken
27. keep	kept	kept
28. hide	hid	hidden
29. hurt	hurt	hurt
30. shed	shed	shed

Grades 6–8

Present	Past	Past Participle
1. bring	brought	brought
2. build	built	built
3. burst	burst	burst
4. choose	choose	chosen
5. dive	dived/doved	dived
6. forbid	forbade	forbidden
7. grind	ground	ground
8. leap	leaped/leapt	leaped/leapt
9. leave	left	left
10. lend	lent	lent
11. lose	lost	lost
12. ring	rang	rung
13. rise	rose	risen
14. shoot	shot	shot
15. shut	shut	shut
16. stand	stood	stood
17. steal	stole	stolen
18. wind	wound	wound

Grades 6–8 (continued)

19. weep	wept	wept
20. throw	threw	thrown
21. tear	tore	torn
22. swing	swung/swang	swung
23. swear	swore	sworn
24. sweep	swept	swept
25. spit	spit	spit
26. string	strung	strung
27. strike	struck	struck
28. sting	stung	stung
29. stick	stuck	stuck

[Read the following story to the class.]

THE MIDNIGHT RIDE OF PAUL REVERE

Paul Revere was a well-known silversmith and manufacturer at the time of the American Revolution. The American Revolution was when the British American colonies decided to declare their independence from England and become the United States of America. That was over 200 years ago in the 1770s.

Paul Revere believed very strongly that America should be independent from England, so he helped fight the British in every way he could. In 1773 he and many other men living in Boston area dressed up like Indians and went on board a British ship. The ship was full of tea for which the British were making the Americans pay a high tax. To protest the tax, Revere and the other men dressed like Indians, threw all the tea into the ocean. Everyone called it the Boston Tea Party.

Two years later England and the Colonies were preparing to go to war with each other. The Colonists had been storing guns and gun powder in a town called Concord. The British found out about it and decided to capture the people and the guns. The Colonists found out what the British were planning, but they didn't know when. On April 18, 1775, Paul Revere saw the British marching to Concord. The silversmith got on his horse and rode through the country, from Boston to Concord, yelling "The British are coming; the British are coming." This woke up all the Minutemen, who got their guns and were ready to fight when the British got to Concord. This was the first battle of the war for independence, and, thanks to the "Midnight Ride of Paul Revere," the Colonists were ready.

[Display the following sentence on the overhead projector.]
Paul Revere knows that the British are on the march, so he must ride his horse to give the warning: "The British are coming."
[Then write this sentence beneath the first one.]
Paul Revere knew that the British were on the march, so he rode his horse and gave the warning: "The British are coming."
[Show which verbs were changed and explain which tense each sentence used.]
[Present the first two paragraphs of the excerpt from *Mr. Revere and I* written by Robert Lawson that appears in Figure 8-2. When the students have

read (or heard) them, ask them to decide if the paragraphs are in present or past tense. Ask them how they knew. The class will then decide which tense will be used in the next two paragraphs to correctly complete them. Keep the last two paragraphs covered until the students have decided. Once you have finished, have the students write in the verbs using the verb tense they feel is appropriate. Then have students compare their choices to those of the author (see Answer Key).

[Students may wish to make a list of the most frequently used words in their previous creative writings or journals. An activity sheet is given (Figure 8-3) for this purpose.]

[Hand out Activity 8-4a or 8-4b, according to grade level, for individual work. Check the work together.]

ANSWER KEY

Figure 8-2:
Third paragraph: had covered, was, was, could, was, was given

Fourth paragraph: had announced, gathered, were, were, was, was, deserved

Activity 8-3a and 8-3b:
(a): was helped, came, rode, fight, went

(b): was, was, felt, were, were, used, knew, were, decided, would, found, were, rode, told, were, were, arrived, began, won

GRADING CRITERIA: _____

MODIFICATIONS FOR GRADE LEVELS AND STUDENT ABILITY LEVELS

You can add additional irregular verbs by selecting from pages 202–204 of Edward Fry, et. al., *The Reading Teacher Book of Lists* (Englewood Cliffs, NJ: Prentice-Hall), 1989.

Students can read more about Paul Revere in a book called *Paul Revere and the World He Lived In* by Esther Forbes or *And Then What Happened, Paul Revere?* by Jean Fritz.

STUDENTS WHO WILL BE WORKING ON OTHER PROJECTS OR LESSONS: _____

NOTES FOR FUTURE USE: _____

FIGURE 8-2 Paul Revere's Ride*

That trip to New York was one which I shall never forget. I feel sure that Mr. Revere will not either. While he had learned to ride fairly well, he had never ridden any great distance. In fact he had never ridden any distance. In fact he had hardly ever been out of sight of Beacon Hill. New York was over two hundred miles away; neither of us knew the route; and, as Mr. Revere had said, it was midwinter. It was snowing slightly as we crossed Boston Neck and headed west and south.

We rode hard all that day. As we passed through each village Mr. Revere shouted out the news of the great Tea Party. Everywhere it was received with the greatest excitement, the villagers crowding about, urging Mr. Revere to tarry, to rest and eat. But he refused to waste a moment, merely inquiring about the route and dashing on to the next town.

By nightfall we _____ (cover) about forty-five miles. I _____ (be) well tired, and poor Mr. Revere _____ (be) so sore and exhausted that he _____ (can) scarcely dismount. Our host for the night _____ (be) the head of the Sons of Liberty and the leading citizen of the Village. I _____ (be) _____ (give) the best of attention, well rubbed down, well fed and watered.

As soon as Mr. Revere _____ (announce) his news the Sons of Liberty _____ (gather) on the village green, celebrating with bonfires and musketry. Before the rejoicings _____ (be) well started, however, the lights in our host's house _____ (be) all extinguished and I _____ (be) sure that Mr. Revere _____ (be) being allowed to sleep soundly. Goodness knows he _____ (deserve) it.

*Taken from *Mr. Revere and I,* by Robert Lawson, 80–81.

FIGURE 8-3 Student Verb Record

<u>My Own List of Irregular Verbs</u>

By_____

Present <u>Tense</u>	Past <u>Tense</u>	Past Participle <u>Tense</u>

1._____
2._____
3._____
4._____
5._____
6._____
7._____
8._____
9._____
10._____
11._____
12._____
13._____
14._____
15._____
16._____
17._____
18._____

MIDNIGHT RIDE OF PAUL REVERE
IN PAST AND PRESENT TENSE

Directions: Change the underlined words to the past verb
              tense. This change will make the actions in the
              story to have occurred in the past.

Paul Revere

Paul Revere <u>is</u> a famous American. He
<u>helps</u> other Americans when the British <u>come</u>.
He <u>rides</u> to tell the Minutemen to <u>fight</u>. He
<u>goes</u> through the countryside.

Paul Revere

Paul Revere _____ a famous American.

He _____other Americans when the British

_____. He _____ to tell the

Minutemen to _____. He _____ through

the countryside.

THE MIDNIGHT RIDE OF PAUL REVERE
IN PAST AND PRESENT TENSE

Change the paragraph from present tense to past tense. Underline the words you changed.

Paul Revere

    Paul Revere is a famous American Silversmith. He is also a patriot who feels the British are not fair in their treatment of the Americans. The British are making the Americans pay high taxes on goods they use, like tea. Paul knows he must do something to show the British that the Americans are unhappy. He decides he will go and throw a shipload of tea into the Boston Harbor. Paul also finds out when the British are going to attack, so he rides his horse and tells the Minutemen that the British are coming. The Minutemen are ready to fight when the British arrive. The War for Independence begins and the Americans later win.

Paul Revere

_____
_____
_____
_____
_____
_____
_____
_____
_____
_____
_____

Finish on Back

Reading Skill Development: Learning the Steps in Inferential Comprehension

TIME REQUIRED

Teacher Directed Exploration (Activity 8-5): 15 minutes

Student Discovery Page (Activity 8-6): 30 minutes

TEACHING STRATEGIES

Students learn by graphing their progress and by finding examples of concept taught.

ACTIVITY 8-5 _____

USING CLUES DURING NATIONAL LIBRARY WEEK

[OBJECTIVE] YOU WILL LEARN TO USE CONTEXT CLUES TO MAKE INFERENCES AND YOU WILL LEARN THE STEPS IN INFERENTIAL COMPREHENSION. YOU WILL KNOW YOU HAVE LEARNED WHEN YOU MAKE INFERENCES AS YOU READ.

National Library Week occurs in April. You can learn to get even more out of your library books.

Context clues help you "read between the lines" and give you opportunities to better understand characters' actions and feelings. It is important for you to learn to use context clues—that is, to use the meaning of other words in a sentence to figure out unknown words, because an author does not always write exactly how characters feel or why they act the way they do.

There are two ways to decide what an author is saying or feeling when he or she doesn't tell us. The first is to pretend that you are the person the author is writing about. Think about the experience the character is having and think of a time you were having similar experiences. Ask yourself:

—What was your appearance?

—What actions did you take?

—How did you feel?

—What characteristic of your personality has been challenged?

—Did you gain any insight?

—What attitude did you have?

By thinking through thoughts like these you can better understand what the author is trying to help you learn.

The second way you can gain understanding of how a character may be feeling is by noting the words an author chooses. For example, an author will convey if he or she likes or dislikes a character through the words used to describe that person. If the author chooses the word "mean" instead of "hard-nosed," you have a clue that the character is not a likable person and may not act favorably in certain situations. Pay close attention to the words used to describe events, ideas, and people.

A third way to understand the author is to look for definitions of words that you don't know. For example, when an author writes a word that is new to you, pay attention to the way the word is used. Here are examples to help you learn what to do. **[You may read a selection from a widely read children's books, which is quite appropriate for National Library Week, or read the following selection about ponderous animals. If you read a library book, do a "think aloud" to show how context clues helped you determine the meaning of a word.]**

Mammoths were ponderous animals. Dinosaurs were ponderous, too. Because they were ponderous, these animals left deep footprints in the mud when they walked near the water holes.

Write the number of the word or phrase that best tells what "ponderous" means.

1. plant-eating
2. prehistoric
3. very heavy
4. four-footed

Number 3 is the correct answer. Dinosaurs and mammoths were plant-eating, prehistoric, four-footed animals. But none of these answers tells why they would leave deep footprints. The phrase "very heavy" is a definition of the word "ponderous."

Listen to the following selection about ambrosia.

According to the Greek and Roman myths, the favorite food of the gods was ambrosia. They ate ambrosia. They ate it at every meal, taking it with them on their travels. The gods liked to eat ambrosia because it was so sweet and delicious.

Write the number of the word that best tells what ambrosia is like.

1. vinegar
2. spinach
3. honey
4. turnip

[Distribute Activity 8-6. Students may complete it alone or in groups. If students work alone, they are to read up to eighteen library books and record the number of inferences they understood in each book. Younger students are to graph the number of paragraphs per book or reading period that they understood before you call time.

If students work in groups, they read the same story or book and record the number of inferences they had that correctly matched the inference the author intended.

The graph in Activity 8-6 can be duplicated and used for other kinds of recordkeeping activities throughout National Library Week.]

GRADING CRITERIA: _____

MODIFICATIONS FOR GRADE LEVELS AND STUDENT ABILITY LEVELS

For Kindergarten through Third Grades and Slower Learning Groups, picture books may be used as well as oral discussion. *For Grades Four through Eight,* use literary works appropriate for grade level.

STUDENTS WHO WILL BE WORKING ON OTHER PROJECTS OR LESSONS: _____

_____

NOTES FOR FUTURE USE: _____

_____

NAME _____   DATE _____

ACTIVITY 8-6

CHECK-OFF SHEET FOR DRAWING INFERENCES

MY PROGRESS CHART

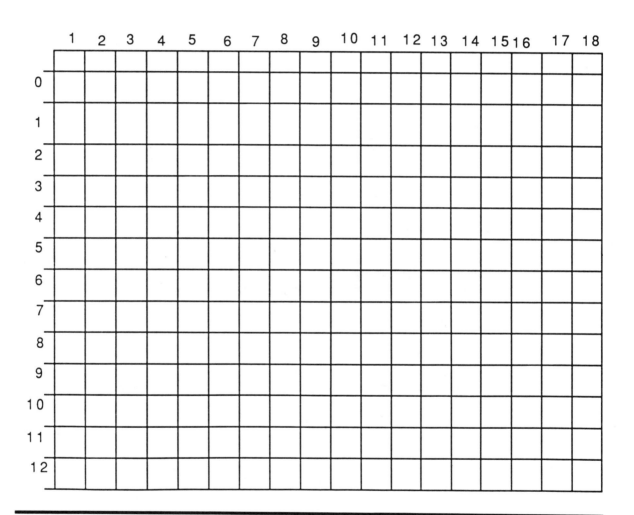

Oral Speaking Skill Development: Learning to Debate and to Defend One's Point of View

TIME REQUIRED

Teacher Directed Exploration (Activity 8-7): 20 minutes

Student Discovery Page (Activity 8-8): 20 minutes per group to prepare and 5 minutes per group to present

TEACHING STRATEGIES

Students will learn a formal debate strategy to improve their ability to defend one's point of view.

ACTIVITY 8-7 _____

THE UNRESOLVED INCIDENT

[OBJECTIVE] TODAY YOU WILL LEARN HOW TO DEBATE AND DE-FEND YOUR POINT OF VIEW. YOU WILL KNOW YOU HAVE LEARNED THE SKILL BY THE NUMBER OF POSITIVE EVALUATIONS YOU RECEIVE ON ACTIVITY 8-8.

[Use Spring Break and wildflowers for the basis of discussion. This lesson can be completed outdoors for visual, tactile, and kinesthetic experiences. Part of the lesson can be done with the whole class and part in groups. Have pictures or, preferably, real samples of wildflowers available. Lead a discussion about differences among wildflowers, their similarities, and ways to preserve them. This subject can be tied to science, signs of spring, and other springtime activities.]

People need to convey thoughts and feelings clearly in work, academics, and social parts of their lives. When people disagree with you, you can use special skills to help them see your position. Before you leave on Spring Vacation we are going to learn five skills that will increase your oral speaking skills.

The first skill is to use sentences that are short and to the point. These are clearer, have more meaning, and are easier to understand than long, rambling sentences.

For example, in discussions about spring I am going to use short, concise sentences to get across our thoughts and feelings. We do not want to ramble or connect several sentences with "and." You will try to be clear and concise, also.

[Have students present their positions concerning either (1) the best thing to do over Spring Break, (2) the best part of Spring, or (3) the best book they have read. During the discussion you will praise students who use short sentences, and show how easy they were to understand. You will stress that when a person uses a different subject he or she needs to start a new sentence. Give the following example of several related sentences run together.] "We went to pick flowers today and the sun was shining and Suzy fell and the teacher read a story to us." What is wrong with this sentence? What could be done to make it easier to understand? Talking in short sentences is the first skill to help people understand your point of view.

The second skill is that when you state a fact, and tell where you found it or who told you. In this way, people can more quickly accept the fact and begin thinking about a way to use it.

Third, if you are going to state an opinion, tell people it is your opinion and tell why you believe as you do. Then follow your reason with a statement about the opposite opinion and why you don't agree with it. In this way, people can more easily accept your opinion. They will see that you have thought about both sides before you formed your opinion.

Fourth, if you are beginning to present your point of view, use concrete facts and events that people know have occurred. Then move to your interpretation of these facts.

Last, listen to other people. Listen completely until they finish. Then begin your response to their statement by telling with which part of what they said you agree. If you do not agree with any of the points, you can say, "I can tell you have given your point a lot of thought."

You are going to practice using these five skills by participating in a debate over a topic or book you select. First, look at the rules you will follow in this and any other debate you ever have.

RULES FOR DEBATE

1. Flip a coin to decide which team starts. That team will be Team A.

2. Opening statements—Team A: Each member presents one aspect of their side of the argument, including some explanation and support. Support can take the form of statistics, cases, quotations by authorities, and so forth. There is a 2-minute time limit for each team member, but the full 2 minutes need not be used. While Team A is presenting these opening statements, Team B should be taking notes for the rebuttal.

3. Rebuttal—Team B: Members take turns pointing out weaknesses in the opening statements made by Team A, including any logical fallacies noted. No students should make a second rebuttal until each student on Team B has made at least one. There is a total time limit of 5 to 8 minutes, rather that a limit on each rebuttal. Members of Team A may not answer now, but they should take notes to pass to the member they selected for the closing statement.

4. Opening statements—Team B (as per Rule 2).

5. Rebuttal—Team A (as per Rule 3).

6. Closing statement—Team A: One member summarizes the best of Team A's arguments and puts to rest any claims made during the rebuttal of Team A's opening statements.

7. Closing statement—Team B: (same as per Rule 6).

[Put this debate format in outline form to be posted during the debate.]

[Depending on the maturity level of the students, you design a question or have them select one of the four following questions concerning the story to be debated. Each side of the question has a team; for example if your class contains twenty-four students, they would divide into eight teams of three, with one team debating the pro side and one team debating the con side of each question.]

[Make the following story into an overhead transparency and write the questions on the board, or make the story and questions into a handout.]

THE UNRESOLVED INCIDENT

What should Lisa and Nancy do?

It all started with an argument between two girls, each of whom insisted she should be first in the lunch line. Betty was from Mr. Mangieri's class, and Margie was from Mrs. Sanchez's class. The girls exchanged angry words. The squabble simmered all day and continued the next morning.

Most of the students in Mr. Mangieri's class sided with Betty; most of the students in Mrs. Sanchez's class sided with Margie.

Two girls, however, refused to take sides: Lisa and Nancy. They argued that Betty and Margie were both wrong for making an issue over a trivial matter. Lisa suggested the two might flip a coin to decide who should be first in the lunch line, but other members of the class refused to go along with this suggestion. Instead, they tore into Nancy and Lisa, accusing them of being wishy washy.

"You should stick up for your friends no matter what!" one girl shouted at Lisa. "What's the matter with you?"

"We won't play with you if you don't take Betty's side," another told Nancy.

Nancy managed to smile at this remark and answered, "OK, don't play with me. But I'm not going to take sides in such a silly argument."

"Neither am I," said Lisa.

Although both Nancy and Lisa were sure they were right to keep out of the squabble, they could see that their classmates were now angrier at them than they'd been at either Margie or Betty. Both Nancy and Lisa realized they'd have some difficult days at school before their classmates forgot about the incident. Meanwhile, what should Lisa and Nancy do?

SIDES TO BE DEBATED

1. Do you think Lisa and Nancy should have avoided trouble by taking sides as the rest of their classmates did? Pro side = YES, Con side = NO

2. Do you think the girls in the argument should have been willing to settle their squabble as Lisa suggested? Pro side = YES, Con side = NO

3. Does the argument "You should stick up for your friends no matter what!" make any sense? Explain. Pro side = YES, Con side = NO

4. Do most fights involve a "silly" question that should be settled quickly? Pro side = YES, Con side = NO

[Go over the story and questions with the class and assign teams and positions. Allow each group to brainstorm, using the brainstorming higher-level thinking skills that they learned in a previous creative writing lesson.]

[Once the teams have generated points to support their positions, they begin the debates, with you serving as monitor.]

[Each student completes a debate sheet (Activity 8-8) for each debate (except for the one in which they participate). These sheets are then given to the debate teams as feedback on how well they have learned the five skills of defending one's point of view and the skills of debating.]

GRADING CRITERIA: _____

_____

MODIFICATIONS FOR GRADE LEVELS AND STUDENT ABILITY LEVELS

For Kindergarten through Grade Three, you may wish to complete the activities as a whole class, one half of the students against the other and use only one of the above questions. _For Fourth through Eighth grades,_ students can debate a real issue concerning their school or a current event.

INDIVIDUAL STUDENT NEEDS: _____

_____

STUDENTS WHO WILL BE WORKING ON OTHER PROJECTS OR LESSONS: _____

_____

NOTES FOR FUTURE USE: _____

_____

ACTIVITY 8-8

DEBATE SCORE SHEET

Directions:
Single points can be awarded for:

1. Opening statements that are short and clearly explained and adquately supported.
2. Use of good fact.
3. Worded opinions correctly.
4. Good rebuttal-can point out poor explanation, faulty support, or a good question about something left unsaid.
5. Listened as was taught as the fifth skill.

TEAM A MEMBER

	OPENING	REBUTTAL	CLOSING	TOTAL POINTS
1.				
2.				
3.				
4.				
5.				

TEAM B MEMBER

	OPENING	REBUTTAL	CLOSING	TOTAL POINTS
1.				
2.				
3.				
4.				
5.				

AFTER HEARING THE DEBATE I VOTED FOR TEAM _____ BECAUSE

_____.

_____
DEBATE JUDGE

Listening Skill Development: Learning to Overcome Listening Roadblocks*

TIME REQUIRED

Teacher Directed Exploration (Activity 8-9): 10–20 minutes

Student Discovery Page (Activity 8-10): 20–35 minutes

TEACHING STRATEGIES

Students will learn through self-assessment.

ACTIVITY 8-9

CELEBRATING THE YOUNG CHILD BY OVERCOMING LISTENING ROADBLOCKS

[OBJECTIVE]   YOU WILL LEARN TO IDENTIFY "ROAD BLOCKS" THAT CAUSE DIFFICULTIES IN REMEMBERING WHAT YOU HEAR. YOU WILL KNOW YOU HAVE LEARNED WHEN YOU ARE ABLE TO FILL IN ACTIVITY 8-10 WHILE LISTENING.

April is designated as the Month of the Young Child, so we will take a reading from stories about youth in our country.

[Brainstorm with students, having them list as many reasons as they can for why they have trouble and how they can overcome these problems in listening. Hand out Activity 8-10.] In Activity 8-10 you see a checklist of listening and hearing roadblocks, and where they occur as you try to remember what you hear. Being aware of different roadblocks where they occur will help you overcome these roadblocks and develop better listening strategies. I would like you to listen to a passage read from a book. Complete the checklist as you listen to this story.

[A list of recorded readings from which you may choose follows.]

Author	*Title*
Paul Galdone	*The Gingerbread Boy*
Margaret Hodges	*St. George and the Dragon*
Trina Schart Hyman	*Little Red Riding Hood*
Gerald McDermott	*Arrow to the Sun*
Anne Grifalconi	*The Village of Round and Square Houses*

[A special benefit of using a recorded reading rather than reading a book aloud yourself is that you could complete a Listening Roadblocks Checklist with the students, modeling how all people can improve their listening strategies. If you can not obtain one of the above recorded readings, tape record a reading from a book students have not heard. As you read, try to incorporate some of the "listening roadblocks" listed in Activity 8-10.]

---

*These activities were created in collaboration with Monica Moore, graduate student from Texas Christian University.

GRADING CRITERIA: _____

_____

MODIFICATIONS FOR GRADE LEVELS AND STUDENT ABILITY LEVELS

For Kindergarten through Third Grades and Slower Learning Groups, choose a book on their level. The teacher may orally present the Activity 8-10 checklist. *For Fourth through Eighth Grades and Gifted Learners,* select more difficult books.

INDIVIDUAL STUDENT NEEDS: _____

_____

STUDENTS WHO WILL BE WORKING ON OTHER PROJECTS OR LESSONS: _____

_____

NOTES FOR FUTURE USE: _____

_____

LISTENING ROADBLOCKS CHECKLIST

Overcoming Problems In Hearing A Speaker:

1. When the speaker talked too softly, I _____
_____
_____.

2. When the speaker talked loudly enough but not clearly
I_____
_____.

3. When I'm trying to hear when a room is noisy I _____
_____
_____.

4. When the speaker repeats "Uh", "O.K.", "and", or another word or phrase repeatedly it did not effect my listening because I _____
_____.

Building My Own Listening Skills:

5. When I have trouble paying attention because something
else is on my mind I _____
_____.

6. When I have trouble paying attention because I was thinking about something I want to say I _____
_____
_____.

7. When I do not understand a word the speaker uses I __
_____
_____.

8. When I get confused and almost quit listening I _____
_____
_____.

9. When I can't figure out what might come next I _____
_____
_____.

Self-Assessment of My Listening:

10. One thing I think I am doing well or am showing impro-
ement in my listening ability is _____
_____
_____.

Spelling Skill Development: Learning To Spell Words with Different Suffixes

TIME REQUIRED

Teacher Directed Exploration (Activity 8-11): 15 minutes

Student Discovery Page (Activity 8-12): 20 minutes

TEACHING STRATEGIES

Students work in cooperative groups and learn groups of words that have the same end changes.

ACTIVITY 8-11

CELEBRATING SPRING BY LEARNING SUFFIXES

[OBJECTIVE] YOU WILL SPELL WORDS THAT CHANGE IN SPELLING WHEN VARIOUS SUFFIXES ARE ADDED TO THE ROOT WORD. YOU WILL KNOW YOU HAVE BEEN SUCCESSFUL IF YOU CAN CORRECTLY PLACE SUFFIXES ON ROOT WORDS TO MAKE NEW WORDS.

In April, with Spring in full swing, you might enjoy writing creative stories about birds, the nice weather, flowers and other Spring topics. Sometimes your stories will involve suffixes, or word endings, that change how a word is spelled. To effectively translate words with different suffixes in your stories, you need a basic understanding and knowledge of suffix rules. **[Cover the basic rules, which follow, after having talked about what suffixes are. Have students identify the suffixes in the examples. The class may want to brainstorm to generate a list of frequently used suffixes.]**

1. Words ending in silent "e" drop the "e" when adding a suffix or ending beginning with a vowel, and keep the "e" when adding a suffix or ending beginning with a consonant.

bake	manage
baking	managing
baker	management

2. When a root word ends in "y" preceded by a consonant, the "y" is changed to "i" in adding suffixes and endings unless the ending or suffix begins with "i."

fly	study
flies	studying
flying	studious
	studies

3. When a root word ends in "y" preceded by a vowel, the root is not changed when adding suffixes or endings.

play	monkey
playful	monkeys

4. When a one-syllable word ends in a consonant with one vowel before it, the consonant is doubled before adding a suffix or ending that begins with a vowel:

run	ship
running	shipping
	shipment

5. In words of more than one syllable, the final consonant is doubled before adding a suffix or ending if: (1) the last syllable is accented, (2) the last syllable ends in a consonant with one vowel before it, and (3) the suffix or ending begins with a vowel.

begin	admit
beginning	admittance

[Hand out Activity 8-12. The students will either work independently or in groups to formulate lists of words for Activity 8-12 that have suffixes. These words should be used in the Springtime creative writing stories. The students can use the rules to ensure correct spellings. After a list is generated the words should be written on index cards (one word per card) and sorted or categorized. For example, the students may have the following six words on index cards:

wolves	**hopping**
popping	**cats**
dogs	**halves**

The students would categorize the six words by the changes that must be made when adding the suffixes or by the suffix itself. In this example "wolves" and "halves" would be in one group, "popping" and "hopping" in another, and "dogs" and "cats" in a third group.]

Why did you put these words together? How are these words alike? How are these words different? Is this a useful category for grouping words? How can grouping words help you to become more aware of spellings when suffixes are added?

[After students become aware of rules for suffix spelling changes, you may wish to have them create Springtime stories that include correctly spelled suffixes. When the stories are finished, have groups met together again. Allow students to plan the next step to view suffixes. They can either create their own way to read each others' stories, or they can choose from one of the following options.]

1. A student reads a peer's story and underlines words that contain a suffix.

2. A student makes a list of at least ten root words to change by giving a new suffix. Another student in the group makes the changes, and the list creator checks the spelling.

3. Students may wish to accumulate many index cards of suffix-ending words to use as references in future writing.

4. Students count the number of words on all their papers that have suffixes spelled correctly, and the team with the most wins.

GRADING CRITERIA: _____

MODIFICATIONS FOR GRADE LEVELS AND STUDENT ABILITY LEVELS

For Younger Students, one rule at a time can be introduced. _For Older and Gifted Students,_ classmates can create their own sentences to challenge each other, following the format of Activity 8-11.

STUDENTS WHO WILL BE WORKING ON OTHER PROJECTS OR LESSONS: _____

NOTES FOR FUTURE USE: _____

ACTIVITY 8-12

THE BIRDS IN SPRING HELP SPELLING SKILLS

Directions: Circle the word that has the correct meaning and spelling for the blank of each sentence.

1. **Mr. Pasto** teaches his dog tricks. His dog is _____ .

   trainible   trainable   trainee

2. The baker is _____ a cake.

   bakeing   baking   baken

3. The monkeys are very _____ .

   playfull   playing   playful

4. The _____ of the title is "The."

   begining   begins   beginning

5. He _____ very hard.

   studies   studious   studing

6. She is _____ a book.

   writing   writeing   writin

7. We're _____ our packages.

   ship   shipping   shiping

8. The _____ rode horses.

   cowboies   cowboys   cowbois

Creative Writing Skill Development: Learning That Paragraphs Are Written for Different Purposes*

TIME REQUIRED

Teacher Directed Exploration (Activity 8-13): 30 minutes

Student Discovery Page (Activity 8-14): 45 minutes per paragraph frame

TEACHING STRATEGIES

Students work in cooperative groups.

ACTIVITY 8-13

CELEBRATING NATIONAL HUMOR MONTH WITH DIFFERENT PARAGRAPHS

[OBJECTIVE] YOU WILL ENHANCE YOUR READING COMPREHENSION AND YOUR WRITING SKILLS BY LEARNING TO USE DIFFERENT TYPES OF PARAGRAPHS. YOU WILL KNOW YOU HAVE BEEN SUCCESSFUL WHEN YOU CORRECTLY IDENTIFY THREE TYPES OF PARAGRAPHS.

April is National Humor Month. To comprehend, identify, and write many kinds of literature, you need to know different types of paragraphs. One of the most distinctive paragraph types is the humorous paragraph, whose purpose is to amuse the reader.

[Review all types of paragraphs listed below with older students. With younger students, focus on only two or three of the most widely used types.]

Type of Material	Purpose
Explanatory	Gives reasons for an event, outcome, justification for a position, and so on
Definition	Provides the meaning of a word or phrase, often by reference to categories
Introductory	Provides an overview or set of purposes
Summarizing or Concluding	Pulls together information very concisely—useful as a preview or as a review
Transitional	Leads the reader smoothly from one idea to another
Narrative	Tells a story—usually in fiction books but sometimes found in content material, especially history
Descriptive	Delineates features or points, as, for example, in the procedural steps of a science experiment
Cause–effect	Presents the results of one or more causative factors, agents, or features
Comparison	Indicates how two or more things, situations, or aspects are alike and different

*These activities were created in collaboration with Monica Moore, a graduate student in the Department of Curriculum and Instruction at Texas Christian University.

Conditional	Specifies what would happen if something else occurred
Inductive reasoning	Presents facts, relationships among the facts, and ultimately a generalization
Deductive reasoning	Presents a generalization first and then supports it with specific details and relationships among details
Time sequence	Relates the order in which particular events occurred
Spatial sequence	Specifies in a certain order where things are in a given space
Problem–Solution	Identifies a problem and then presents one or more solutions
Question–Answer	Sets up a question and then proceeds to give answers

Certain words and phrases signal particular types of writing. For example:

Type of Writing	*Signal Words*
Descriptive, Definitional, Explanatory	for example, specifically, for this reason
Summarizing, Concluding	hence, therefore, as a result, thus, in summary, in conclusion, accordingly, so, consequently, finally
Cause–effect	because, since, so that
Comparison–contrast	whereas, while, however, nevertheless, on the other hand, both . . . and, neither
Conditional	if . . . then, unless, although, only if
Sequence	first, second, third, then, finally, next, before, after, as, during, while, and another, also, in addition

[You can bring newspapers and humorous books for students to use in identifying different paragraph types. After you have presented the different types of paragraphs, you can present paragraph frames (Activity 8-14).] Paragraph frames serve the same function as skeletons in our body; they shape the form ideas will take. Sentence starters and sequence words often signal the type of paragraph. **[The example in Activity 8-14 is a sequentially organized paragraph.]**

GRADING CRITERIA

Students should be able to identify three paragraph purposes correctly.

MODIFICATIONS FOR GRADE LEVELS AND STUDENT ABILITY LEVELS

For Kindergarten through Third Grade, students may take a longer time to complete their paragraph frames. *For Fourth through Eighth Grades,* the paragraph frames may be more detailed in writing and artwork.

Activity 8-14 can be extended by having younger students draw scenes from paragraphs and identifying types of paragraph you read. Older students can create their own paragraph fames. These frames can be shared in class, with students deciding which type of paragraph each classmate chose.

STUDENTS WHO WILL BE WORKING ON OTHER PROJECTS OR LESSONS: _____

_____

NOTES FOR FUTURE USE: _____

_____

ACTIVITY 8-14

PARAGRAPH FRAMES*

Before a frog is grown, it goes through many changes.*
First, the mother frog _____
_____

Next, _____
Then, _____
Finally, _____
Now they _____

Before a frog is grown,
it goes through many stages.
First the mother frog lays
the eggs. Next the eggs hatch
and turn into a tadpole. Then
slowly the tadpoles legs begin
to grow. Finally the tadpole
turns into a frog. Now and then
they have to go into the water
to keep their skin moist.

*Taken from Evelyn T. Cudd and Leslie Roberts, *Using Writing to Enhance Content Area Learning in the Primary Grades.* *The Reading Teacher*, V. 46, NO. 2, p. 392–405. Reprinted with permission of Evelyn T. Cudd and the International Reading Association.

Student Groups Form

The student groups form can be used to record a wide variety of information about the make-up and progress of cooperative learning groups that you use in language arts activities.

Student Groups

CHAPTER

9 *May*

May is a very festive month. It is the end of the school year for many districts, and has many other events to celebrate as well. During the month, people go to baseball games, flowers start to bloom, May Day celebrations abound, and, of course, Mother's Day occurs. People begin to be restless because of the warm air and sunshine. This month's activities are designed to help keep restless children motivated and to end the year on a good note.

May is Physical Fitness and Sports Month, and students will shape up their proofreading skills by writing stories and allowing their classmates to check them. They will commemorate Be Kind to Animals Week by increasing their speaking abilities. Activities in May also focus on Cinco de Mayo, National Police Week, the All-American Buckle Up, Mother's Day, National Teacher's Day, and Memorial Day.

Scope and Sequence of Language Arts Skills Taught in May

Handwriting (Activities 9-1 and 9-2): Students will learn how to make letters correctly in manuscript, cursive, or calligraphy so other people can read their work with ease.

Spelling (Activities 9-3 and 9-4): Students will learn to use compound words to increase their spelling power.

Reading (Activities 9-5 and 9-6): Students will learn how to recognize the elements of classical literature.

Listening (Activities 9-7 and 9-8): Students will learn to take good notes while listening.

Grammar (Activities 9-9 and 9-10): Students will learn how to correctly use colons, semicolons, apostrophes, and periods.

Composition (Activities 9-11 and 9-12): Students will learn how to state a topic sentence and support it with descriptions, examples, and nonexamples so they write paragraphs that are cohesive.

Speaking (Activities 9-13 and 9-14): Students will learn how to express themselves better orally by cutting out redundancies.

SUPPLEMENTAL ACTIVITIES

1. Students can write to the following addresses for information on this month's activities.

American Humane Association
9725 E. Hampde
Denver, CO 90231

Indiana State Police
Attn: David Bartle
100 N. Senate Ave.
Indianapolis, IN 46204

American Police Hall of Fame
14600 S. Tamiami Trail
North Port, FL 33595

The President's Council on Physical
  Fitness and Sports
Attn: Dr. Matthew Guidry
450 Fifth St., N.W.
Suite 7103
Washington, DC 20021

Trader's Village
2602 Mayfield Rd.
Grand Prairie, TX 75051

2. The following notable people were born in May. Students whose birthdays fall in May can write to those who were born on or near their birth date. They or their classmates could also read autobiographies or biographies about their favorite person.

1. Kate Smith, Glenn Ford, Steve Carlton

2. Bing Crosby, Theodore Bikel, Benjamin Spock

3. Sugar Ray Robinson, Christopher Cross, Golda Meier

4. Audrey Hepburn, William Bennett

5. Michael Murphy, Tammy Wynette

6. Willie Mays, Sigmund Freud

7. Gary Cooper, Robert Browning

8. Harry S. Truman, Melissa Gilbert

9. Mike Wallace, Billy Joel

10. Fred Astaire, Sir Thomas Lipton, Gary Owens

11. Phil Silver, Rupert Merdock, Martha Graham

12. Kim Fields, Florence Nightingale, Yogi Berra

13. Stewart Granger, Beatrice Arthur, Joe Louis

14. George Lucas, Bobby Darin

15. James Mason, Trini Lopez

16. Liberace, Henry Fonda, Olga Korbut

17. Maureen O'Sullavan, Benjamin Disraeli

18. Robert Morse, Jack Paar, Frank Capra

19. Malcom X, Grace Jones, David Hartman

20. Cher, Moshe Dayan

21. Fats Waller, Dennis Day, Alexander Haig

22. Laurence Olivier, Peter Nero, Judith Christi

23. Douglas Fairbanks, Joan Collins

24. Queen Victoria, Bob Dylan, Coleman Young, Priscilla Presley

25. Ralph Waldo Emerson, Beverly Sills

26. Al Jolson, John Wayne, Stevie Nicks

27. Isadora Duncan, Henry Kissinger, Vincent Price

28. The Dionne Quintuplets, Gladys Knight, Carrol Baker

29. John F. Kennedy, Bob Hope, Anthony Geary

30. Mel Blanc, Benny Goodman, Keir Dullea

31. Joe Namath, Prince Rainier, Edward Williams, Gregory Harrison

3. Designate one day as Summer Birthday Day and celebrate the birthdays of all students whose birthdays fall during the summer vacation.

4. Could a group of students read the directions and learn to make homemade ice cream or frozen yogurt in class?

5. Compile an end of the year "Reverse Slam Book," in which every student in class writes something nice in every other person's book, so that each student has a pleasant remembrance of this year's classmates.

The May calendar can be used in many ways, as detailed in Chapter 1.

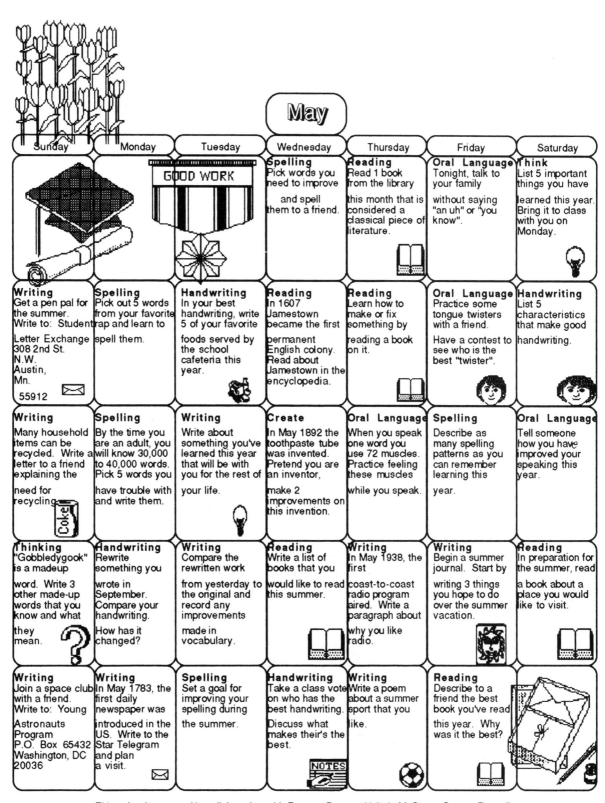

May

Sunday	Monday	Tuesday	Wednesday	Thursday	Friday	Saturday
	GOOD WORK		**Spelling** Pick words you need to improve and spell them to a friend.	**Reading** Read 1 book from the library this month that is considered a classical piece of literature.	**Oral Language** Tonight, talk to your family without saying "an uh" or "you know".	**Think** List 5 important things you have learned this year. Bring it to class with you on Monday.
Writing Get a pen pal for the summer. Write to: Student Letter Exchange 308 2nd St. N.W. Austin, Mn. 55912	**Spelling** Pick out 5 words from your favorite rap and learn to spell them.	**Handwriting** In your best handwriting, write 5 of your favorite foods served by the school cafeteria this year.	**Reading** In 1607 Jamestown became the first permanent English colony. Read about Jamestown in the encyclopedia.	**Reading** Learn how to make or fix something by reading a book on it.	**Oral Language** Practice some tongue twisters with a friend. Have a contest to see who is the best "twister".	**Handwriting** List 5 characteristics that make good handwriting.
Writing Many household items can be recycled. Write a letter to a friend explaining the need for recycling.	**Spelling** By the time you are an adult, you will know 30,000 to 40,000 words. Pick 5 words you have trouble with and write them.	**Writing** Write about something you've learned this year that will be with you for the rest of your life.	**Create** In May 1892 the toothpaste tube was invented. Pretend you are an inventor, make 2 improvements on this invention.	**Oral Language** When you speak one word you use 72 muscles. Practice feeling these muscles while you speak.	**Spelling** Describe as many spelling patterns as you can remember learning this year.	**Oral Language** Tell someone how you have improved your speaking this year.
Thinking "Gobbledygook" is a madeup word. Write 3 other made-up words that you know and what they mean.	**Handwriting** Rewrite something you wrote in September. Compare your handwriting. How has it changed?	**Writing** Compare the rewritten work from yesterday to the original and record any improvements made in vocabulary.	**Reading** Write a list of books that you would like to read this summer.	**Writing** In May 1938, the first coast-to-coast radio program aired. Write a paragraph about why you like radio.	**Writing** Begin a summer journal. Start by writing 3 things you hope to do over the summer vacation.	**Reading** In preparation for the summer, read a book about a place you would like to visit.
Writing Join a space club with a friend. Write to: Young Astronauts Program P.O. Box 65432 Washington, DC 20036	**Writing** In May 1783, the first daily newspaper was introduced in the US. Write to the Star Telegram and plan a visit.	**Spelling** Set a goal for improving your spelling during the summer.	**Handwriting** Take a class vote on who has the best handwriting. Discuss what makes their's the best.	**Writing** Write a poem about a summer sport that you like.	**Reading** Describe to a friend the best book you've read this year. Why was it the best?	

This calendar created in collaboration with Frances Dornan, Valarie McGarry, George Russell.

Handwriting Skill Development: Learning to Write with a Variety of Writing Utensils

PREREQUISITE

Gather scratch paper, pencils, erasers, poster board, a variety of writing materials (crayons, colored pencils, paint, felt tip pens, glitter, sequins, fabric, buttons, glue, scissors, magazines, pudding, shaving cream and whipped cream).

TIME REQUIRED

Teacher Directed Exploration (Activity 9-1): 20 minutes

Student Discovery Page (Activity 9-2): 25 minutes

TEACHING STRATEGIES

Students will learn through kinesthetic experiences.

ACTIVITY 9-1

CELEBRATING CINCO DE MAYO BY WRITING WITH MANY WRITING UTENSILS

[OBJECTIVE] YOU WILL LEARN TO BECOME MORE ADEPT AT WRITING WITH A WIDE VARIETY OF WRITING UTENSILS. YOU WILL KNOW YOU HAVE LEARNED WHEN YOUR WRITING IS AS CLEAR AS IF IT IT HAD BEEN WRITTEN WITH A PENCIL OR PEN.

It is important for other people to be able to read your handwriting if you want to convey your ideas through such things as posters, stories, or letters to family and friends—or even so others can read your name!

[Read the following information about Cinco de Mayo. Have students use all that they can remember from the story to make a pamphlet about the day, or use the story of Cinco de Mayo in other ways to meet your students' needs.]

Cinco de Mayo: Celebrating a Mexican Holiday

One of the great days in Mexican history is Cinco de Mayo, which is the Fifth of May. It is the anniversary of the 1862 battle of Puebla, when Mexican forces defeated French invaders. The victory was only a temporary setback for the French troops. It appealed to the imagination of the Mexicans, however, and gave them what they needed to eventually win in September.

May 5 is a national holiday in Mexico. It is celebrated by Mexicans all over the world. In the United States it is celebrated importantly in Texas, Arizona, and California.

In many places in Arizona, Mexican people have local celebrations each May 5. The most impressive are held in the twin border cities of Nogales, Arizona and Nogales, Sonora, Mexico. Here, at the 100th anniversary celebration, there were parades with bands, floats, and people marching from both cities. Every year this celebration goes on for several days. There are fireworks, the crowning and announcing of the Fiesta Queen, Indian dances, bull and cock fights, barbecues, balls, street dancing, and strolling mariachis.

San Diego and Los Angeles observe the holiday with orchestras and bands, banners and flags, speeches, and dances. In San Antonio, Texas, there are chicken barbecues, Mexican dances, and music at the city parks. On the morning of May 5 there are official flag-raising ceremonies. After flags have been raised, the important officials meet at Goliad, General Zaragoza's birthplace. General Zaragoza was a hero of the 1862 battle and was born in Goliad on March 24, 1829. His birthplace is now a state park.

If you have trouble forming any of your letters, you can refer to the handwriting chart posted at the front of the room.

[Students should collect necessary materials from the supply area and work independently on transferring their sketches to poster board or other materials. When they are finished with their projects, they should be turned in to be checked before they are distributed.]

[Some teachers enjoy having students use their fingers and practice forming letters on paper plates that are filled with pudding or whipped cream. If you decide to do so, buy ready-to-make pudding (non-cooked variety) or aerosol canned whipped cream. Approximately two tablespoons of pudding or whipped cream is placed in the center of each child's paper plate. Students spread their pudding/whipped cream and use their forefinger to write words. They enjoy licking their fingers after writing each word.]

[Approximately 10 to 15 minutes will be required for the children to clean up and put away the campaign materials and supplies. Shelf or cabinet space should be set aside for all posters, and other creations to keep them from becoming damaged while students are working on them. Boxes should also be supplied to keep all supplies organized and in one place.]

[Students practice using different types of writing materials and utensils during Activity 9-2. You may want to bring a can of shaving cream on a second day of handwriting practice. By covering student desks with shaving cream, students can use their fingers to practice writing sentences. A side benefit of using shaving cream is that when the practice session is over students remove the shaving cream with paper towels. When they rub their desks, students will notice that the shaving cream has removed dirt and pencil marks. Their desks will be cleaned in the process of the lesson!]

___

GRADING CRITERIA: _____

___

MODIFICATIONS FOR GRADE LEVELS AND STUDENT ABILITY LEVELS

These activities can be done on a smaller, less complicated scale for younger children. Instead of writing pamphlets beginning writers can write their names on thin strips of construction paper after practicing their handwriting with one of the other mediums described in this lesson.

STUDENTS WHO WILL BE WORKING ON OTHER PROJECTS OR LESSONS: _____

___

NOTES FOR FUTURE USE: _____

___

HANDWRITING IN THE MONTH OF MAY

A student may want to describe a story she/he read about the winter time within this design.

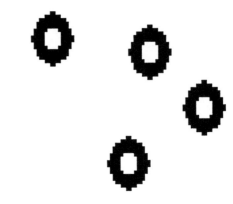

Within this seal a student can describe a story about animals.

Name ——————————

Author ——————————

This design can be used to write
a report for a book about magic.

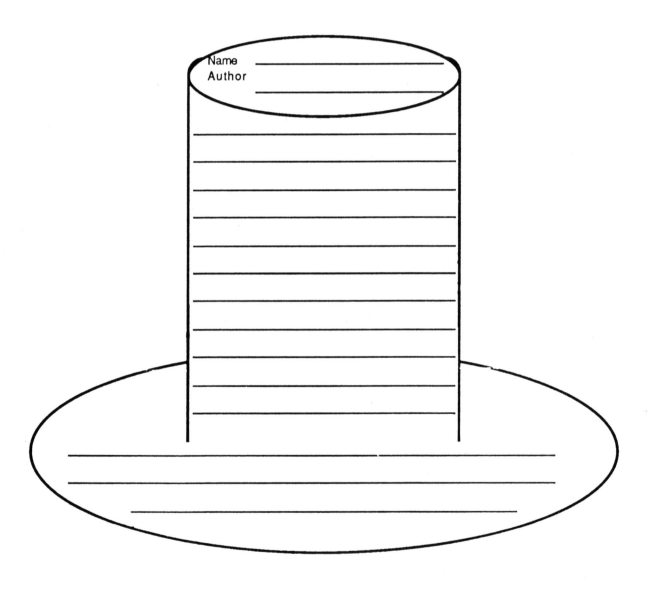

Name _____

Author
_____

This design may be used to tell about a story about a musician

Title: _____

Author: _____

Spelling Skill Development: Learning to Identify Compound Words and Word Parts*

TIME REQUIRED

Teacher Directed Exploration (Activity 9-3): 30 minutes

Student Discovery Page (Activity 9-4): 30 minutes

TEACHING STRATEGIES

Students will learn through creating their own words and dramatical re-enactments.

ACTIVITY 9-3 _____

CELEBRATING THE OSCARS WITH COMPOUND WORDS

[OBJECTIVE]   YOU WILL BECOME AWARE OF SMALLER, FAMILIAR WORD PARTS WITHIN WORDS AND TO USE COMPOUND WORDS TO IN-CREASE YOUR WORD POWER. YOU WILL KNOW YOU HAVE LEARNED WHEN YOU SCORE 80% OR BETTER ON THE TEST.

We are going to celebrate the anniversary of the first Oscars being given. The Academy of Arts and Science awarded the first Academy Awards on May 16, 1929. Another famous event occurred in that same week. On May 20th, Levi Strauss patented denim pants and the first blue jeans were made. Do you think blue jeans were first made in a year before the first Oscars were given, or in some year later than 1929? **[The class may be surprised when you tell them that blue jeans were invented in 1878!]**

You will be using these two events to learn a new spelling skill. We know that many actors wear blue jeans pants. If you wanted to remember how to spell "actor," you could look at the word and see that it has two smaller words in it: "act" and "or." You can spell the two smaller words and get the larger word correct. With any new words you study, look to see if there are words within a word that you already know how to spell. Spell these parts correctly, and you are able to spell larger words. Let's try again. What can help you remember to spell the word "pants" correctly? That's right—the word "ants."

[Distribute one of the words lists in Figure 9-1 as appropriate for the class level. Have the students identify the two words within each word on the list, perhaps by shading with two different colors. Give a test on selected words from the list. Hand out Activity 9-4a when finished.]

[Hand out Activity 9-4b. To make sure students cannot only identify but also use words within larger words, they will create words from suffixes, prefixes, and root words to increase their word power. In the first and second parts of Activity 9-4, students underline words within words to help them learn words from their spelling book and then use the words in a paragraph. Toy trophies or statuettes or miniature blue jeans can be given for "Best Word Creator in a Compound Role" and "Best Paragraph Writer" to the students who generate the most responses to each part. (An "Oscar" or a denim patch

*These activities were created by Monica Moore, a graduate student at Texas Christian University.

can also be given for the highest test score in Activity 9-3 and 9-4b, to commemorate the two occurrences that serve as the theme for this lesson.)]

_____

GRADING CRITERIA: _____

_____

MODIFICATIONS FOR GRADE LEVELS AND STUDENT ABILITY LEVELS

For Kindergarten through Third Grades, students work in groups and use more familiar words. For Fourth through Eighth Grades and Gifted Learners, individualize the lesson and choose more difficult compound words.

INDIVIDUAL STUDENT NEEDS: _____

_____

STUDENTS WHO WILL BE WORKING ON OTHER PROJECTS OR LESSONS: _____

_____

NOTES FOR FUTURE USE: _____

_____

FIGURE 9-1   Compound Word Lists

lookout			downstairs
nobody	storeroom	airplane	outside
wildlife	birthday	watermelon	grandmother
anything	overnight	greenhouse	bedroom
daytime	somebody	snowman	grownup
sunlight	steamship	broomstick	downtown
snowball	someday	cardboard	everyone
everybody	something	starfish	pancake
horseshoe	fisherman	milkman	playground
schoolyard	baseball	barnyard	campfire
Sunday	football	watchdog	anywhere
upstairs	basketball	chairman	footprint
eyesight	doorway	roadside	without
housewife	footsteps	postman	overcoat
homemade	lifetime	highway	playtime
someone	butterfly	strawberry	afternoon
waterfall	doghouse	anybody	goldfish
bedtime	doorbell	driveway	runaway
moonlight	flashlight	farmland	springtime
boxcar	salesman	birdhouse	overlook
mousetrap	houseboat	downfall	cannot
sidewalk	wintertime	sunflower	horseback
storybook	dishpan	workday	workshop
lighthouse	dishwasher	wintertime	evergreen
workman	newspaper	firewood	into
fireplace	beehive	policeman	bedroom
raindrop	earthquake	dollhouse	newspaper
shoemaker	weekend	sunburn	farmhouse

FIGURE 9-1 (Continued)

snowshoe	fishhook	policeman
snowman	seashore	footman
snowflake	seaport	watchman
snowfight	seashell	fisherman
snowstorm	seaplane	milkman
snowplow	oceanfront	doorman
icehouse	oceanside	chairman
doghouse	bedtime	typewriter
greenhouse	nighttime	whichever
playhouse	daytime	whenever
courthouse	anytime	notebook
birdhouse	rainbow	schoolbook
farmhouse	clockwise	pocketbook
lighthouse	counterclockwise	workbook
henhouse	baseball	cookbook
schoolhouse	basketball	textbook
schoolyard	football	bookmark
playground	neighborhood	bookworm
playpen	handwriting	bookcase
today	supermarket	bookkeeper
tonight	handbag	bookstore
into	filmstrip	storybook
something	cowboy	everything
sometimes	cowgirl	everyone
somewhere	pigsty	drugstore
somehow	sandbox	paperback
someone	hatbox	horseback
anybody	playmate	bareback
anything	teammate	nowhere
anyway	classmate	cupcake
anyhow	classroom	shortbread
anyplace	cannot	gingerbread
anywhere	tiptoe	grandfather
bedside	lunchroom	grandmother
butterfly	bedroom	sidewalk
battlefield	bathroom	inside
firearms	stoplight	outside
fireside	meanwhile	beside
sailboat	barnyard	mountainside
lifeboat	proofread	cornfield
mailman	firewood	armchair
fireman	sildworm	fireplace
spaceman	championship	blacksmith
sandman	worldwide	broomstick
bellhop	bathtub	rainstorm
motorboat	redcap	nightmare

AN OSCAR FOR BEST SPELLING OF COMPOUND WORDS

Choose words that you do not know how to spell in your spelling book and underline word parts that will aid you. Then write a paragraph using at least ten of these words.

antiwar
autobiography
rearm
international
microfilm
microchip
bicycle
triangle
unseal
underground
unicycle
telephone
centimeter
overdo
arms
happiness
civility
childlike
thankful
restless
teacher
fastest
happily
honestly
pressed
sized
tiring

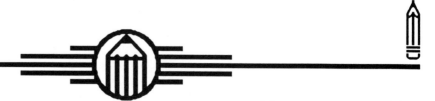

Reading Skill Development: Learning to Identify Elements of Classical Literature

TIME REQUIRED

Teacher Directed Exploration (Activity 9-5): 15 minutes

Student Discovery Page (Activity 9-6): 30 minutes

TEACHING STRATEGIES

Students learn through examples and by applying new information to familiar topics. Students also learn through self-selection.

ACTIVITY 9-5 _____

CELEBRATING MOTHER GOOSE DAY WITH CLASSICAL LITERATURE

[OBJECTIVE] YOU WILL LEARN TO RECOGNIZE THE ELEMENTS OF CLASSICAL LITERATURE SO YOU CAN INCREASE YOUR LITERARY AP-PRECIATION. YOU WILL KNOW YOU ARE SUCCESSFUL WHEN YOU BEGIN TO APPLY WHAT YOU HAVE LEARNED BY SELECTING MORE BOOKS TO READ AND BY APPRECIATING A WIDER VARIETY OF BOOKS.

Can you tell me why some book favorites are considered very important for many years? **[That is, you ask students to list reasons why a book or poem stands out. As students give reasons, list them on the overhead projector or chalkboard. After the list is complete, share with the class the following characteristics of classical literature. As you note each item, ask them either to tell you an example that illustrates that element or to tell you why the item would make a book more valuable. Students can suggest a book they have read that contained one of the following elements. You write that book in parenthesis after the element.]**

ELEMENTS OF CLASSICAL LITERATURE

1. Author has a writing style that is different from other writers.

2. Characters are so well described that they will never be forgotten by the reader. They seem as if they are alive and known by the reader.

3. Character(s) in the book is respected and teaches us how to be a better person.

4. Character(s) in the book introduces us to new feelings and helps us learn about new values, technology, and/or cultures.

5. The strength of the character is that the actions and thoughts recorded are timeless truths that give us insight into dilemmas that are hard to resolve alone.

6. The plan of the writing is well thought through. We can repeatedly analyze it from different perspectives and levels of specificity.

7. The author uses the rhythm of words and phrases to make a point.

8. The writing stimulates different levels of meanings for readers, such as giving vivid details so literal meaning is memorable; and, contains an implied meaning so we see the author's different meanings and purposes.

9. The writing is creative, creating a mood or emphasis. For example, in classical literature, authors often introduce new scenes and emotions by beginning in the middle of a series of events so the reader becomes curious and uses imagination.

10. Classics can bring new visions of the world to the reader's consciousness.

11. The writing unite sensual sensations and ideas so the reader remembers the ideas when similar situations occur in his or her life.

12. Authors of classical literature seem to create a momentum and slight chaos, so that readers can leave their own world and create a new arrangement, discover a new law, or reach a new interpretation of truth that they would not have been able to create alone.

13. Classical literature describes human emotions and events in such a way that they become universal, magnetic, and relevant for many generations.

14. Classical literature helps society more clearly identify its weaknesses.

[Once this list has been introduced, read aloud an excerpt from *The Wind in the Willows* or another piece of classical literature appropriate to the class level. In pairs or groups, the class identifies which of the above characteristics the selection contained. Each pair describes their choice of characteristics in paragraphs. Then, for second through fourth grade students, this large group sharing is followed with students writing a description of reasons why one of their favorite library books will or will not become a classic.]

[Older students can read selections from the Junior Great Books Series or watch a filmstrip of a classical literary work. They then answer the questions on Activity 9-6.]

GRADING CRITERIA: _____

MODIFICATIONS FOR GRADE LEVELS AND STUDENT ABILITY LEVELS

For Kindergarten through Third Grades and Slower Learning Groups, complete both activities orally as a large group. *For Fourth through Eighth Grades and Gifted/Most Able Learners,* students could extend this activity by writing a sequel to their favorite book to create a new piece of classical literature or by selecting a new book that they judge could become a classical piece of literature and tell why they judged as they did.

STUDENTS WHO WILL BE WORKING ON OTHER PROJECTS OR LESSONS: _____

NOTES FOR FUTURE USE: _____

CLASSICAL LITERATURE IS JUST MY STYLE

Directions: Answer in the space provided.

1. What elements of classical literature did you identify?

2. Why is it important to read books that have been read for generations?

3. Write three sentences that capture a memorable event or emotion from the literature. As you write, pretend you are the author of the work and try to write the sentences in the same way he or she might.

4. Tell what you changed about your writing style as you answered question 3. Why did you change it in that way?

5. What type of book that might be written in the year 1995 do you think will become a classic?

Listening Skill Development: Learning to Take Good Notes

TIME REQUIRED

Teacher Directed Exploration (Activity 9-7): 15 minutes

Student Discovery Page (Activity 9-8): 15–25 minutes

TEACHING STRATEGIES

Students will learn through practicing note-taking skills and receiving immediate feedback concerning objective to be learned.

ACTIVITY 9-7 _____

CELEBRATING MEMORIAL DAY AND BETTER HEARING MONTH

[OBJECTIVE] TODAY YOU WILL LEARN HOW TO TAKE GOOD NOTES WHILE LISTENING. YOU WILL KNOW YOU HAVE LEARNED WHEN YOUR NOTES ENABLE YOU TO REMEMBER FIVE SPECIFIC PIECES OF INFORMATION THAT YOU HEARD.

When you listen to information about something that is new to you, you need to take notes to help you remember it. Good notetaking has three parts. You use shortcuts, you indent less important ideas, and you only write key words.

Let me show you what I mean. **[Show Figure 9-2 on the overhead projector. Read the passage aloud and discuss the notes they could take on the material.]**

[Distribute Activity 9-8. Read aloud the passage in Figure 9-3 and ask the class to take notes. Then have them answer the following questions using their notes. Discuss personal symbols and abbreviations for a few minutes first, so that they are relying on their notes, not on short-term memory.]

1. What state observes Memorial Day on April 26?
2. Is Memorial Day a legal holiday in all states?
3. Flags are at half mast until what time?
4. Where is the Tomb of the Unknown Soldiers in Arlington Cemetery located?
5. What is the last ceremony conducted on Memorial Day?
6. What is the last Monday in May called in Virginia?

_____

ANSWER KEY

1. Georgia
2. No
3. Noon

4. Virginia

5. Placing a wreath at the Tomb of the Unknown Soldier

6. Confederate Memorial Day

GRADING CRITERIA: _____

_____

MODIFICATIONS FOR GRADE LEVELS AND STUDENT ABILITY LEVELS

For Kindergarten through Third Grades and Slower Learning Groups, a notetaking activity should not be used. Read the Figure 9-3 passage aloud, asking them to use all the listening skills they've learned. Ask the questions immediately after reading. Tell the students if they get five of the six correct, they have learned how to be good listeners this year. _For Fourth through Eighth Grades and Gifted/Most Able Learners,_ the activity can be expanded. Spend 2 days for gifted learners. On the first day they create personal symbols and think of additional notetaking aids. They share these with the rest of the class on the second day.

STUDENTS WHO WILL BE WORKING ON OTHER PROJECTS OR LESSONS: _____

_____

NOTES FOR FUTURE USE: _____

_____

FIGURE 9-2   Memorial Day Passage for Activity 9-7

Memorial Day is a very special day in America. It is a day to honor Americans who gave their lives for their country. The soldiers who died in the Spanish-American War, World Wars I and II, the Korean War, the Vietnam War, and Persian Gulf War are honored on this day. Memorial Day is sometimes called Decoration Day.

On Memorial Day flowers and flags are placed on the graves of soldiers. In order to honor those who died at sea, some U.S. ports arrange ceremonies in which tiny ships filled with flowers are set afloat on the water. Boy Scouts, Girl Scouts, and fraternal groups march in military parades. Soldiers march and take part in special programs.

The people of Waterloo, New York, first observed Memorial Day on May 5, 1866, to honor soldiers who had died in the Civil War. Major General John A. Logan served as Commander in the Republic. His units were in charge of Memorial Day celebrations in the northern states for many years. The American Legion took over the duty after World War I.

FIGURE 9-3 Memorial Day Passage for Activity 9-8

After World War I, Congress voted to have a national holiday. This holiday was to honor every American who served in a war. This holiday was to pay special tribute to those who died in a war. This holiday, called Memorial Day, also pays homage to relatives and friends of those who lost their lives.

Every Memorial Day flags are flown at half mast until noon. Beginning in 1971, Memorial Day was changed from May 5 to become the last Monday in May each year. One of the most important ceremonies of this day is the placing of a wreath on the Tomb of the Unknown Soldier. This ceremony is held at Arlington National Cemetery in Washington, D.C., our nation's capitol.

A few states in the southeastern section of the country also hold a Confederate Memorial Day. Confederate Memorial Day honors all men who fought in the Civil War. This holiday is held on April 26 in Georgia and the last Monday in April in Alabama and Mississippi. In Virginia they combine Confederate Memorial Day with Memorial Day and celebrate both on the last Monday in May. South Carolina, Virginia, Florida, Louisiana, Tennessee, West Virginia, and Kentucky do not celebrate Confederate Memorial Day.

ACTIVITY 9-8

TAKING NOTES ON NEW INFORMATION

MY NOTES ON MEMORIAL DAY

Answers to questions:

1. _____

2. _____

3. _____

4. _____

5. _____

6. _____

Grammar Skill Development: Learning to Use Colons, Periods, and Apostrophes

TIME REQUIRED

Teacher Directed Exploration (Activity 9-9): 20 minutes

Student Discovery Page (Activity 9-10): 20 minutes

TEACHING STRATEGIES

Students will learn by seeing nonexamples and correcting them.

ACTIVITY 9-9 _____

USING CORRECT PUNCTUATION IN A MOTHER'S DAY MESSAGE

[OBJECTIVE] TODAY YOU WILL LEARN TO USE COLONS, PERIODS, AND APOSTROPHES. YOU WILL KNOW YOU HAVE LEARNED IF YOU COMPLETE ACTIVITY 9-10 WITHOUT ANY ERRORS.

You are going to learn uses for three punctuation marks. If you can use the marks correctly, you will be able to send a special message correctly written to your mother or someone special in celebration of Mother's Day.

[Give older students a review of all the following rules; for younger students review only two or three.]

There are three uses of the period.

1. At the end of a sentence—The books are here.

2. After abbreviations in titles—Dr. James

3. After initials in proper names—J. J. Hill

The question mark is used:

1. At the end of a direct question—Is this your balloon?

2. After a direct question within a sentence—"Will you be ready?" the man asked.

[The first use of a question mark can be understood and used by beginners in the first grade. The second should not be presented until late in the third grade. This form is less difficult: He asked, "Will you be ready?"]

[For older students, go on to present the following information.] Have you ever wondered how punctuation marks came to be? In Chinese writing there is no punctuation, and as recently as 1945 no punctuation was used in the Korean language either. However, when the Koreans decided to write horizontally rather than vertically, they recognized the need for such marks.

The ancient Greeks and Romans frequently wrote without separating their words, let alone separating sentences, with punctuation. It was orators who made the first separations, in order to emphasize the thoughts they were expressing. Originally punctuation was based on how the words would be spoken aloud: semicolon for a two-unit pause, a colon for a three-unit pause, and a period for a four-unit pause. The question mark was a sign to raise the voice at the end of a word. The explanation point was a little dagger drawn to resemble the real dagger used to post important notices to buildings.

It is thought that human beings learned to talk about a million years ago. Alphabetic writing has been used for several hundred years, but punctuation in the modern sense came into use in our language less than 300 years ago, and the system is far from perfect. In English as it stands, punctuation marks are used as follows:

1. For linking, use:

> ; semicolon
> : colon
> —linking dash
> - linking hyphen

2. For separating, use:

> . period
> ? question mark
> ! exclamation mark
> , separating comma

3. For enclosing, use:

> , . . . , paired commas
> - - . . . - - paired dashes
> (. . .) paired brackets
> ". . ." paired quotation marks

4. For indicating omission, use:

> ' apostrophe
> . omission period in abbreviations (or dot)
> - omission dash
> . . . triple periods (or dot)

It is easy to remember how to use the colon because it is used only in three ways:

1. After the greeting in a business letter—Dear Sir:

2. Before a long series—Mother bought the following: oranges, lemons, bread, jam, and cake.

3. To separate the hour from the minutes—2:30 A.M.

The apostrophe receives a great deal of attention in spelling. It is used in four ways.

1. With the letter "s" to show possession—Mary's coat, boy's coats

2. To show where letters have been omitted—don't (do not), o'er (over)

3. To show the omission of numbers from a date—Class of '84.

4. As quotation marks with a quotation—"Is your 'Super Dooper Special' still in progress?" he asked.

[Present the paragraph in Figure 9-4, either as individual copies or on the chalkboard or overhead projector. Have the students fill in the missing punctuation marks.]

[Hand out Activity 9-10.] On this activity sheet you will write a Mother's Day message for someone special. You can tell what you have learned about Mother's Day, if you want, or tell why that person is special to you. Try to use many of the punctuation marks we have talked about. After you finish writing your message, read it out loud to yourself as a way to check where pauses and punctuation might be needed. Then exchange papers with someone and help each other by proofreading each other's message.

GRADING CRITERIA: _____

_____

EARLY FINISHERS

Those who finish early (or gifted learners) can have a contest to see who can find the most examples of different types of punctuation marks as they read the next section in one of their textbooks. As they read, they are to number their paper, list the type of punctuation they found, and then tell the purpose the punctuation mark serves. The person with the most correct wins.

MODIFICATIONS FOR GRADE LEVELS AND STUDENT ABILITY LEVELS

For Kindergarten through Third Grades, proofread messages that could be carefully rewritten to be given as gifts. *For Fourth through Eighth Grades and Gifted/Most Able Learners,* gifted students could be introduced to the uses of the semicolon.

Victor Borge's audible punctuation system can add liveliness to your discussion and help the students remember how punctuation marks are used. Play a record or videotape of this comic's discourse, or demonstrate the system yourself, using a short story with a wide variety of punctuation. The students will enjoy the silly noises (especially the "plop" of the period). Let them use audible punctuation in proofreading their Activity 9-10 message.

INDIVIDUAL STUDENT NEEDS: _____

_____

STUDENTS WHO WILL BE WORKING ON OTHER PROJECTS OR
LESSONS: _____

_____

NOTES FOR FUTURE USE: _____

_____

PUNCTUATING A MOTHER'S DAY MESSAGE

MY MOTHER'S DAY MESSAGE

Do all my sentences end with a period or a question mark?

Proofread by _____

FIGURE 9-4   Filling in Punctuation

Mother s Day as we know it was first celebrated on May 10 1908 Anna M Jarviss initiated this day of remembrance in honor of her own mother and because she felt adult children were not attentive to their mothers in general The idea caught on and on May 7 1914 a federal resolution was adopted that made the second Sunday in May officially Mother s Day

Creative Writing Skill Development: Learning How to Describe

TIME REQUIRED

Teacher Directed Exploration (Activity 9-11): 15 minutes

Student Discovery Page (Activity 9-12): 30 minutes

TEACHING STRATEGIES

Students will learn from teacher modeling.

ACTIVITY 9-11

CELEBRATING TEACHER APPRECIATION DAY WITH GOOD DESCRIPTIONS

[OBJECTIVE]   YOU WILL IMPROVE YOUR WRITING BY LEARNING TO MAKE MORE VIVID DESCRIPTIONS. YOU WILL KNOW YOU HAVE IMPROVED YOUR WRITING ABILITY WHEN YOU CORRECTLY USE ONE OF THE DESCRIPTIVE METHODS IN YOUR WRITING TODAY AND IN THE FUTURE.

Writing is one way people can relate their ideas, experiences, and feelings to others. We want to be good writers so that others will understand our thinking. This week is Teacher Appreciation Week. We will learn how to write better descriptions by writing about things teachers or others have done that meant a lot to you.

I want you to learn to describe things by (1) writing examples of what you are describing, (2) telling about things that are *not examples* of what you are describing, (3) making comparisons to nature or life that illustrate your description, and **[fourth option for older students only]** (4) drawing analogies to something that has similar characteristics to what you are describing.

[Present Figure 9-5 on an overhead projector or as individual copies.]

[Hand out Activity 9-12. Have students describe the eight concepts using one of the techniques discussed and then write a descriptive paragraph on page 341.]

GRADING CRITERIA: _____

MODIFICATIONS FOR GRADE LEVELS AND STUDENT ABILITY LEVELS

For Younger Children, it may be necessary to write some short stories together on the chalkboard or chart paper, underlining the descriptions. This can be followed by another lesson having them draw pictures of a favorite pet and then dictating descriptors to go underneath. *For Older Students,* longer, more detailed stories can be written, following guidelines you set. Poems could also be written following the same format (see "Mice" by Rose Fyleman or "Mr. Rabbit" by Dixie Wilson).

STUDENTS WHO WILL BE WORKING ON OTHER PROJECTS OR LESSONS: _____

_____

NOTES FOR FUTURE USE: _____

_____

FIGURE 9-5   Four Ways to Describe

1.   EXAMPLE

I like a teacher who gives good
instructions before we work. <u>My
teacher works a sample and tells us
how she thinks to arrive at the
correct answer.</u>

2.   NONEXAMPLE

My teacher lets me know how much I'm
learning. She doesn't <u>keep our
papers for a long time without
grading them.</u>

3.   COMPARISON TO NATURE OR LIFE

My teacher is <u>like sunshine to me.
Her smile makes me feel wanted and
happy.</u>

4.   ANALOGY TO SOMETHING THAT HAS
SIMILAR CHARACTERISTICS

Whenever I do good work I feel like
a colt who has just learned to walk.
<u>My teacher is standing close by, and
watching me.</u>

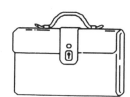

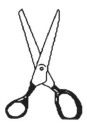

ACTIVITY 9-12

NATIONAL TEACHER APPRECIATION DAY:
LEARNING TO WRITE GOOD DESCRIPTIONS

Use one of the ways we studied to describe each balloon

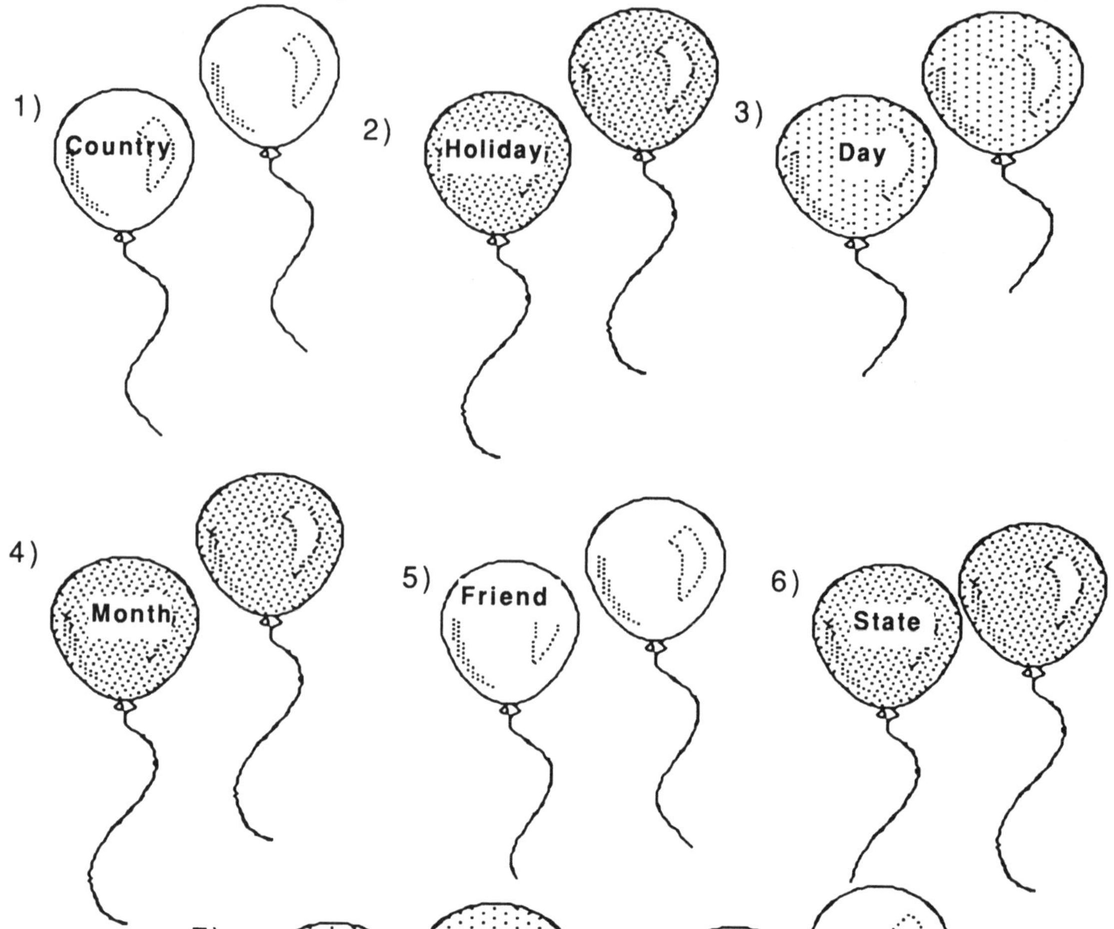

1) Country

2) Holiday

3) Day

4) Month

5) Friend

6) State

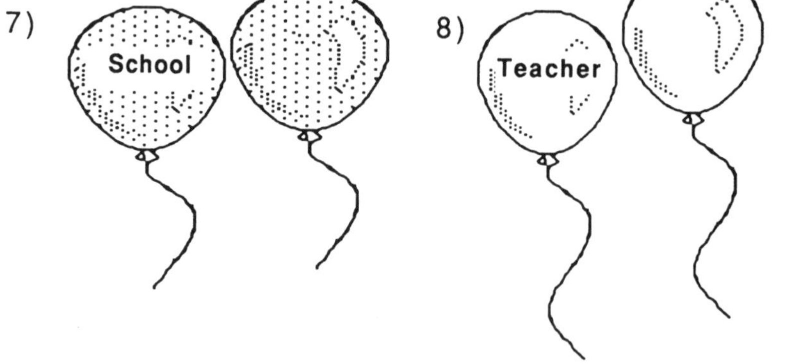

7) School

8) Teacher

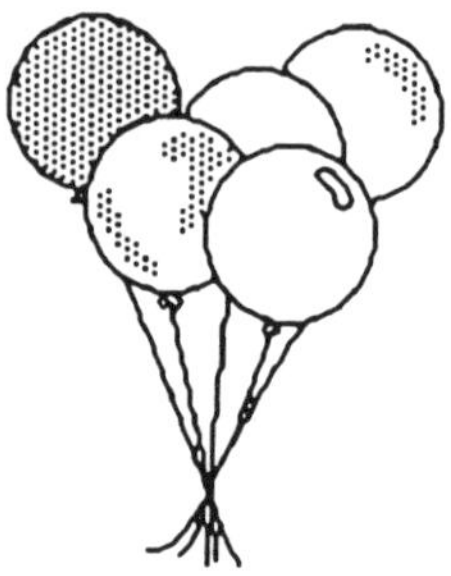

National Teacher Day:
A Description of My Teacher

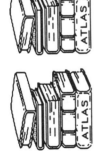

Oral Language Skill Development: Learning to Avoid Redundancy

TIME REQUIRED

Teacher Directed Exploration (Activity 9-13): 10 minutes

Student Discovery Page (Activity 9-14): 20 minutes

TEACHING STRATEGIES

Students hear their improved speaking abilities through comparisons of taped pre- and postinstruction presentations.

ACTIVITY 9-13 _____

CELEBRATING NATIONAL FITNESS MONTH WITH BETTER SPEAKING

[OBJECTIVE]   YOU WILL IMPROVE YOUR ORAL SPEAKING ABILITIES AND LEARN TO EXPRESS YOURSELF BETTER IN CONVERSATIONS BY LEARNING TO REMOVE REDUNDANCIES. YOU WILL KNOW YOU ARE SUCCESSFUL WHEN YOU EITHER HEAR A COMPARISON OF AUDIO TAPES THAT DEMONSTRATES IMPROVEMENTS OR YOU RECEIVE AN IMPROVEMENT SCORE.

May is the month set aside to celebrate National Physical Fitness and Sports. Many events have occurred in May that demonstrate the effects and importance of being physically fit.

- Roger Bannister became the first athelete to run the mile in less than 4 minutes in 1954.

- The Kentucky Derby is held.

- The first major league night baseball game was played at Cincinnati, Ohio in 1935.

- Jesse Owens made sports history in 1935.

- Olympic champion Jim Thorpe was born in 1888.

- The Indianapolis 500 Race is held.

- Sir Edmund Hillary and Tenzing Norkay reached the summit of Mt. Everest in 1953.

Just as athletes must learn skills and practice, you must learn skills and practice to become a good speaker. Today we are going to learn to speak better and to become more interesting to listen to because we will learn how to speak without repeating points. The way we are going to do it is to combine short sentences into longer, more specific and detailed ones. For example, I could say "The girl was happy. The girl was laughing," or I could remove the repeated words and say the same thing in a more interesting way: "The laughing girl was happy."

Before class is over you will write ten sentences. Then you will remove the extra words and rearrange your thoughts so that you can develop the habit of not repeating yourself.

[Present Figure 9-6 on an overhead projector or as individual copies.] To practice, I am giving you four sets of sentences that relate to May's special Physical Fitness theme. What I want you to do is to write the sets of sentences without repeating words and by rearranging the order in which they appear. You can end up with one, two, or three sentences. **[For younger students you can consolidate the sentences as a whole-class activity, and the class can practice the speech described at the bottom of the activity in pairs, with you, one on one, or in small groups.]**

[Hand out Activity 9-14.]

GRADING CRITERIA

Either (audio) tape each student's speaking ability before and after instruction and allow the student to hear the improvements, or give each student an improvement score based on a speaking sample you grade following this lesson.

MODIFICATIONS FOR GRADE LEVELS AND STUDENT ABILITY LEVELS

For Kindergarten through Third Grades and Slower Learning Groups, do the lessons as large-group activities. *For Fourth through Eighth Grades and Gifted/Most Able Learners,* allow them to practice Activity 9-14 twice using different topics.

STUDENTS WHO WILL BE WORKING ON OTHER PROJECTS OR LESSONS: _____

NOTES FOR FUTURE USE: _____

Activity 9-14

Healthy! Exciting! Educational!

Enjoyable! Friendly! Great!

<u>Physical Fitness Is Important As Is Speaking Without Repeating Myself</u>

Name ———————————— Date ————————————

Directions: Make the following sets of sentences more interesting by omitting words and reordering as shown in the first example.

Example:

    The boys are running. The boys are fast.

Changed to:

    The boys are running fast.

    1. I got a new bike.
      The bike is shiny and red.
       The bike is a ten-speed bike.
      I got the bike for my tenth birthday.
      I will ride the bike every day.

    2. The girls are going to camp.
      The camp is a physical fitness camp.
      The girls are Girl Scouts.
      The camp is in the mountains.
      The camp is one of the best in America.

    3. It is good exercise to plant flowers and vegetables.
      I like to grow things and I am going to make a garden.
      I like the tomatoes and green pepper plants best.
      I grow peanuts and onions also.

    4. It was the first game of the season.
      The White Sox were playing the Rangers.
      The White Sox were playing the Rangers in Chicago.
      The Rangers won the game.
      After the games, we played baseball.

On the next page, write ten topics or sentences you will use on your posttest of speaking ability. Use what you have learned to remove all repetition to make your speech interesting.

Fun!

!nuƒ

ACTIVITY 9-14

SHAPING UP SPEAKING ABILITIES

Write ten related sentences to use on your posttest of speaking ability. Use what you have learned to remove repetition, and to make your speech interesting.

Healthy! Exciting! Educational!

Enjoyable! friendly! Great!

fun!

fun!

Form to Aid in Planning

The long-term planning form can be used as you begin to map out activities for teaching language arts concepts in the coming school year.

LONG TERM PLANNING

SEPT.	OCT.
NOV.	DEC.
JAN.	FEB.
MAR.	APRIL
MAY	JUNE

CHAPTER
10 *Summer Months*

This chapter includes birthday lists and activity calendars for June, July, and August. The birthday lists can be used during the school year by students with summer birthdays who want to find out about notable people with whom they share a birth date. The calendars can be sent home with students at the end of the school year to encourage them to continue exploration and practice in language arts skills. The calendars and birthday lists can also be used in a summer school or year-round classroom, in the ways described in previous chapters.

June Birthdays

1. Pat Boone, Andy Griffith, Molly Picon
2. Stacy Keach, Charles Haid
3. Tony Curtis, Allen Ginsberg
4. Gene Barry, Robert Merrill
5. Bill Moyers, Robert Lansing
6. Bjorn Borg, George Denkmejian
7. Prince, Peter Orodino
8. Emmanuel Ax
9. Michael J. Fox
10. F. Lee Bailey, Maurice Sendak, Prince Phillip
11. Joe Montana, Gene Wilder
12. Peter Hayes, Jim Nabors
13. Ralph Edwards, Ben Johnson
14. Marla Gibbs, Burl Ives, Dorothy McGuire
15. Morris Udall
16. Billy "Crash" Craddock, Roberto Duran
17. Barry Manilow, Joe Piscopo
18. Paul McCartney

19. Mildred Natwick, Alan Cranston

20. Cyndi Lauper, Anne Murray

21. Micheal Gross, Meredith Baxter

22. Joseph Papp, Bill Blass

23. James Levine, Bob Fosse

24. Phil Harris, Al Molinaro

25. June Lockhart

26. Eleanor Parker

27. John McIntire

28. Mel Brooks, John Elway

29. Rafael Kubelik

30. Lena Horne, Tony Musante

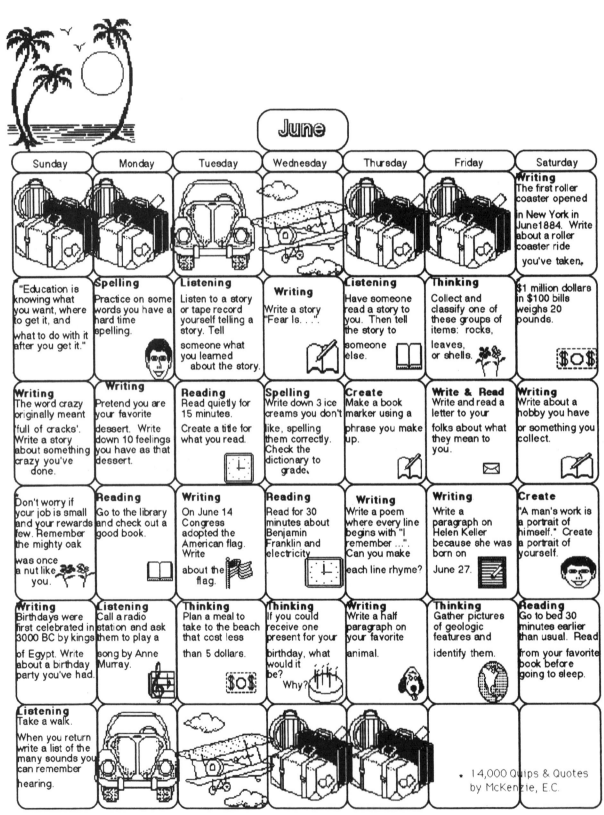

June

Sunday	Monday	Tuesday	Wednesday	Thursday	Friday	Saturday
						Writing The first roller coaster opened in New York in June 1884. Write about a roller coaster ride you've taken.
"Education is knowing what you want, where to get it, and what to do with it after you get it."	**Spelling** Practice on some words you have a hard time spelling.	**Listening** Listen to a story or tape record yourself telling a story. Tell someone what you learned about the story.	**Writing** Write a story "Fear Is. . . .".	**Listening** Have someone read a story to you. Then tell the story to someone else.	**Thinking** Collect and classify one of these groups of items: rocks, leaves, or shells.	$1 million dollars in $100 bills weighs 20 pounds.
Writing The word crazy originally meant 'full of cracks'. Write a story about something crazy you've done.	**Writing** Pretend you are your favorite dessert. Write down 10 feelings you have as that dessert.	**Reading** Read quietly for 15 minutes. Create a title for what you read.	**Spelling** Write down 3 ice creams you don't like, spelling them correctly. Check the dictionary to grade.	**Create** Make a book marker using a phrase you make up.	**Write & Read** Write and read a letter to your folks about what they mean to you.	**Writing** Write about a hobby you have or something you collect.
Don't worry if your job is small and your rewards few. Remember the mighty oak was once a nut like you.	**Reading** Go to the library and check out a good book.	**Writing** On June 14 Congress adopted the American flag. Write about the flag.	**Reading** Read for 30 minutes about Benjamin Franklin and electricity.	**Writing** Write a poem where every line begins with "I remember ...". Can you make each line rhyme?	**Writing** Write a paragraph on Helen Keller because she was born on June 27.	**Create** "A man's work is a portrait of himself." Create a portrait of yourself.
Writing Birthdays were first celebrated in 3000 BC by kings of Egypt. Write about a birthday party you've had.	**Listening** Call a radio station and ask them to play a song by Anne Murray.	**Thinking** Plan a meal to take to the beach that cost less than 5 dollars.	**Thinking** If you could receive one present for your birthday, what would it be? Why?	**Writing** Write a half paragraph on your favorite animal.	**Thinking** Gather pictures of geologic features and identify them.	**Reading** Go to bed 30 minutes earlier than usual. Read from your favorite book before going to sleep.
Listening Take a walk. When you return write a list of the many sounds you can remember hearing.					• 14,000 Quips & Quotes by McKenzie, E.C.	

This calendar created in collaboration with Frances Dornan, Valarie McGarry, George Russell.

July Birthdays

1. Mary Calderon, Dan Aykroyd
2. Ken Curtis, Polly Holliday
3. Ken Russell
4. Virginia Graham, Gina Lollobrigida
5. Huey Lewis, James Lofton
6. Fred Dryer, Nancy Reagan, Della Reese
7. Roz Ryan, Shelly Duval, Ralph Lee Sampson
8. Cynthia Gregory, Kim Darby
9. Ed Amos, Tom Hanks, O.J. Simpson
10. Ron Glass, William Brock
11. Gene Evans, Nicolai Gedda
12. Mark Hatfield, Richard Simmons
13. Harrison Ford
14. Gerald R. Ford, Missy Gold
15. Ken Kercheval, Alex Karras
16. Barnard Hughes, Ginger Rogers, Stewart Copeland
17. Art Linkletter, Phyllis Diller
18. John Glenn, Harriet H. Nelson
19. Pat Hingle, Roosevelt "Rosey" Grier, Vikki Carr
20. Sally A. Howes, Diana Rigg
21. Edward Hermann, Don Knotts
22. William Schallert, Don Henley, Bobby Sherman
23. Gloria de Havilland, Robert Hayes
24. Chris Sarandon, William Ruckelshaus
25. Jack Gilford, Barbara Harris
26. Jason Robards, Mick Jagger
27. Maureen McGovern, Bobbie Gentry
28. Jacqueline Onassis, Ricardo Multi
29. Elizabeth Dole, Robert Horton
30. Ken Olin, Paul Anka
31. Curt Gowdy, Don Murray

July

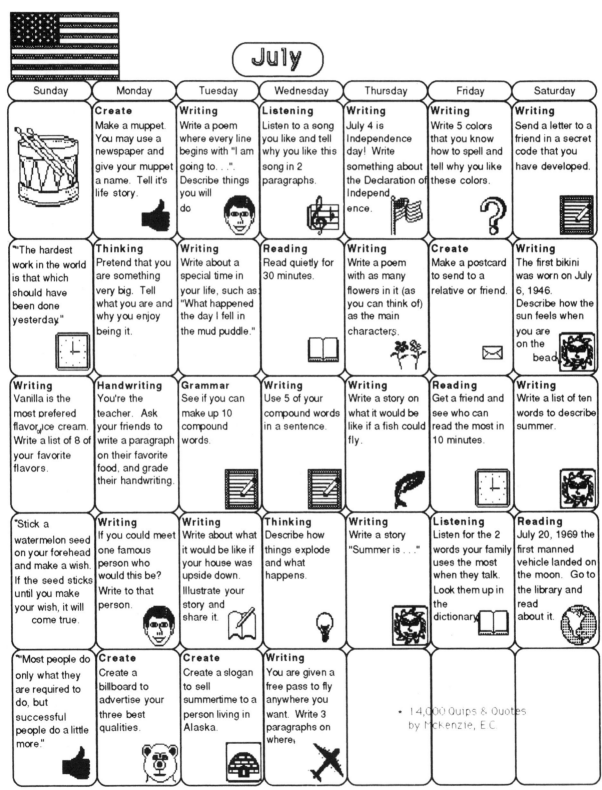

Sunday	Monday	Tuesday	Wednesday	Thursday	Friday	Saturday
	Create Make a muppet. You may use a newspaper and give your muppet a name. Tell it's life story.	**Writing** Write a poem where every line begins with "I am going to. . .". Describe things you will do	**Listening** Listen to a song you like and tell why you like this song in 2 paragraphs.	**Writing** July 4 is Independence day! Write something about the Declaration of Independence.	**Writing** Write 5 colors that you know how to spell and tell why you like these colors.	**Writing** Send a letter to a friend in a secret code that you have developed.
"The hardest work in the world is that which should have been done yesterday."	**Thinking** Pretend that you are something very big. Tell what you are and why you enjoy being it.	**Writing** Write about a special time in your life, such as "What happened the day I fell in the mud puddle."	**Reading** Read quietly for 30 minutes.	**Writing** Write a poem with as many flowers in it (as you can think of) as the main characters.	**Create** Make a postcard to send to a relative or friend.	**Writing** The first bikini was worn on July 6, 1946. Describe how the sun feels when you are on the beach.
Writing Vanilla is the most prefered flavor of ice cream. Write a list of 8 of your favorite flavors.	**Handwriting** You're the teacher. Ask your friends to write a paragraph on their favorite food, and grade their handwriting.	**Grammar** See if you can make up 10 compound words.	**Writing** Use 5 of your compound words in a sentence.	**Writing** Write a story on what it would be like if a fish could fly.	**Reading** Get a friend and see who can read the most in 10 minutes.	**Writing** Write a list of ten words to describe summer.
"Stick a watermelon seed on your forehead and make a wish. If the seed sticks until you make your wish, it will come true.	**Writing** If you could meet one famous person who would this be? Write to that person.	**Writing** Write about what it would be like if your house was upside down. Illustrate your story and share it.	**Thinking** Describe how things explode and what happens.	**Writing** Write a story "Summer is . . ."	**Listening** Listen for the 2 words your family uses the most when they talk. Look them up in the dictionary	**Reading** July 20, 1969 the first manned vehicle landed on the moon. Go to the library and read about it.
"Most people do only what they are required to do, but successful people do a little more."	**Create** Create a billboard to advertise your three best qualities.	**Create** Create a slogan to sell summertime to a person living in Alaska.	**Writing** You are given a free pass to fly anywhere you want. Write 3 paragraphs on where	* 14,000 Quips & Quotes by McKenzie, E.C.		

This calendar created in collaboration with Frances Dornan, Valerie McGarry, George Russell.

August Birthdays

1. Dom DeLuise, Giancarlo Giannini
2. Paul Laxalt, Gary Merrill
3. Tony Bennett, Martin Sheen
4. Helen Thomas, Roger Clemens, Queen Elizabeth
5. John Huston, Neil Alden Armstrong, Patrick Ewing
6. Robert Mitchum, Lucille Ball
7. Garrison Keillor, Loni Anderson
8. Esther Williams, Dustin Hoffman, Mel Tills
9. Richard Anderson, Sam Elliott
10. Rhonda Fleming, Jimmy Dean
11. Arlene Dahl, Alegra Kent
12. John Derek, George Hamilton
13. Pat Harrington, Jr., Dan Fogelberg
14. Buddy Greco, Susan St. James, Neal Anderson
15. Jim Dale, Signe Hasso
16. Eydie Gorme, Anita Gilette, Frank Gifford, Madonna
17. Robert DeNiro, Maureen O'Hara, Sean Penn
18. Roman Polanski, Rosalyn Carter, Patrick Swayze, Malcolm Jamal Warner
19. Gerald McRaney, Jill St. John
20. Isaac Hayes, Henry Cisneros, Connie Chung
21. Kenny Rogers, Jim McMahon, Wilton Chamberlain
22. Kathy Lennon, Valerie Harper, Cindy Williams
23. Barbara Eden, Gene Kelly, Shelly Long
24. Durward Kirby, Gerry Cooney, Steve Guttenberg
25. Mel Ferrer, Don Defore, Sean Connery
26. Geraldine Ferraro, Ronny Graham
27. Martha Raye, Helen Walter
28. Peggy Ryan, Emma Samms, David Soul
29. George Montgomery, Richard Attenborough, Michael Jackson
30. Regina Resnik, Timothy Bottoms
31. Warren Berlinger, Buddy Hackett, Debbie Gibson

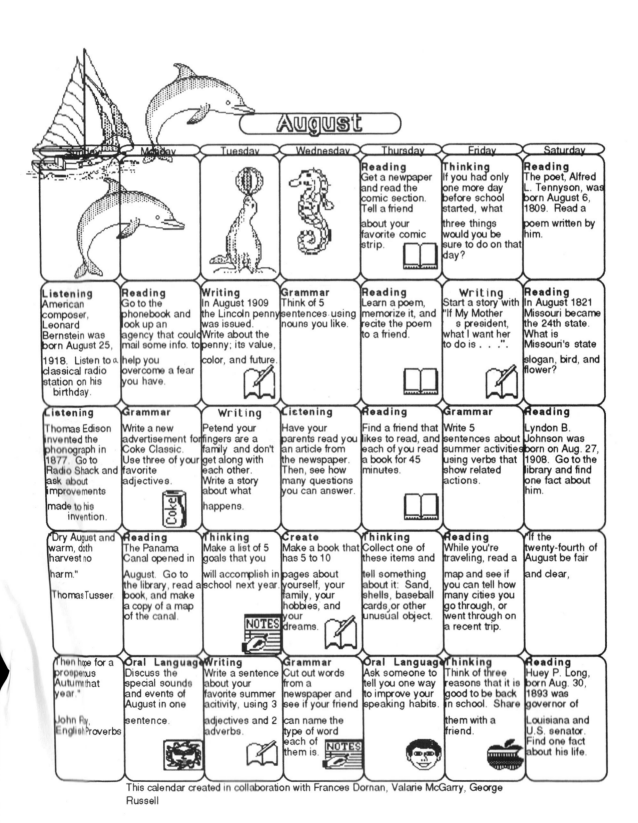

August

Sunday	Monday	Tuesday	Wednesday	Thursday	Friday	Saturday
				Reading Get a newpaper and read the comic section. Tell a friend about your favorite comic strip.	**Thinking** If you had only one more day before school started, what three things would you be sure to do on that day?	**Reading** The poet, Alfred L. Tennyson, was born August 6, 1809. Read a poem written by him.
Listening American composer, Leonard Bernstein was born August 25, 1918. Listen to a classical radio station on his birthday.	**Reading** Go to the phonebook and look up an agency that could mail some info. to help you overcome a fear you have.	**Writing** In August 1909 the Lincoln penny was issued. Write about the penny; its value, color, and future.	**Grammar** Think of 5 sentences using nouns you like.	**Reading** Learn a poem, memorize it, and recite the poem to a friend.	**Writing** Start a story with "If My Mother s president, what I want her to do is . . .".	**Reading** In August 1821 Missouri became the 24th state. What is Missouri's state slogan, bird, and flower?
Listening Thomas Edison invented the phonograph in 1877. Go to Radio Shack and ask about improvements made to his invention.	**Grammar** Write a new advertisement for Coke Classic. Use three of your favorite adjectives.	**Writing** Petend your fingers are a family and don't get along with each other. Write a story about what happens.	**Listening** Have your parents read you an article from the newspaper. Then, see how many questions you can answer.	**Reading** Find a friend that likes to read, and each of you read a book for 45 minutes.	**Grammar** Write 5 sentences about summer activities using verbs that show related actions.	**Reading** Lyndon B. Johnson was born on Aug. 27, 1908. Go to the library and find one fact about him.
"Dry August and warm, doth harvest no harm." Thomas Tusser	**Reading** The Panama Canal opened in August. Go to the library, read a book, and make a copy of a map of the canal.	**Thinking** Make a list of 5 goals that you will accomplish in school next year.	**Create** Make a book that has 5 to 10 pages about yourself, your family, your hobbies, and your dreams.	**Thinking** Collect one of these items and tell something about it: Sand, shells, baseball cards, or other unusual object.	**Reading** While you're traveling, read a map and see if you can tell how many cities you go through, or went through on a recent trip.	"If the twenty-fourth of August be fair and clear,
"Then hope for a prosperous Autumn that year." John Ray, English Proverbs	**Oral Language** Discuss the special sounds and events of August in one sentence.	**Writing** Write a sentence about your favorite summer acitivity, using 3 adjectives and 2 adverbs.	**Grammar** Cut out words from a newspaper and see if your friend can name the type of word each of them is.	**Oral Language** Ask someone to tell you one way to improve your speaking habits.	**Thinking** Think of three reasons that it is good to be back in school. Share them with a friend.	**Reading** Huey P. Long, born Aug. 30, 1893 was governor of Louisiana and U.S. senator. Find one fact about his life.

This calendar created in collaboration with Frances Dornan, Valarie McGarry, George Russell

REACTION FORM

NAME:

SCHOOL/ORGANIZATION:

ADDRESS:

1. How would you change the format of this book?

2. How would you change the content of this book?

3. How could we make this book easier for you to use and more effective?

4. What did you like most about this book?

5. Is there any comment that you would like to make?

6. If you have any activities you would like to submit for consideration in the second edition of *The Almanac*, please attach them with your name and address. You will be credited if a second edition is completed.

Mail them to:

Dr. Cathy Collins
School of Education
Texas Christian University
P.O. Box 32925
Fort Worth, TX 76129